IMAGES
of America

LANCASTER

I0793003

On the Cover: The town square of Lancaster was the center of the community from the beginning. It was a gathering place for settlers in horse-drawn implements, transitioning to automobiles by 1915. (Courtesy of the Lancaster Historical Society.)

IMAGES
of America

LANCASTER

Lancaster Historical Society

ARCADIA
PUBLISHING

ISBN 978-0-7385-7876-7

Published by Arcadia Publishing
Charleston SC, Chicago IL, Portsmouth NH, San Francisco CA

Printed in the United States of America

Library of Congress Control Number: 2009932092

For all general information contact Arcadia Publishing at:
Telephone 843-853-2070
Fax 843-853-0044
E-mail sales@arcadiapublishing.com
For customer service and orders:
Toll-Free 1-888-313-2665

Visit us on the Internet at www.arcadiapublishing.com

To those brave souls who settled the Lancaster community as early as 1844 and to those who led our town as it grew, we dedicate this book.

Contents

ACKNOWLEDGMENTS

The Lancaster Historical Society has been involved in preserving the history since 1969. The society's first president, Judge Newton Fitzhugh, authored several publications describing the events in Lancaster's development. Since this early beginning, a *History of Lancaster* was published in 1978 spearheaded by Ellen Bain (Clark). This current publication is not a replacement for the *History of Lancaster* book, but a pictorial history of the early days up to 1915.

Unless otherwise noted, all images in this book came from the Lancaster Historical Society collection and from the Strain family collection.

Many thanks go to those who helped with pictures for the initial book as well as for this book. Most of the information in this publication has been verified through census, birth records, and other records found on historical sites when available. It is the purpose of this society to help preserve the history of Lancaster for future generations through publications like this and through public displays of historical information. The society welcomes citizens to bring us material, which we can scan and save for future publications and displays. Please contact us with additional data.

Lancaster Historical Society
Mary Sykes, Author
Box 173
Lancaster, Texas 75146
www.lhsweb.org

Introduction

Texas became a republic in 1836 around the same time that the United States was experiencing poor crops and economic problems. This opened the door for immigration to Texas. The rush began about 1837 and continued until 1842 when Mexico threatened to reclaim Texas. Few Native Americans lived in the area at this time. Prior to 1841, the Texas Rangers, led by Gen. E. H. Tarrant and Gen. James Smith, organized to clear the Native Americans from this area. On September 23, 1843, a treaty was signed stating that Native Americans would stay west of the junction of the West and Clear Forks of the Trinity River, some 30 miles west of Bryan's settlement (Dallas).

On February 1, 1841, an act of the Congress of the Republic of Texas authorized the president to enter into an impresario contract with William S. Peters and 19 associates. In return for their services in procuring immigrants from outside Texas to settle specific areas of North Texas, they would be granted certain lands within the same area. The Peters Colony introduced about 600 families to Texas from 1841 until 1844. The Peters Colony contract was altered three times between August 31, 1841 and January 20, 1843 to give more land.

Lancaster came after the final area was granted. It was bounded on the north by the Red River and on the east beginning at the mouth of Big Mineral Creek. The southern edge was expanded several times but the eventual edge was near Ten Mile Creek close to Ellis County. The southern boundary went west 164 miles through what is now Johnson, Hood, Erath, and Eastland Counties and half of Callahan County. The western line went north for about 140 miles back to the Red River.

The Peters Colony included all of Dallas County except a 3-mile strip on the east boundary. Various Native American hunting parties searched for game in the Ten Mile Creek area. The Tawakonis, possibly the Cherokee, and some nomadic tribes had campsites along Ten Mile Creek.

Much of the land around Lancaster lay in the Robertson District formed in 1837. This district was famous for its black land, rich and well adapted for growing small grains. Wild grass grew to the height of an ordinary man and covered much of the range. While the grass was tall, trees were generally short and scrubby, except along waterways. This meant cultivation was easy because little timber had to be cleared.

The Peters' group advertised heavily in Kentucky, Illinois, Missouri, and Tennessee, and for that reason, many of the early settlers to Lancaster were from those states. The Republic of Texas had several categories for land grants. Most Lancaster immigrants fell into the category that gave a married man 640 acres and a single man 320 acres of land. It was up to the grantee or his assignee to locate the land, survey it, and secure his patent. The story of Peters Colony contains inaccurate surveys, boundary disputes, and problems with getting title to lands, but through it all, the settlement of Lancaster began.

Hardscrabble was the first settlement and the origin of Lancaster. The settlement was established in December 1844. Eventually Hardscrabble took supremacy over a settlement farther north called Pleasant Run due to the 1860 untimely death of its founder, M. M. Miller.

Roderick Rawlins brought the first settlers to South Dallas County. He was 68 years old in 1844 and had already lived an extraordinary life before arriving in the county. Rawlins and two of his sons-in-law came ahead to select the general area in which they would settle. The group passed through Dallas to Ten Mile Creek, which was void of inhabitants, and chose this as the site of their settlement. In December, the three men went back to Lamar County near the Red River to bring the rest of their wagon train.

Their settlement was located on the high point just southwest of present-day Nokomis Road and Beltline Road intersection. They chose this base because it was in easy walking distance to a flowing spring on Keller Branch; it had sufficient drainage in all directions; there was timber for construction and fuel; grazing land, such as it was in wintertime, was near the campsite; and the area had good visibility to the open prairie.

All settlers had arrived by January 2, 1845. Their crude cabins were erected in a double row with a street between, running north and south. The people in this first settlement were Roderick Rawlins and family, Valentine Wampler and children (his deceased wife was a daughter of Rawlins), Pleasant Taylor and family, David Lewis Hall and family, Samuel Keller and family, Carlos Wise, John Kiser and family, John Mullican and family, and maybe Benjamin Cox. In total were 30 men, women, and children in Hardscrabble.

Soon to follow were Middleton Perry and Jones Greene with their wives. Following them were their wives' parents, Thomas McKee Ellis and Mary "Polly Witt Ellis and their children. Shortly after came the William Lavender family and his wife's kin, the John Little family. Archibald Lavender and his family were also early settlers.

The main trail went from the Trinity River west towards Johnson's Station, which is now Arlington, Texas, and then on to Fort Worth. People who traveled this way had to cross the Trinity River on Mr. Dawdy's Ferry, now known as Dowdy Ferry Road. This road is north of Pleasant Run Road in Lancaster. It was along this road that Madison Moultrie Miller opened a general store in 1846 and established Pleasant Run, Texas. It was a two-room structure with one room as the store and another for living. Miller was very ambitious, and by 1848, the building had grown to 15 rooms, a separate store, and a warehouse. There was soon a stage stop with hotel rooms, a blacksmith shop, a tin shop, a woodworking shop, and a power gristmill, as well as the Miller General Store. Miller was appointed postmaster and received mail biweekly at Pleasant Run. The nearest post office to Pleasant Run was White Rock, Texas. Miller died unexpectedly in 1860, but the rival to Pleasant Run—Lancaster—continued to grow.

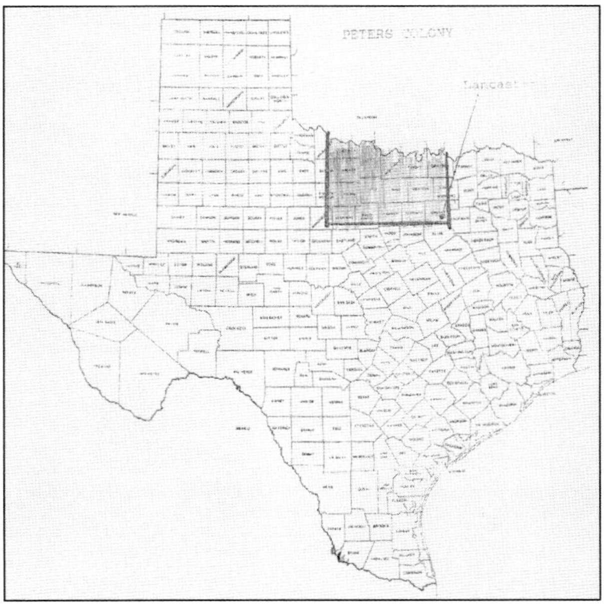

Lancaster is located in the southeast corner of Peters Colony. The black line denotes the entire area given to Peters Colony. Most people who took advantage of the offer for free Texas land came from Illinois, Arkansas, Missouri, Kentucky, and Tennessee. The early settlers often lived near major creeks and rivers. Peters Colony was over 11 million acres.

One

In the Beginning, Lancaster was Named Hardscrabble

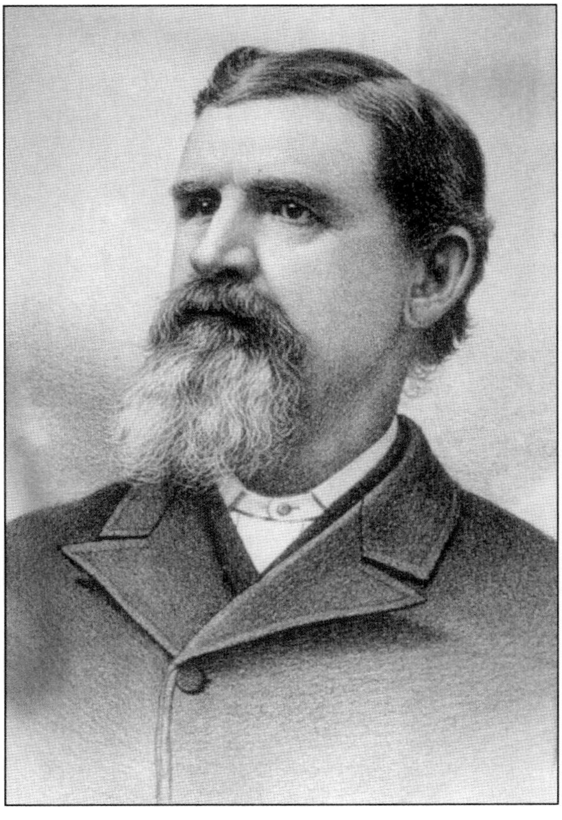

Capt. Roderick Alexander Rawlins (1883–1910) was the youngest son of elder Roderick Rawlins (1776–1848) and Milly Parks (1793–1875). R. A. Rawlins came to Lancaster in 1844 as a youth of 11 years with his father's group of 30 Texas pioneers. In 1853, he married his former teacher, Virginia Bledsoe (b. 1829), a union that joined the Rawlins family with A Bledsoe's family. Together the two families executed a plan to start a town they would name Lancaster. As the Civil War was waged, two units were formed from the Lancaster area. Roderick Alexander Rawlins would become the leader of Company F, 6th Cavalry and return as Captain Rawlins. When he returned to Lancaster, he found his house in disarray. He rebuilt not only the house but the fences as well as reestablishing his livestock herds. He farmed and was in the cattle business until his death. Many cattle drives started at the captain's home. It is assumed that he traveled north to what is now Preston Road and joined up with others on the Chisholm Train.

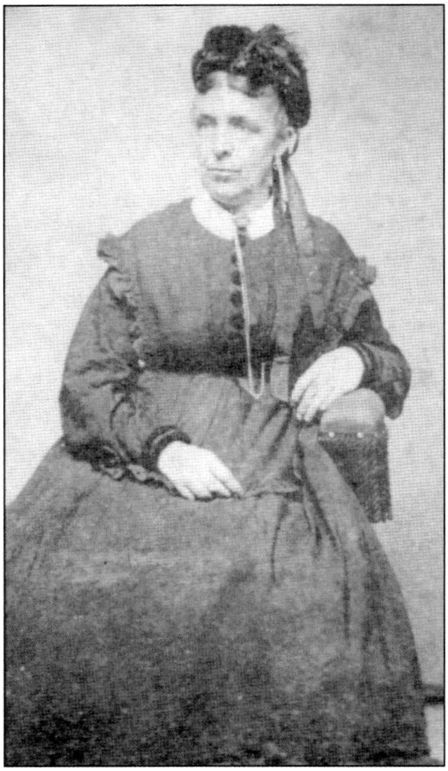

Nancy Rawlins (1820–1891) was the daughter of Roderick Alexander Rawlins and Milly Parks Rawlins. Nancy Priscilla Rawlins-Taylor and her husband, Pleasant King Taylor, arrived in Lancaster in the Rawlins group. They sold their original Texas headright (land given to each settler) on East Beltline Road to Thomas McKee Ellis and moved northward toward Hampton Road. They had four children: R. A., John A., Amelia A., and Joseph F. Taylor.

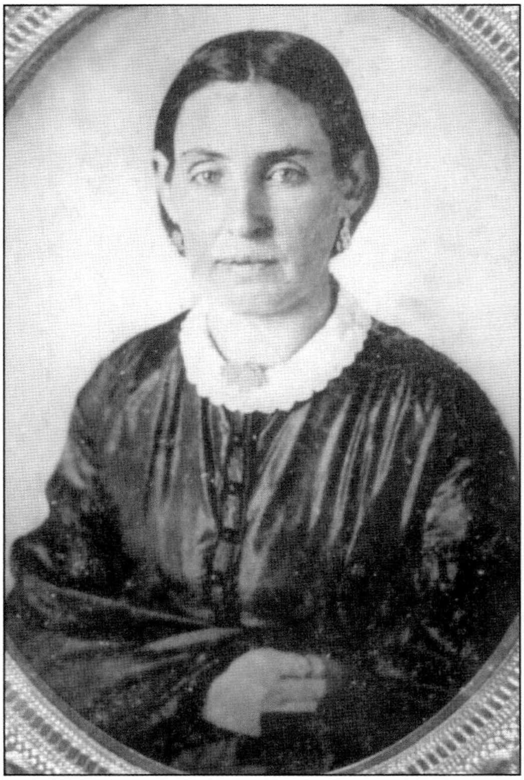

Mildred Talithia Rawlins (1828–1890), daughter of Roderick Rawlins, married Carlos Wise (1819–1899). Their marriage was said to be the first wedding in the community of Hardscrabble. After their marriage, they did not stay long in Lancaster but moved to Fort Byrd, now Birdville. The couple had six children: Julia A., Moulton, Ida V., Sallie F., Tera A., and Ruth E. Wise.

Lucinda Rawlins Keller was the daughter of Roderick and Milly Parks Rawlins. She married Samuel Keller and came to Lancaster in 1845. Although he could only see with one eye, he was able to shoot as well as men with excellent sight. Samuel Keller ran a mill on the north side of Lancaster on a creek that is known as Keller Branch. The ground flour was lifted to the third floor by an elevator belt with cups attached to bolting cloth, which separated the bran and shorts to make two grades of flour. This was the first mill in this region to create fine flour. The Kellers had 11 children: William V. (1843–1864), Sarah A. (b. 1847), James A. (1848–1925), John Roderick (1851–1880), Mary V. (1853–1885), Joseph K. (b. 1845), Samuel Paris (b. 1857), Oliver W. (b. 1859), Milly E. (1846–1846), James B. (b. 1851), and William H. (b. 1860).

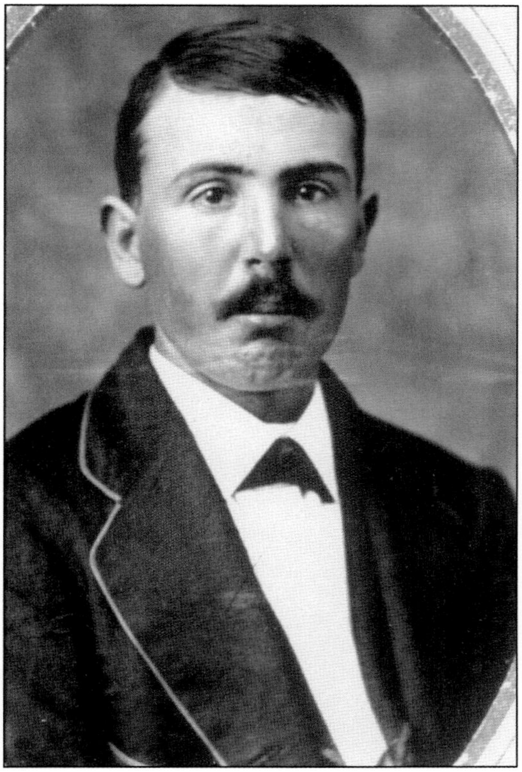

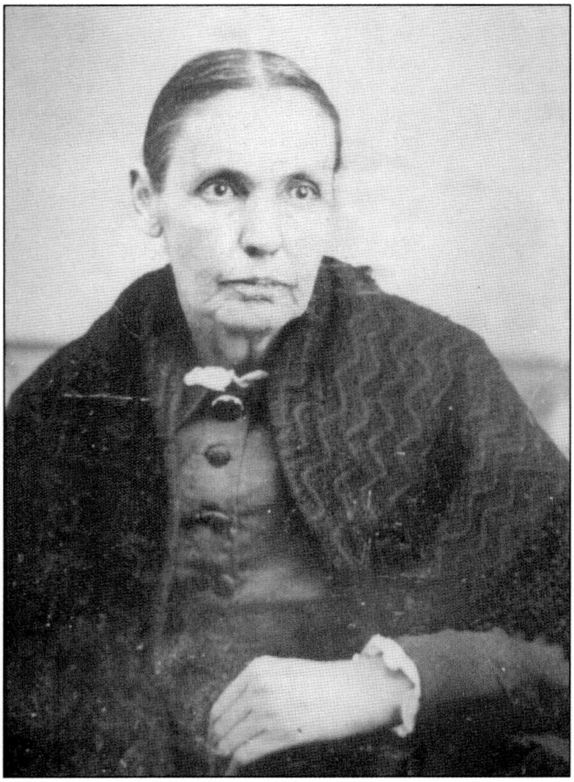

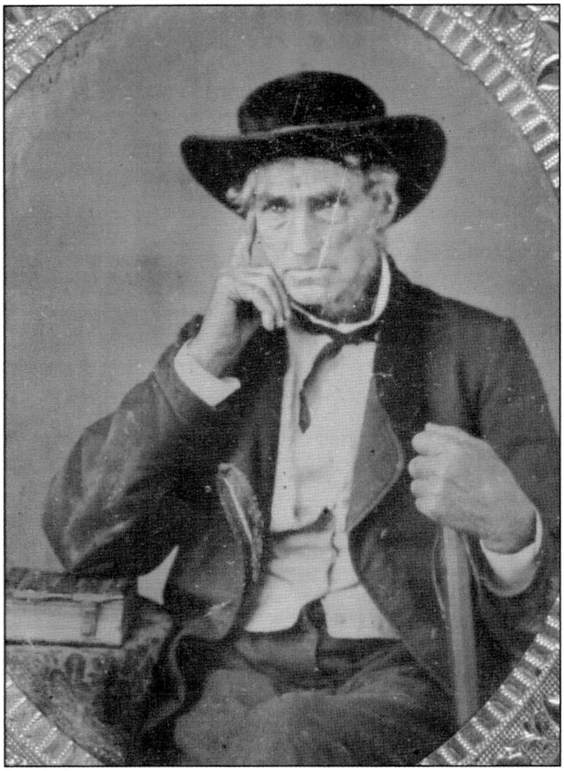

Thomas McKee Ellis (1799–1890) was born in South Carolina to James Lindsay Ellis (1774–1830) and Mary McKee (1776–1849). His grandfather arrived in South Carolina in 1776 from Ireland. Thomas married Mary "Polly" Witt (1803–1890) in Illinois. Two of their married daughters and husbands arrived in Lancaster in 1844. They were Ellen Ellis Perry, Middleton Perry, Mary Ann Ellis Greene, and Jones Greene. Thomas McKee and Polly came from Illinois with eight unmarried children. Most of their children married locals and remained in the area with their families. Ellis was a farmer and community leader. Polly's ancestors were black Huguenots who were forced to flee France in 1705. Her mother, Eleanor Penny Witt, moved here later to live with her daughter.

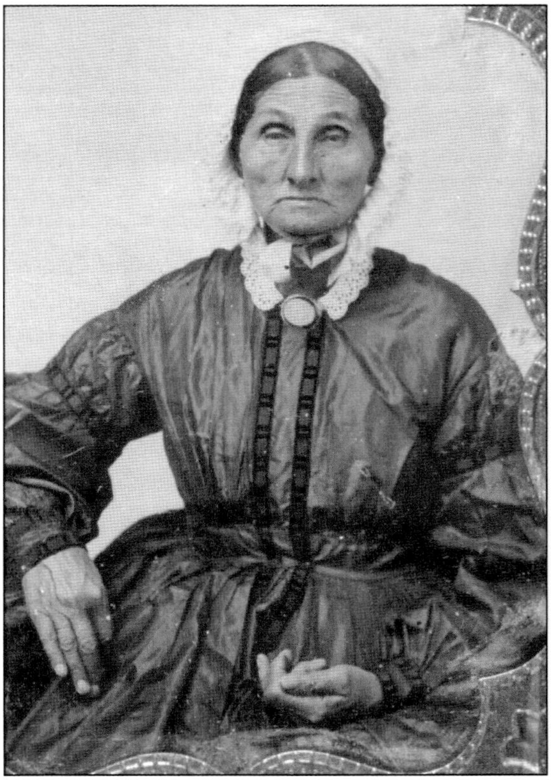

Madison Moultrie Miller (1813–1860) arrived in Texas in 1845 to select his home site. He returned to Texas in 1846 with two children, Cordelia (1828–1921) and William (1839–1849). While he had been away, his wife, Isabell McClusky died. After settling near Bear Creek, Miller married Mary (Polly) Parks Rawlins (1826–1856), another daughter of Roderick Rawlins. They eventually moved to an area north of Lancaster and established the community known as Pleasant Run. Miller ran a very successful trading and mercantile store, which rivaled Lancaster as a trade center. The Miller house consisted of two rooms in 1846 but grew to 15 rooms by 1848. The workers in Miller's flour and gristmill boarded here. Pleasant Run had a post office, and travelers boarded at the Miller's house. Lancaster outgrew Pleasant Run due to Miller's early death in 1860.

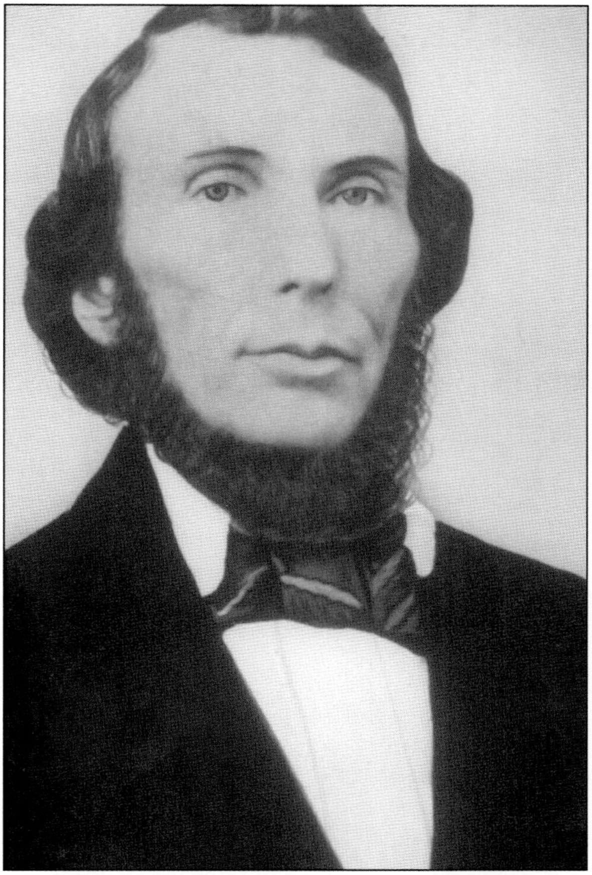

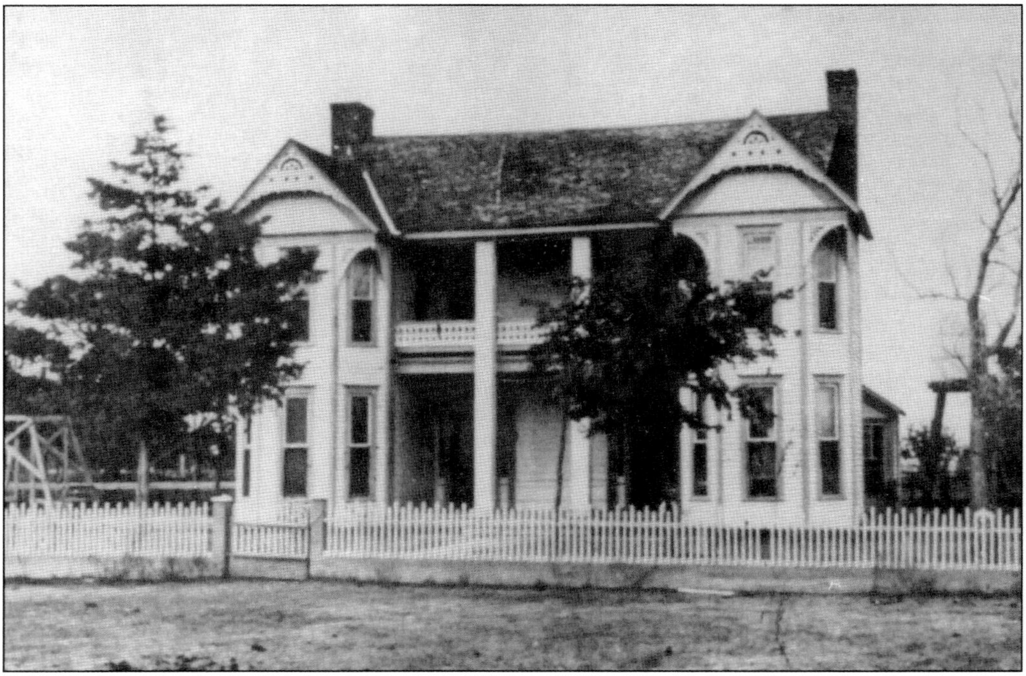

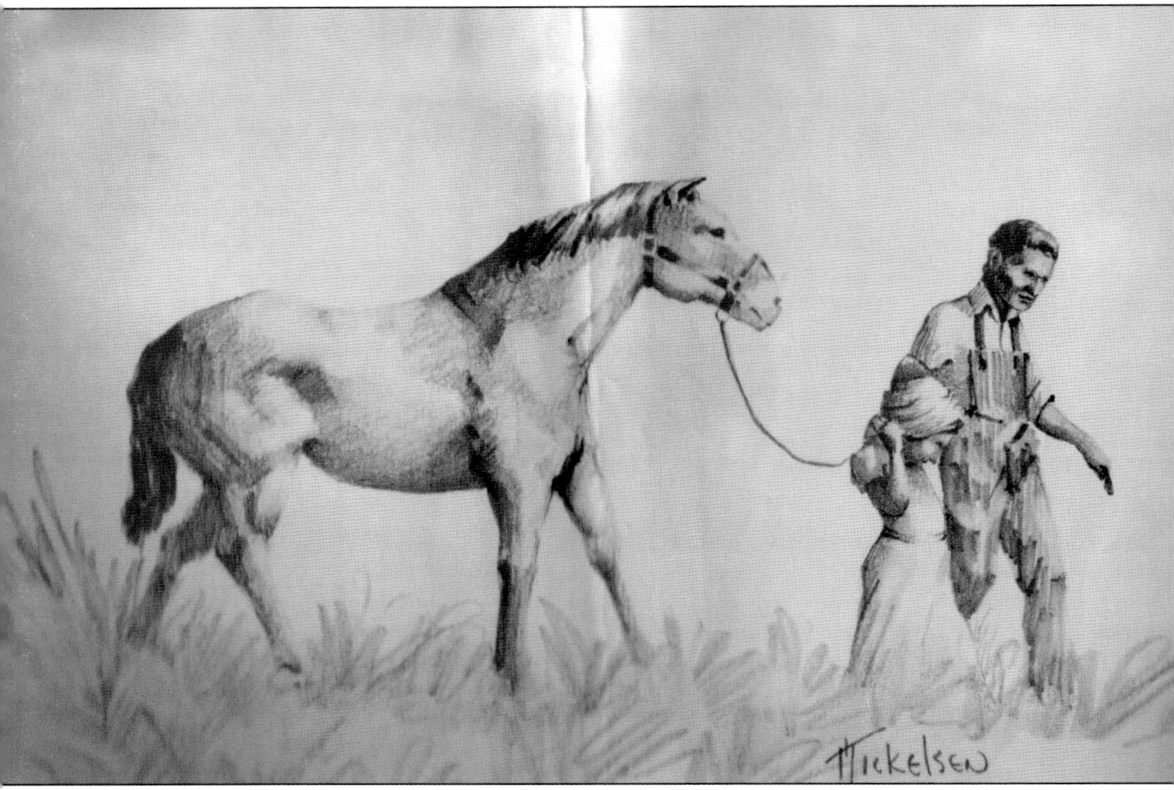

Steel Dust, the father of the Quarter Horse breed, is depicted here by Leo Mickelsen as he is led by Tom McKnight. Steel Dust was brought to Lancaster as a colt by Jones Greene and Middleton Perry. Steel Dust raced other horses, a common entertainment on Saturdays in early pioneer towns. As the winner of the races around Lancaster, Steel Dust's fame grew. It was not long before McKinney, Texas, challenged Lancaster to bring Steel Dust to race their horse, Mammoth. Excitement abounded and young Tom Ellis was set to ride Steel Dust in the big event. The mother of Tom Ellis was a staunch Baptist, though, and refused to let him ride in a horse race on Sunday. Tom McKnight, a young African American, was picked to make the ride. At the end of the race, many Lancaster citizens went home with their pockets heavy with gold while McKinney citizens saw their money and next year's crops lost. Steel Dust sired many other horses during his life and gained the honor of being named the father of the Quarter Horse breed.

Two

A Bledsoe Plans Lancaster's Growth

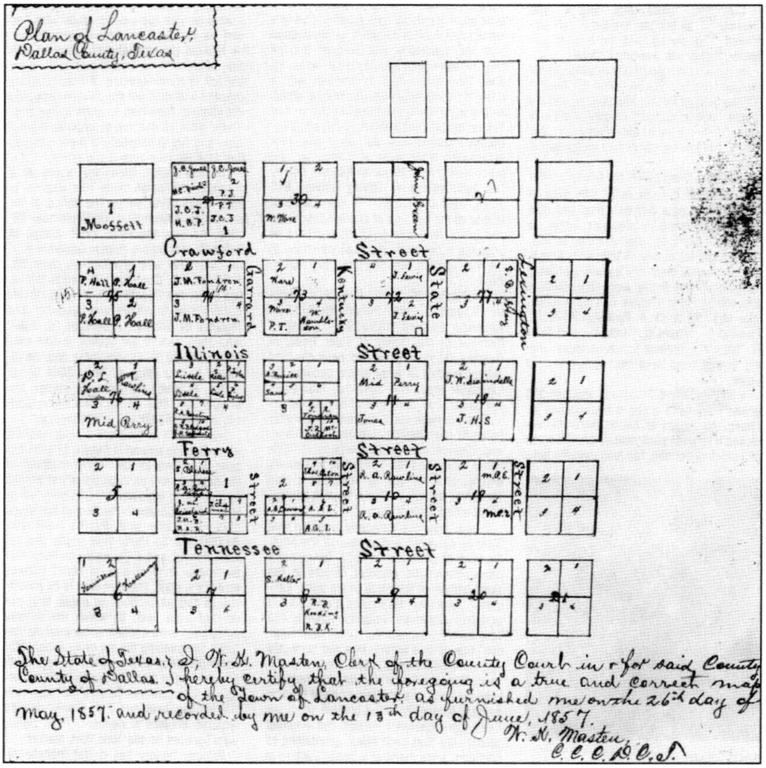

Lancaster was laid out by A Bledsoe to resemble the center of Lancaster, Kentucky. The square has streets that enter from four sides with a center medium. As many as two-thirds of the lots were given away in order to lure settlers from nearby Pleasant Run. The town occupied 1 square mile.

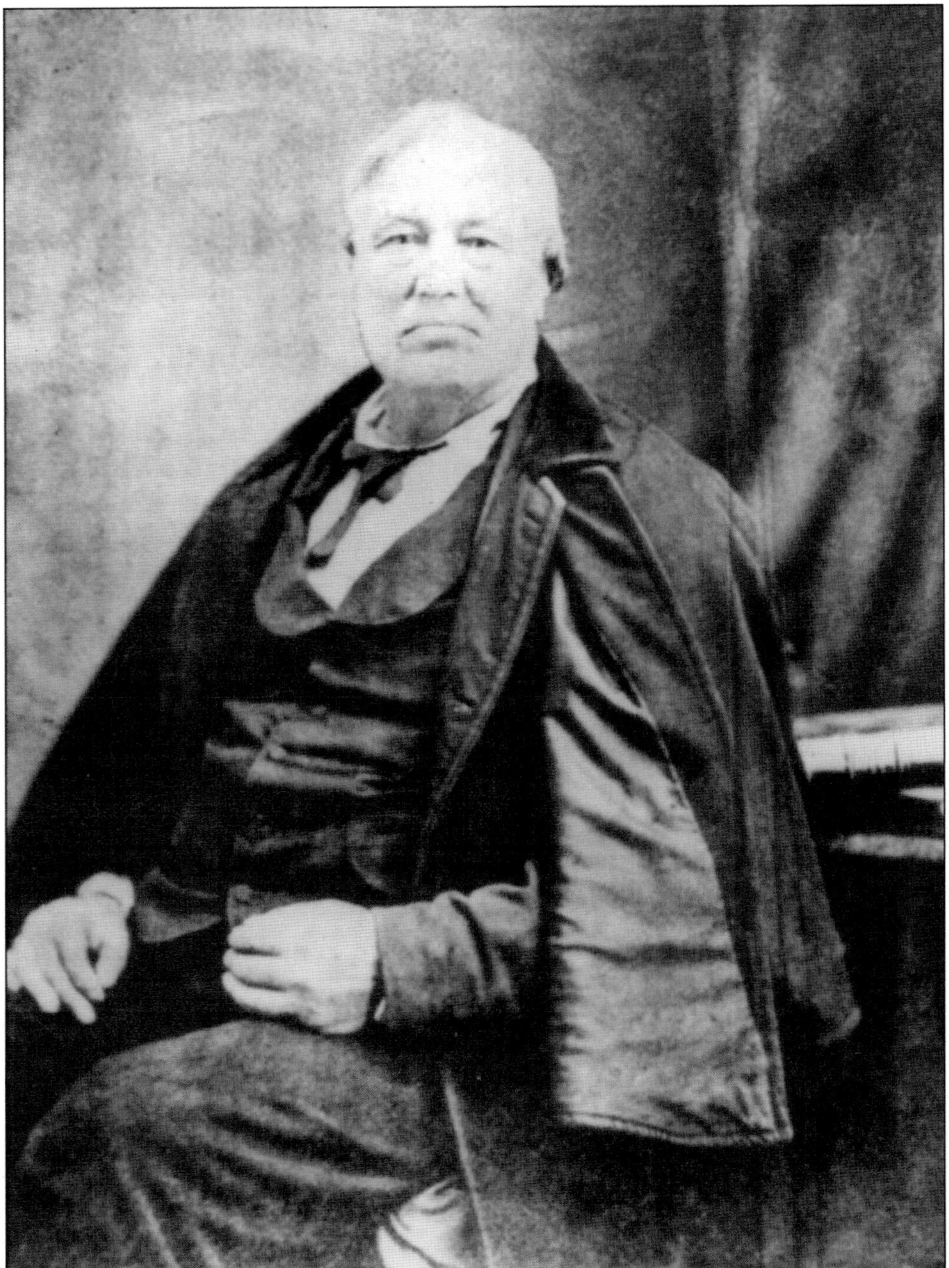

A Bledsoe (1801–1882) was born in Lancaster, Kentucky, to Moses Bledsoe who declared that he looked like a Bledsoe thus naming the baby "A Bledsoe." He married Margaret R. George (1806–1873). In 1846, he explored Texas and selected a 640-acre tract east of Lancaster. His family, including six children, came to Texas. A Bledsoe was 6 feet, 7 inches tall and weighed about 300 pounds. He had massive hands, wore a size eight hat, and size 11 shoes. Bledsoe's daughter, Virginia, married Roderick Alexander Rawlins (1833–1910), son of Roderick Rawlins. This marriage connected the Rawlins and Bledsoe families. The widow of the elder Rawlins and Bledsoe entered into a pact to create a town to compete with M. M. Miller's Pleasant Run trading post just north of them. The official filing date for this plan was 1857.

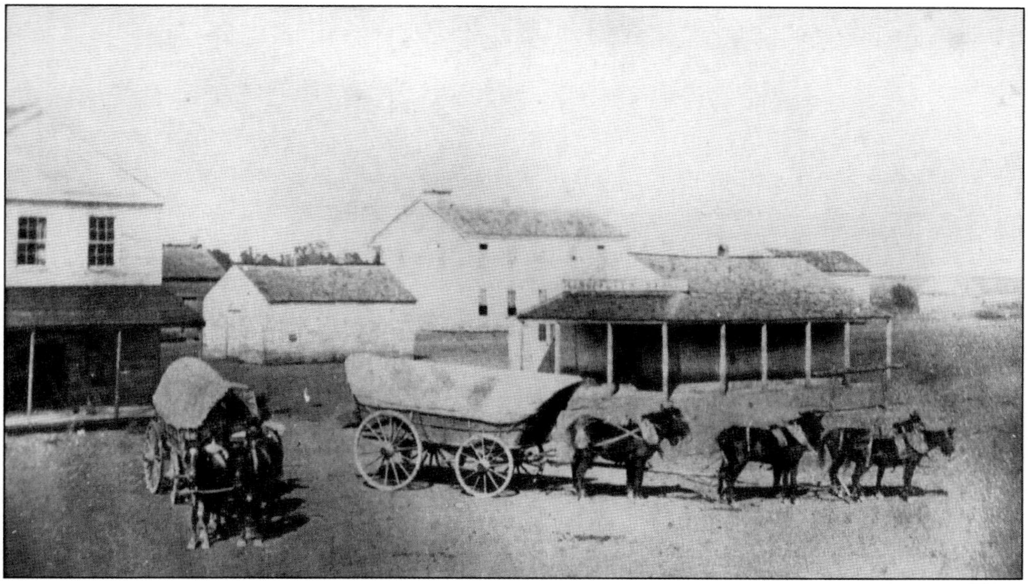

Lancaster Square was the place to shop in the 1860s. In this picture, Nick Groves's store is on the left with Moffett's General Merchandising on the right. In the background is the Masonic hall, which also served as the school and as church on Sunday. Wagons delivered goods from as far away as Galveston. With the unexpected death of M. M. Miller in 1860, the rival settlement of Pleasant Run was no longer competition for Lancaster.

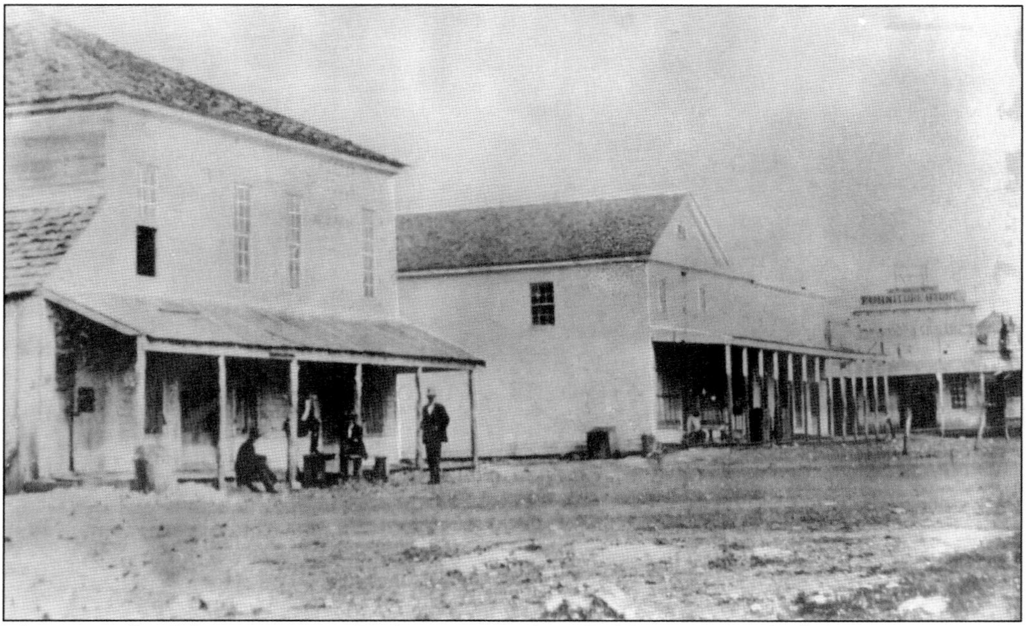

The west side of the square in 1870 shows an unidentified business on the left. Next to it is the White and Ellis General Store, and on the corner is the W. R. Green Furniture Store. Green made caskets as well as furniture. Other businesses were the Holloway General Merchandise, Dr. H. J. Moffett's Drug Store, Porter's Harness Shop, the Sherrard and Carey's Blacksmith Shop plus two grocery stores.

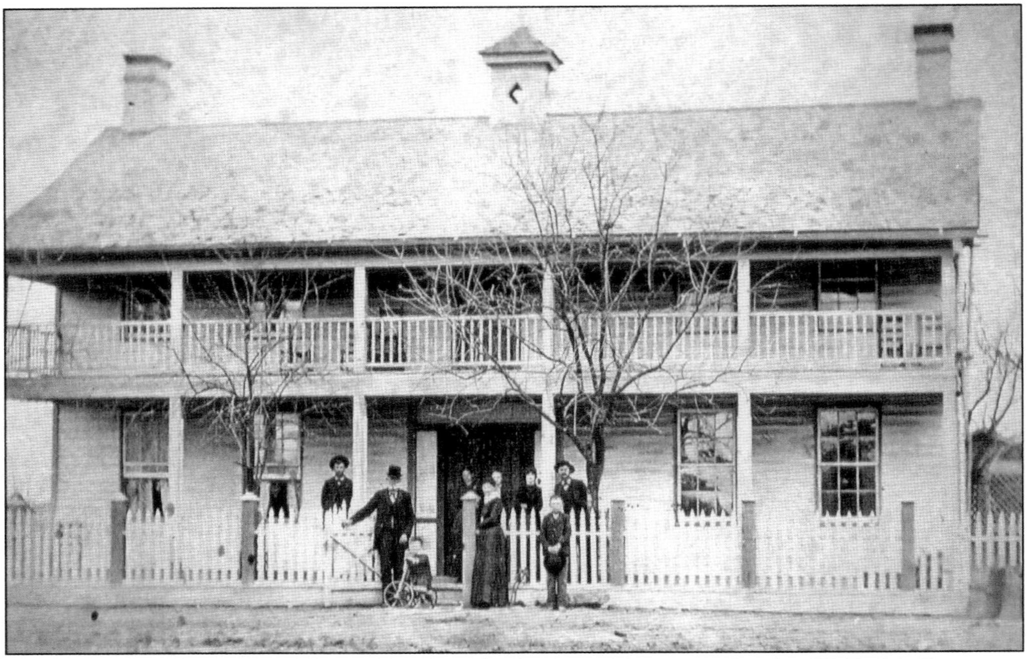

The original part of the Moffett House was built in 1856 by Major Jacobs. W. R. Moffett came to Lancaster from Illinois and was listed as a hotel keeper on the 1860 census. Twice-a-day stagecoaches stopped and were met in true Southern style. The famous meals were served from long board tables lighted by candles. In 1861, the mail was carried by the Sawyer Stage Line that extended from Clarksville to Austin via McKinney, Dallas, and Lancaster.

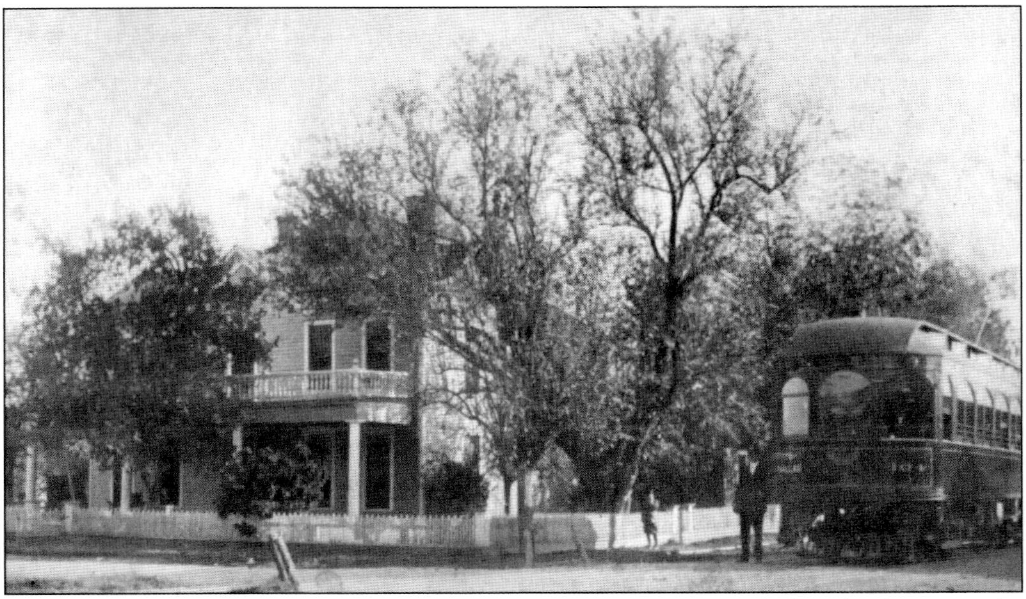

Henry E. Head and his wife, Lucy Francis Jeffries, born in 1840, opened a boardinghouse on the northwest corner of Dallas Avenue and First Street in 1891. Her husband died sometime after 1900 but she continued to run this successful establishment. The food was thought to be the finest around. Electricity came to Lancaster in 1911 with the electric interurban tracks going down the center of Texas Highway 342. The interurban station was only one block from Head House.

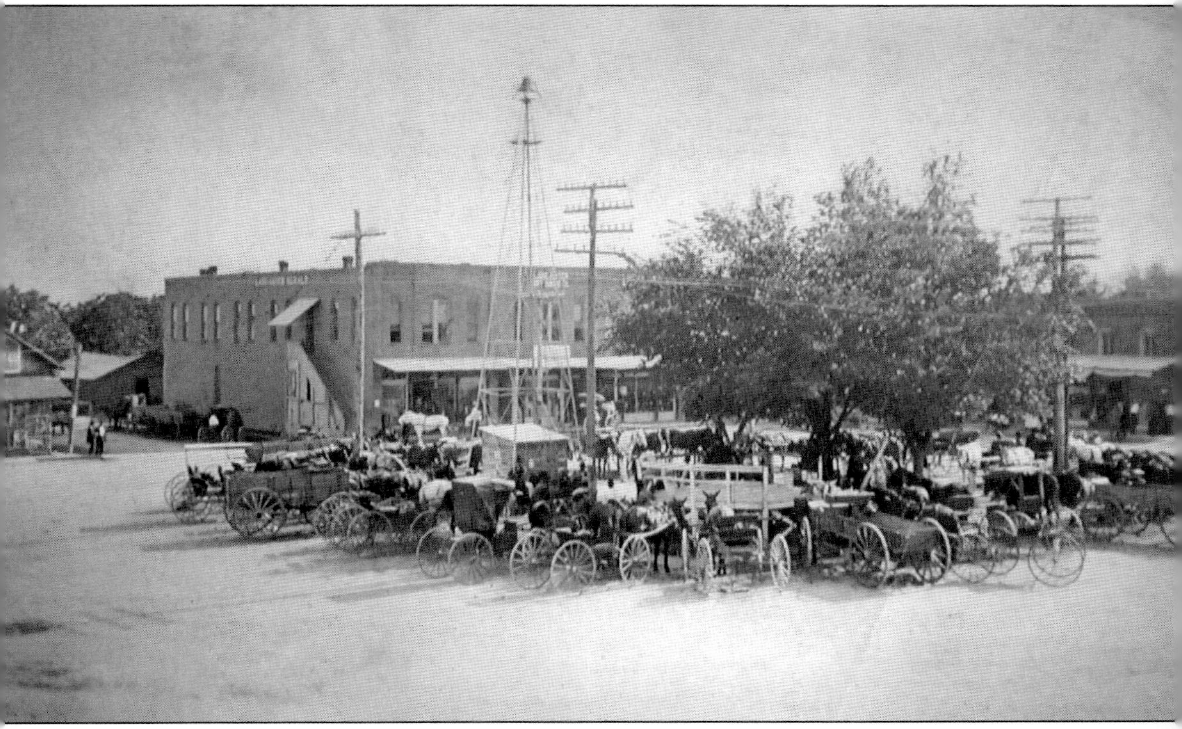

Lancaster in the 1890s hosted two railroads; W. P. Johnson's General Store; J. H. Moffett's General Merchandising; W. P. Coolidge and Company General Merchandising; R. E. Taylor and Company Druggist; W. A. Strain Drugs; John A. Rogers druggist; two roller mills; three cotton gins; R. P. Henry Bank; F. M. Hammond General Merchandise Store; the first soda fountain in Soloman Brundage's shop; Methodist, Baptist, Christian, and Presbyterian churches with large buildings; two schools (the Lancaster Masonic Institute and Female Institute); two fraternal lodges (Masonic and Odd Fellows); and others. The poles are for telephone wires and the taller tower is the fire pole. Lancaster had a volunteer fire department for another 50 years.

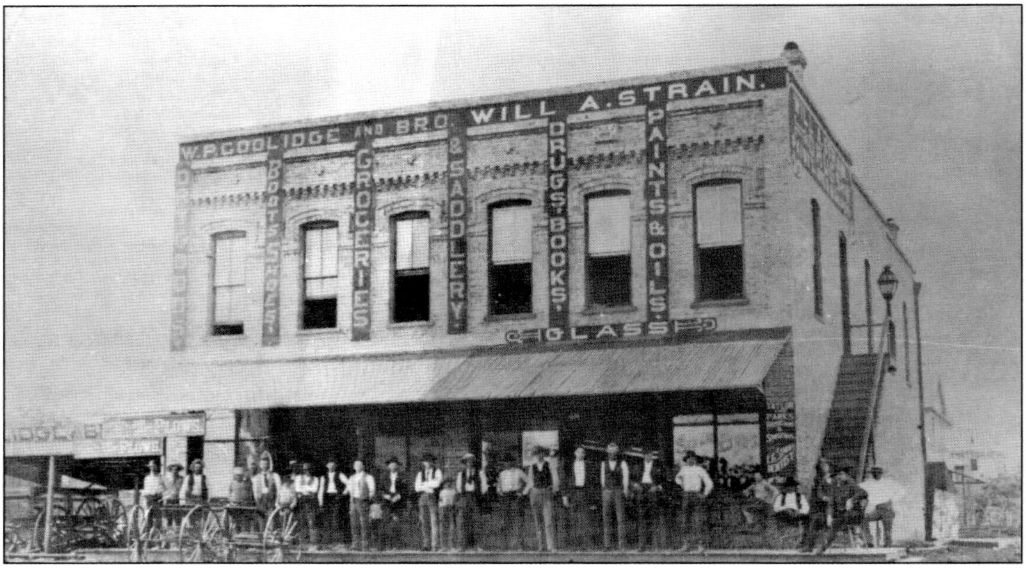

Buildings on the northwest side of the square still exist. In 1890, the W. P. Coolidge and Brothers Mercantile and the Will A. Strain Drug Store occupied the lower levels. Above the drugstore were the offices of Dr. Taylor and Dr. George Parks. In the rear was a photography shop. There is a gas light on the stairs going up to the doctor's offices. The northwest side of the square burned in 1889, and these are relatively new buildings at the time.

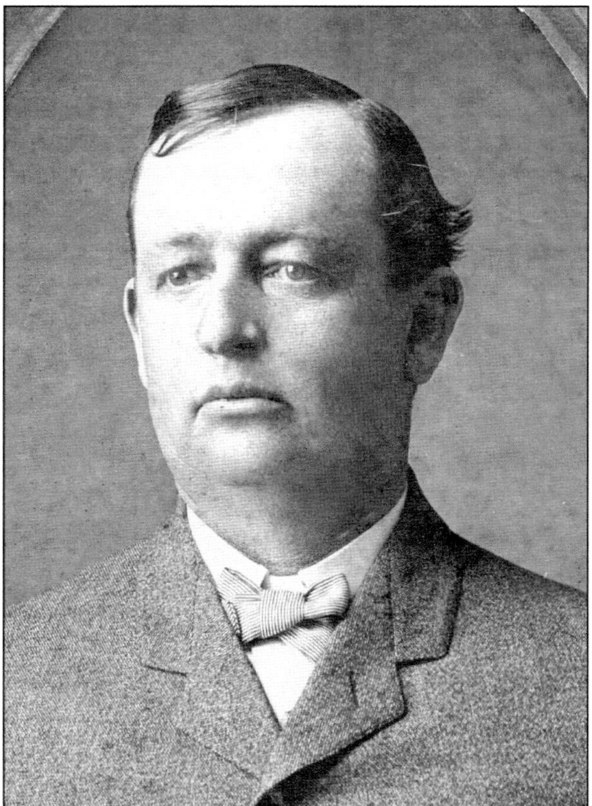

Dr. George T. Parks was born on December 23, 1861, in Lancaster, Texas, and died there on February 24, 1917. According to a granddaughter, he died during a flu epidemic, having contracted the disease while treating others. He received his medical degree from the University of Tennessee Center for Health Sciences in 1887, specializing in allopathy. The community remembered him for a long time. (Courtesy of Carolyn Fulton.)

William A. Strain came to Lancaster from Leesburg, Tennessee, around 1885. He worked in the Lyon Drug Store and learned the pharmaceutical business. As a result, C. M. Lyon took him in as a partner. His nickname, "Strainer," must have been well known. Will later owned his own drugstore in Lancaster and also opened one in Waxahachie.

Having this day taken into partnership W. A. Strain (better known as Strainer), who has been in my employ over two years, and as this day ushers in the new year, so this Greeting introduces to our many friends the new firm of Lyon & Strain.

We will keep in stock a full line of Drugs and Chemicals, Patent Medicines, Perfumery, Dye Stuffs, Paints, Oils, Varnishes, School Books, Stationery, etc.

Physicians Prescriptions and Family Receipts a Specialty.

Thanking my friends for past favors and soliciting the same liberal patronage for the new firm, who will endeavor to merit, by fair dealing and prompt attention, a continuance of the same.

I remain, yours truly,

C. M. LYON.

LANCASTER, TEXAS, January 1, 1886.

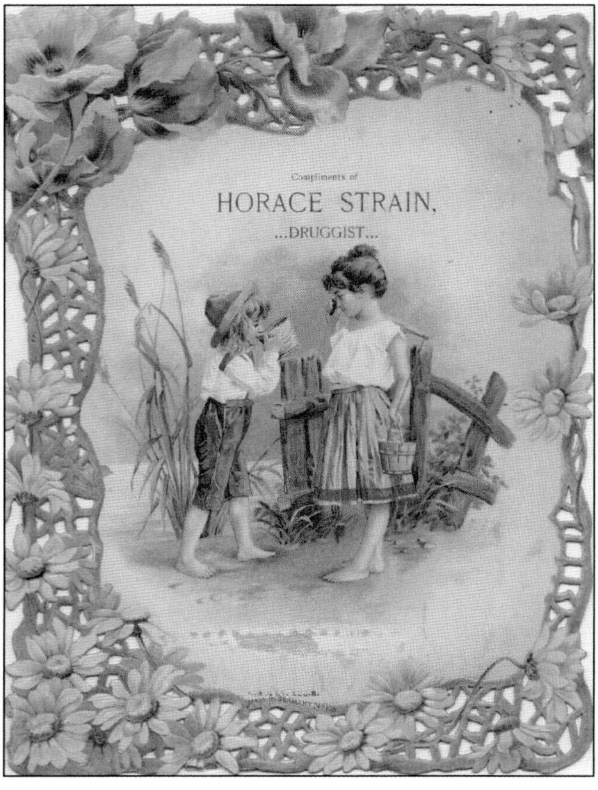

The Strain Drug Store was run by Horace Strain in 1900. There were several drugstores on the square and owners found items to lure shoppers into their business such as calendars. Drugstores, in the early 1900s, also sold perfumes, stationary, books, dyes, paints, and oil. Horace Strain was a half brother to W. A. Strain.

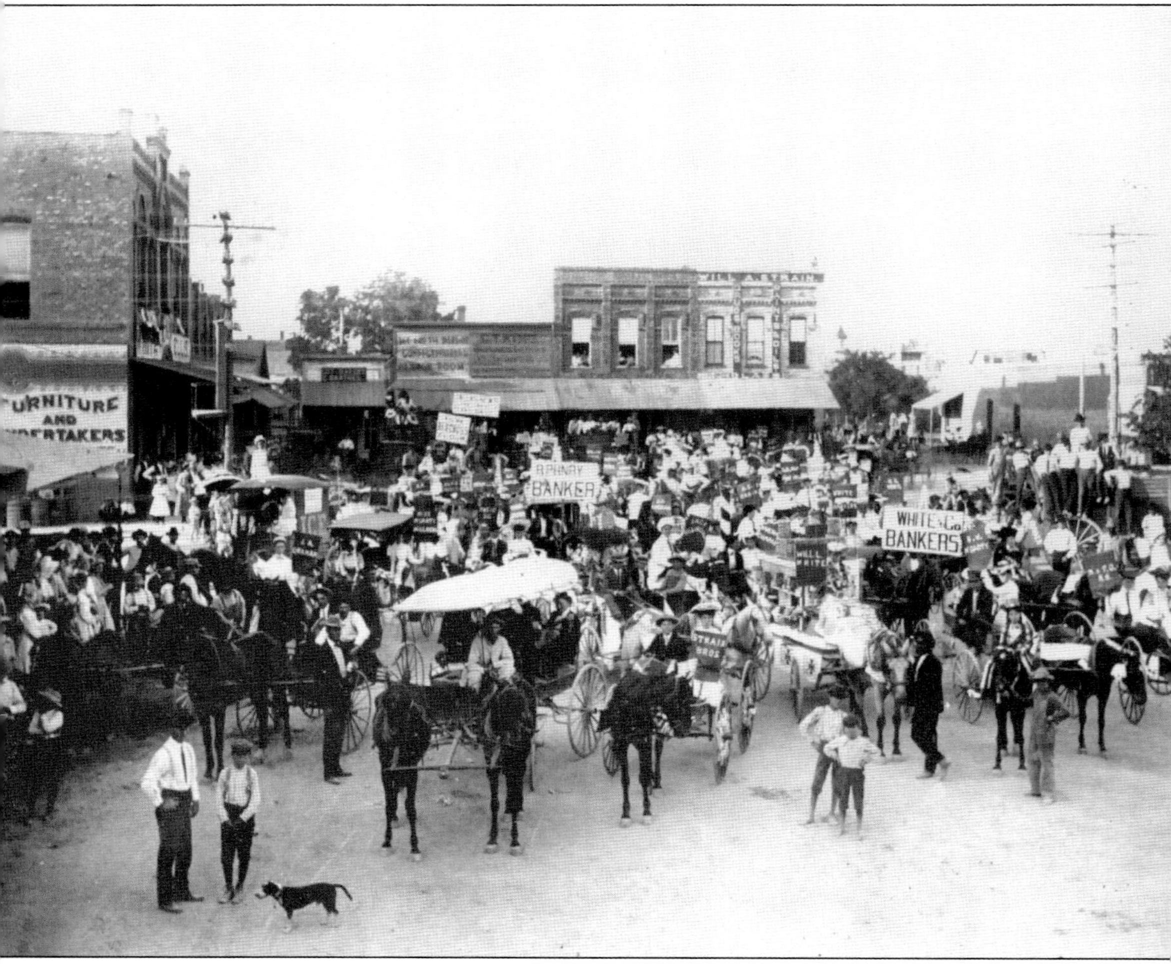

A view of the northwest side of the square around 1905 indicates the popularity of the town. On the left, not fully seen, is a furniture store, and to the right are two confectionery stores and the W. A. Strain Drug Store. The drugstore building still stands. Above the Strain building is the Independent Order of Odd Fellows (IOOF) meeting room. In the background is the First Baptist Church (1903). Other improvements in the town besides telephones included an artesian well built in 1895. The well had a depth of 1,100 feet and flowed at the rate of 128,000 gallons per day. A bathhouse was built at the well where citizens enjoyed warm baths. Men and boys went one day and the women and children another. Fires destroyed parts of the square in 1877 and 1889. A horse-drawn fire engine was purchased in the late 1890s or early 1900s.

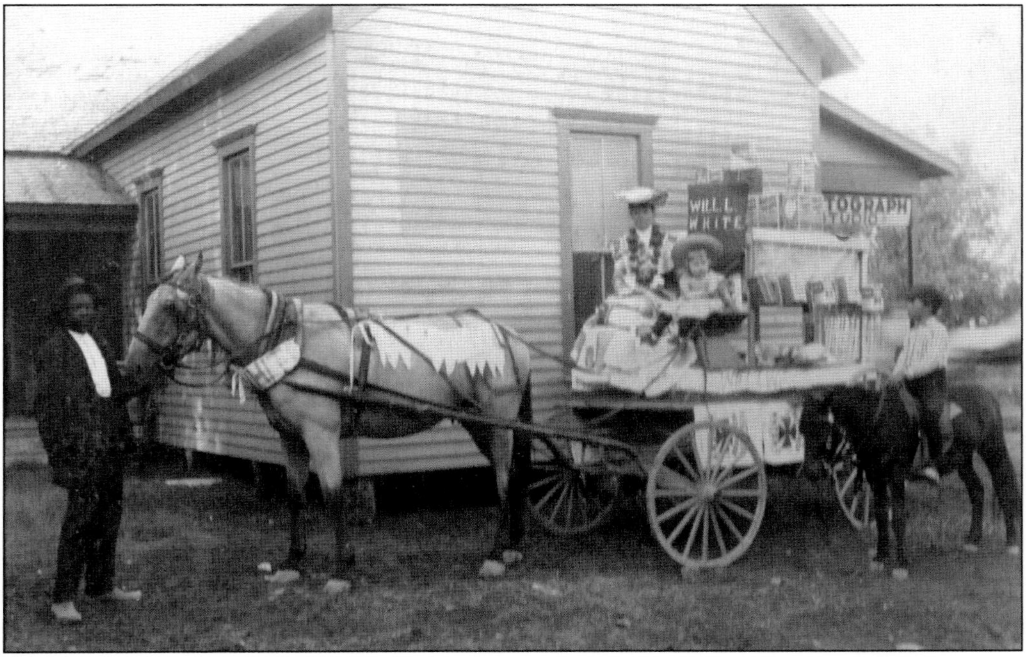

The Trades Day in 1905 brought many people to Lancaster. Wagons were decorated for various businesses on the square. On this wagon is Maude Greene (later Mrs. Alex Mitchell) but the identity of the others is unknown. The business is the Will L. White Grocery Store. Greene and Will L. White were cousins.

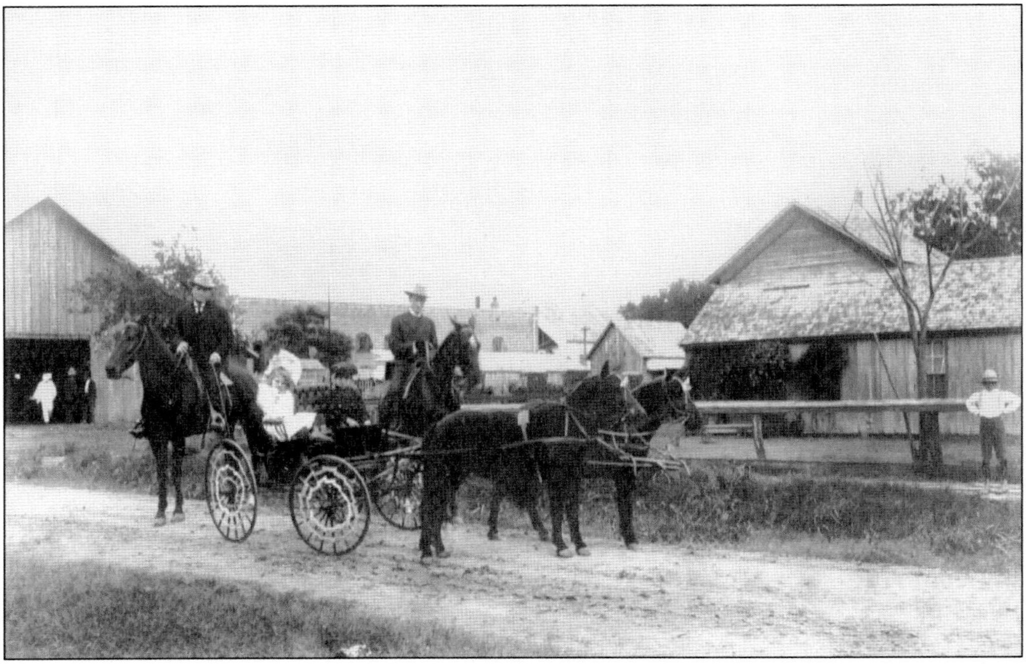

Another wagon gets ready for Trades Day around 1905. Riding in the pony cart are Laura White and Ellis Strain, who are about five years old. On the horse behind the wagon is Hal White, father of Laura. The other rider is unidentified. The citizens of Lancaster were very involved in the community.

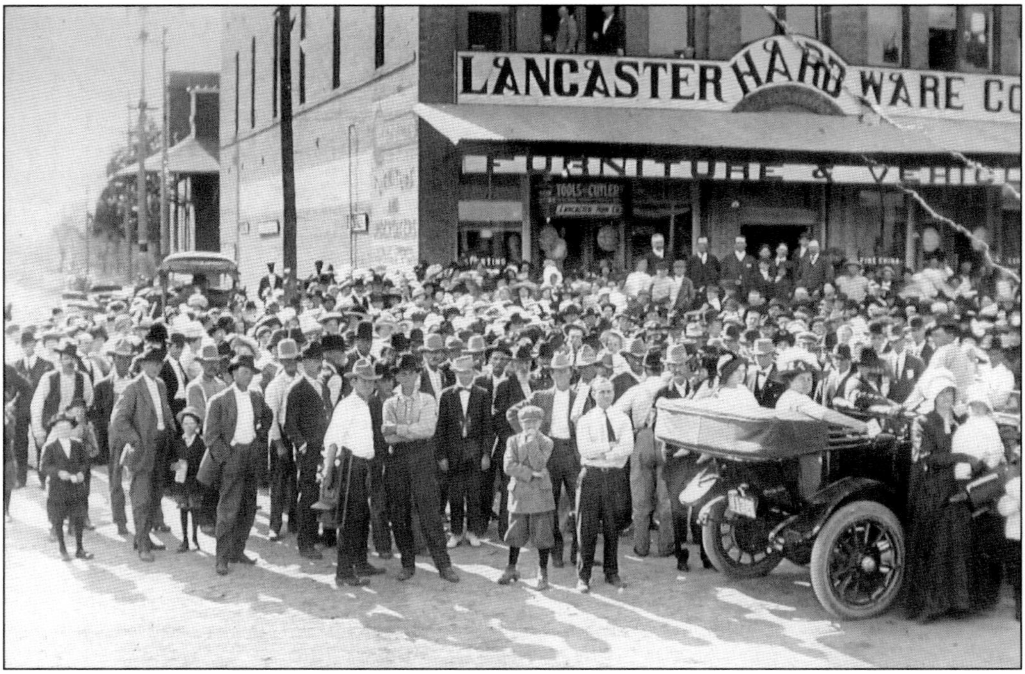

Unlike earlier Trades Days, this one featured cars. Lancaster Hardware sold furniture and vehicles, which were probably wagons and buggies. Cars were not common vehicles yet, and most citizens still had horses and buggies. By 1909, several cars were in Lancaster. It also appears that electricity may have been in use, arriving around 1911.

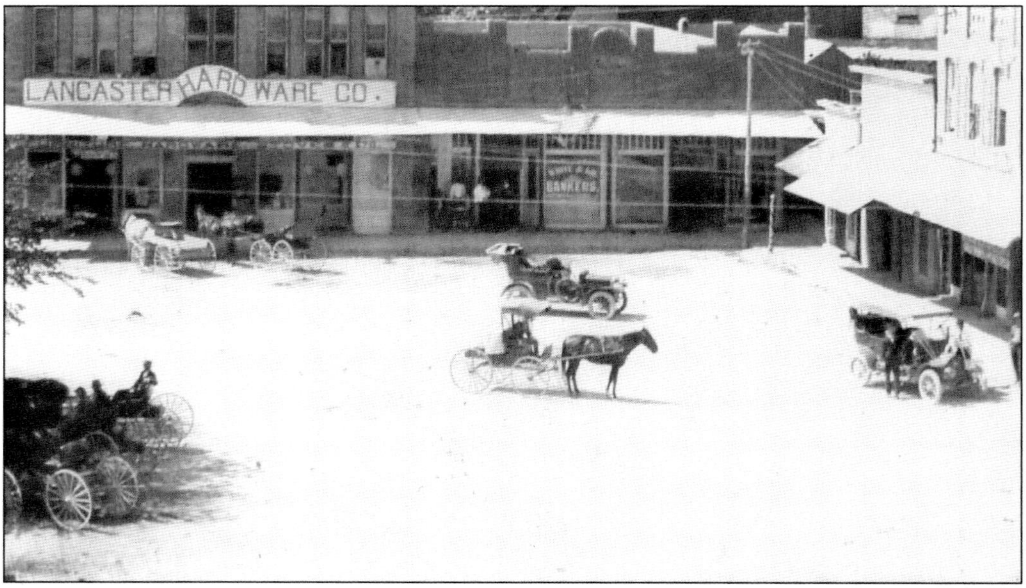

The Lancaster Hardware Company was bought in 1890 by S. L. Randlett from L. S. Beckley. To the right of the hardware store is White and Company Bankers, which opened in 1898. Lou F. White was president while her sons, Hal E., Karl, and Byrd White, served as vice presidents. It was very unusual for a female to own and run a business, but White was a very unusual person. The two cars probably belonged to Karl White and Hal E. White.

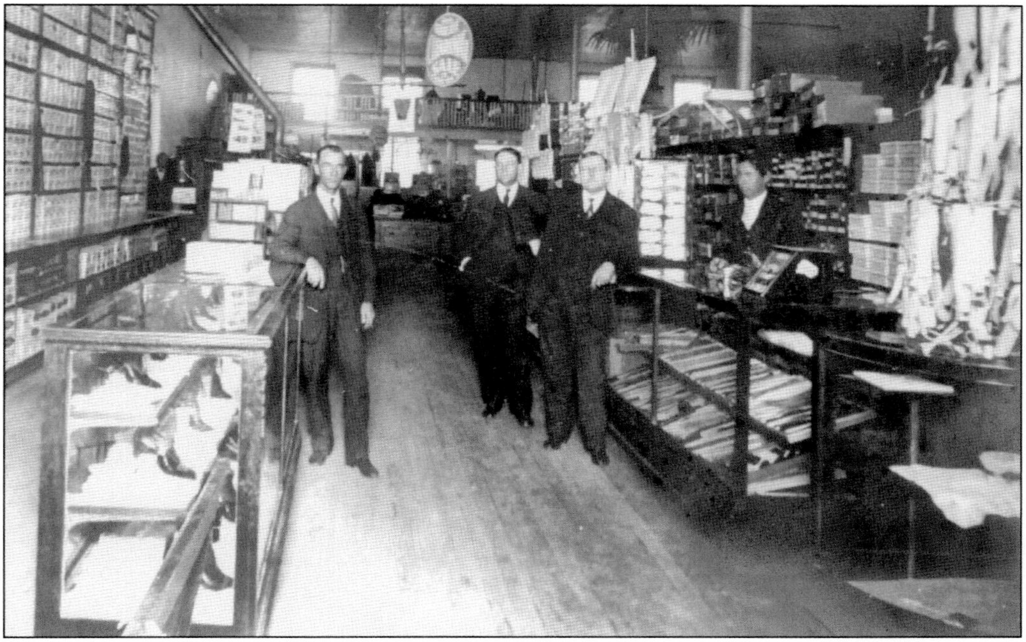

F. M. Hammond came to Lancaster in 1889 and opened a store. He arrived with two wagons of dry goods and a slogan, "satisfaction guaranteed." This store was reorganized several times but eventually became Heads and Son. This scene was before electricity and money exchanges were done on a sliding wire called cash carriers.

L. S. Beckley owned the Lancaster Hardware Store on South Dallas Avenue. In 1890, newcomer Sam Randlett bought this hardware store, promising new stock. Randlett and his partner, W. L. White, constructed a new building in 1891 and, as promised, new stock arrived several times a month. Upstairs was a mortuary. Many a Lancaster citizen was carried to his final resting place on Lancaster Hardware's horse-drawn hearse.

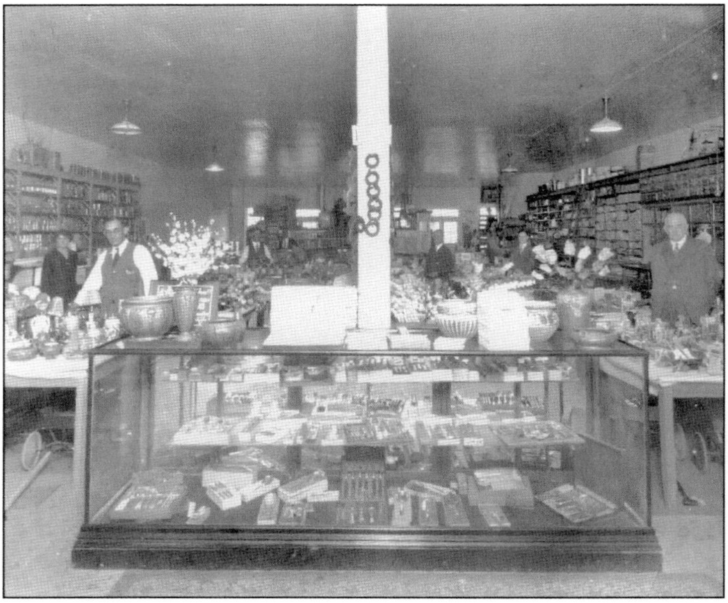

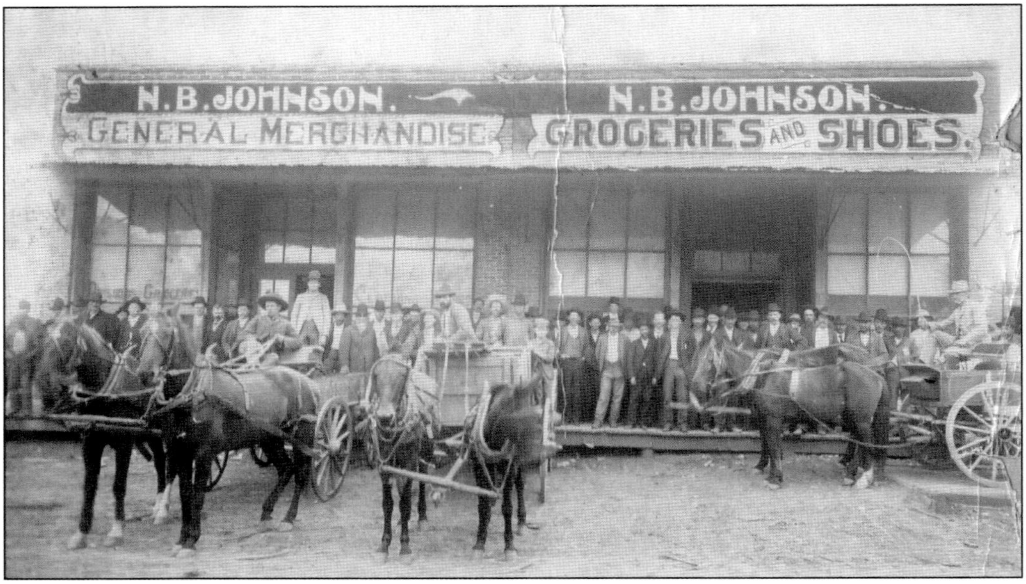

N. B. Johnson opened a general merchandising firm in 1889 on the southwest corner of the present Henry Park. In the fall, he moved into the site of the Hammond building where he stayed for about three years. He then moved to a brick building where he continued in business for 8 to 10 years. W. G. Howell, his partner, later ran a business known as the Lancaster Dry Goods Company.

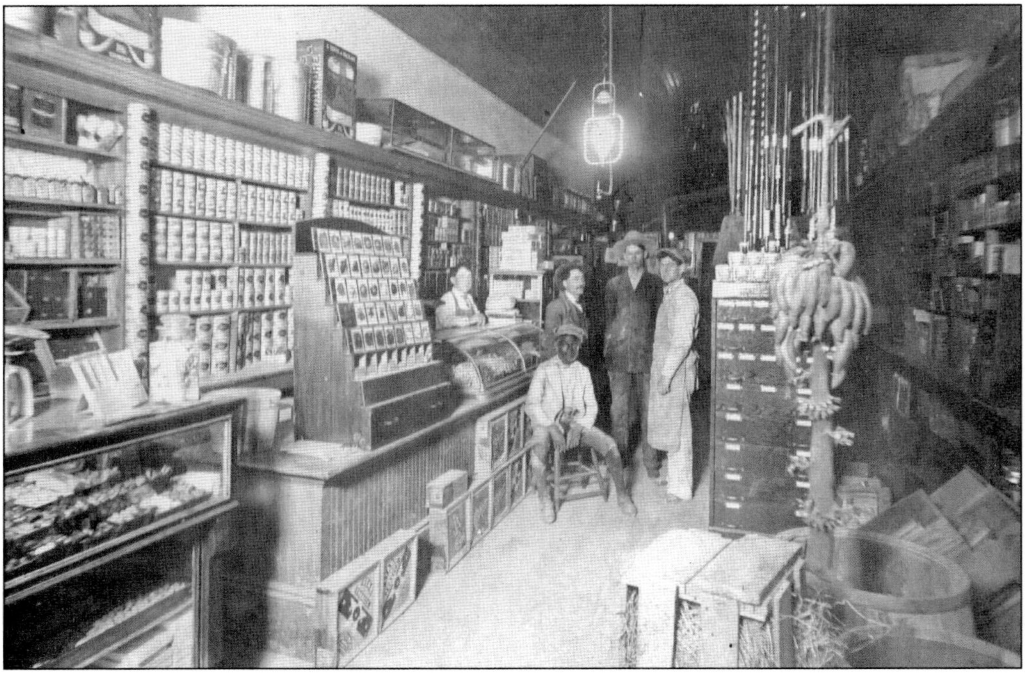

George C. Rawlins was the owner of a grocery store around 1914. Otto Chiles is sitting in front on the stool. Others in the picture are, from left to right, Rawlins's son—John A. Rawlins—behind the counter, Rawlins (mustache), Edgar L. Parker, and Velpeau Denton (son of the school principal). Credit was often extended to their customers and was not due until crops were harvested. Rarely were doors locked, and some businessmen allowed customers to pick up merchandise and leave notes on what they bought.

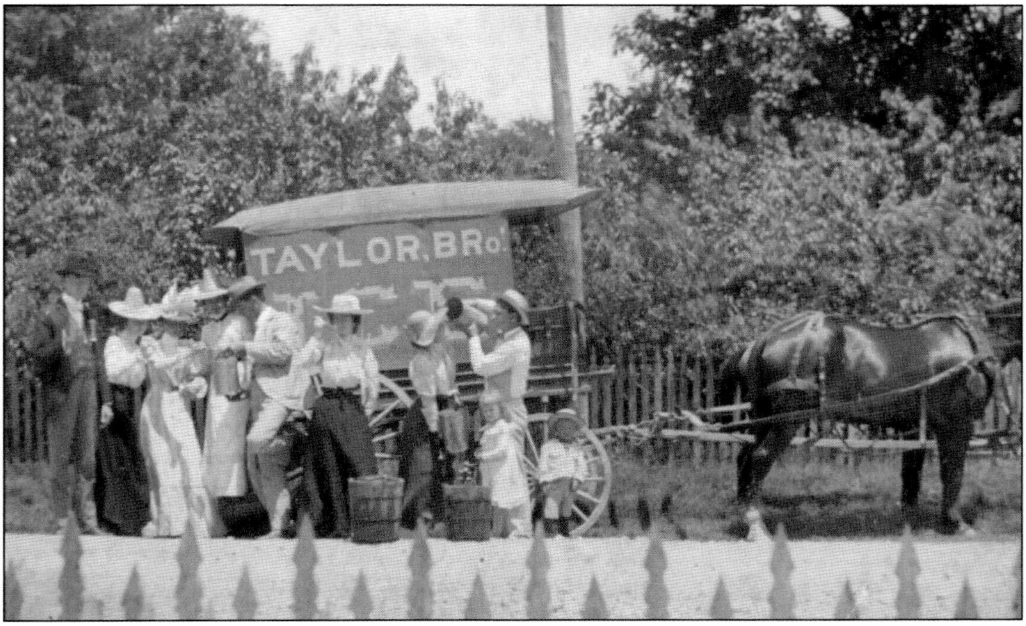

Home iceboxes depended on the ice man delivering blocks of ice to keep the food cold. From time to time, they had other treats to sell. At a church social, if all the ice cream was not sold, Taylor Brothers Ice Company took the leftovers to sell on their ice run the next day.

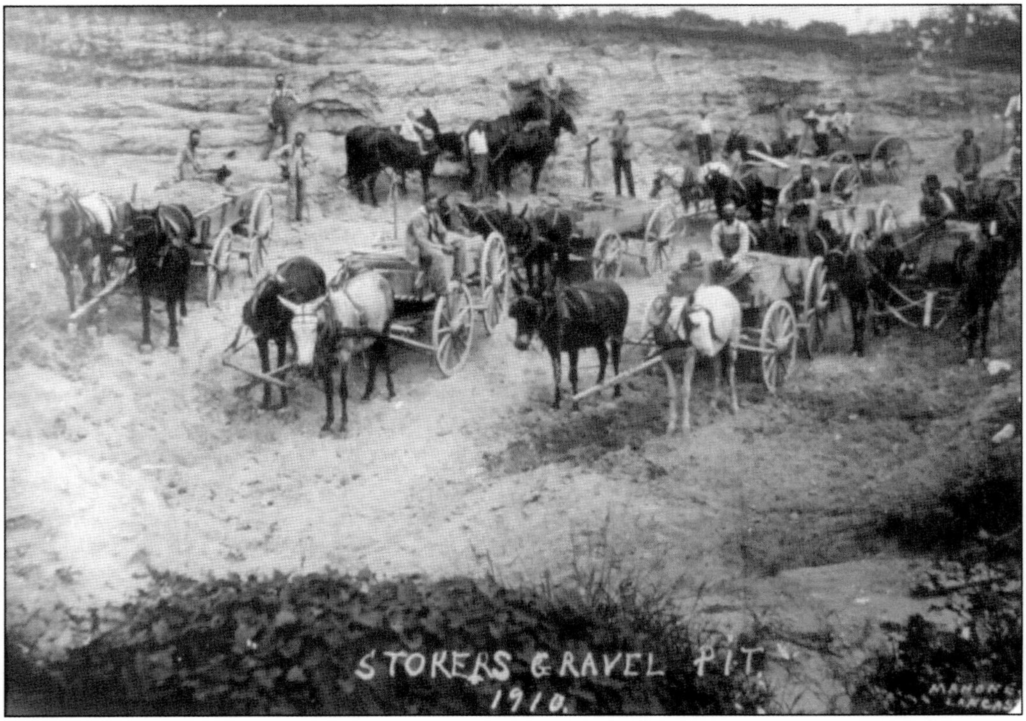

Towns are dependent on roads to connect homes and businesses. Early roads were made from gravel. There were gravel pits along the Trinity River bottom, which was less than 10 miles from Lancaster, and on nearby Ten Mile Creek. Gravel was also used for sidewalks and house foundations. Men had to dig the gravel and load it by hand.

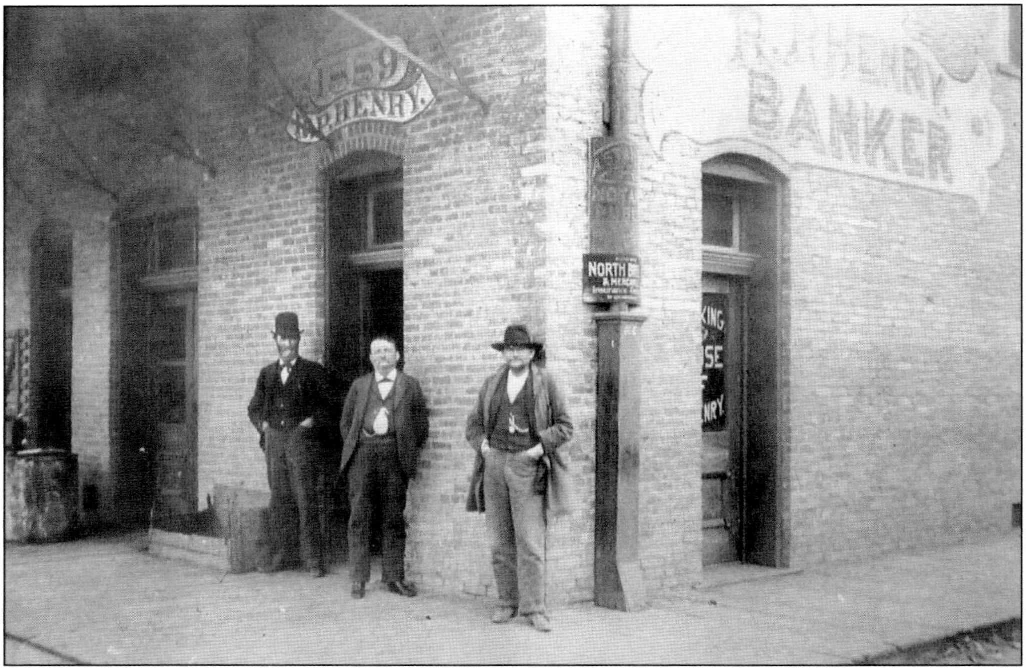

R. P. Henry opened the first official bank in 1889 on the southwest corner of Main Street and Henry Street where it stood until all private banks were forced to close in 1933. Rene Paul Henry was ambitious and eager to take advantage of his opportunities. He built his bank with money earned from other business endeavors.

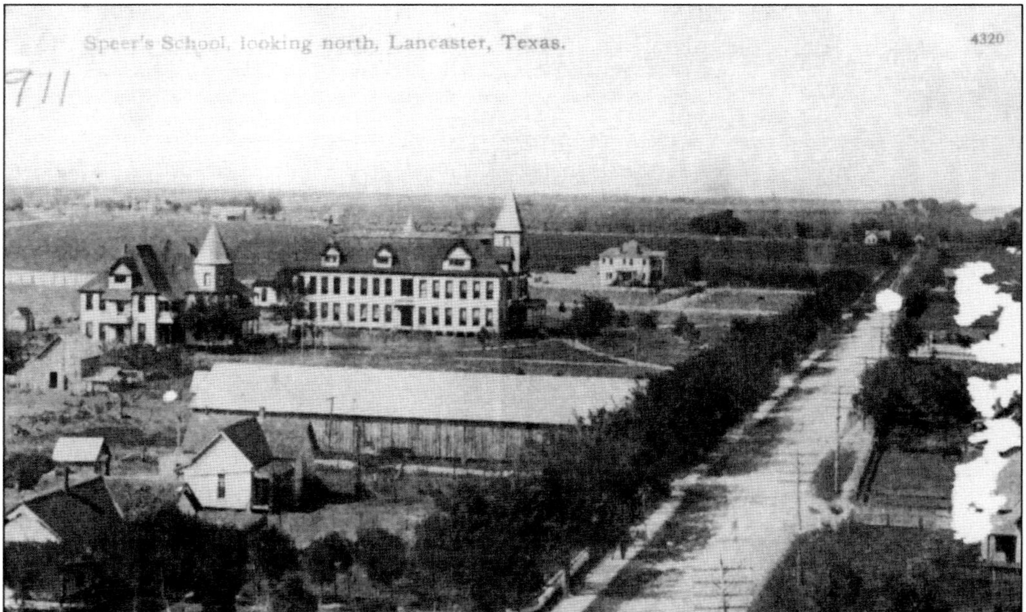

This picture, from around 1904, was made from the Lancaster water tower looking north. The house below the long building is the Roddy home on Dallas Avenue. The long building is the skating rink. The large buildings are the Randolph College campus. The F. M. Hammond home is to the left of Randolph College.

Three
FARMING, THE CORE BUSINESS

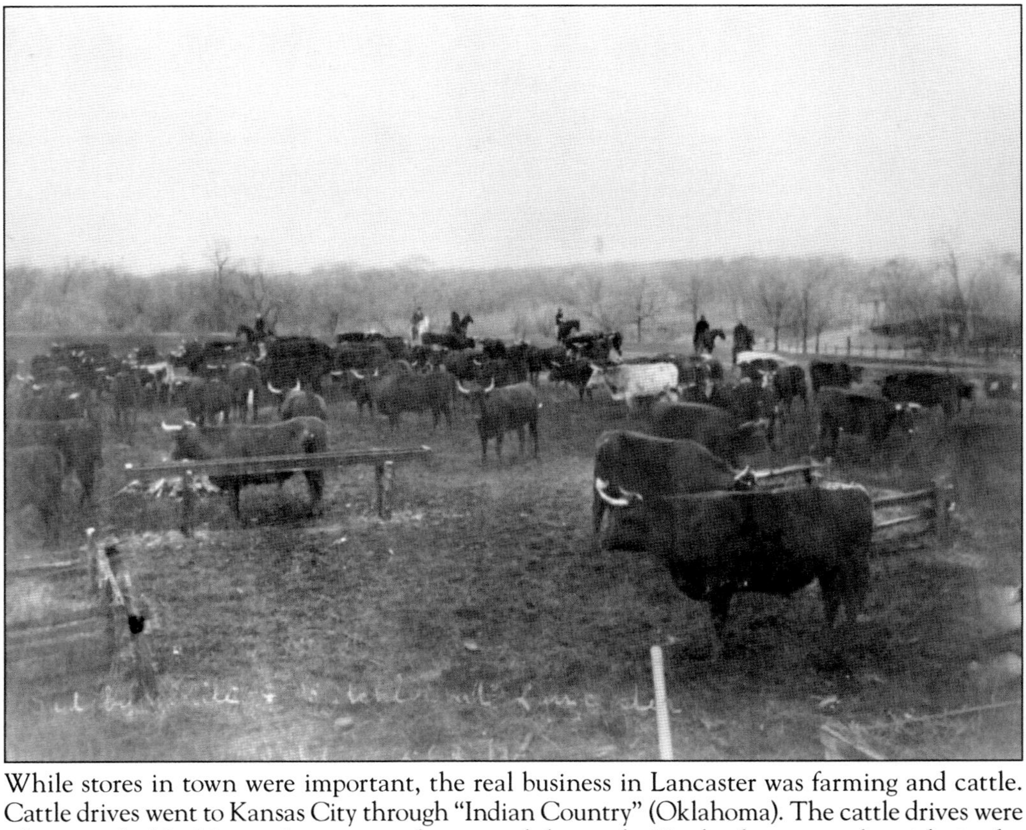

While stores in town were important, the real business in Lancaster was farming and cattle. Cattle drives went to Kansas City through "Indian Country" (Oklahoma). The cattle drives were often attacked by Native Americans who wanted the cattle. Herds often spent the night in the low spot south of the Rawlins home.

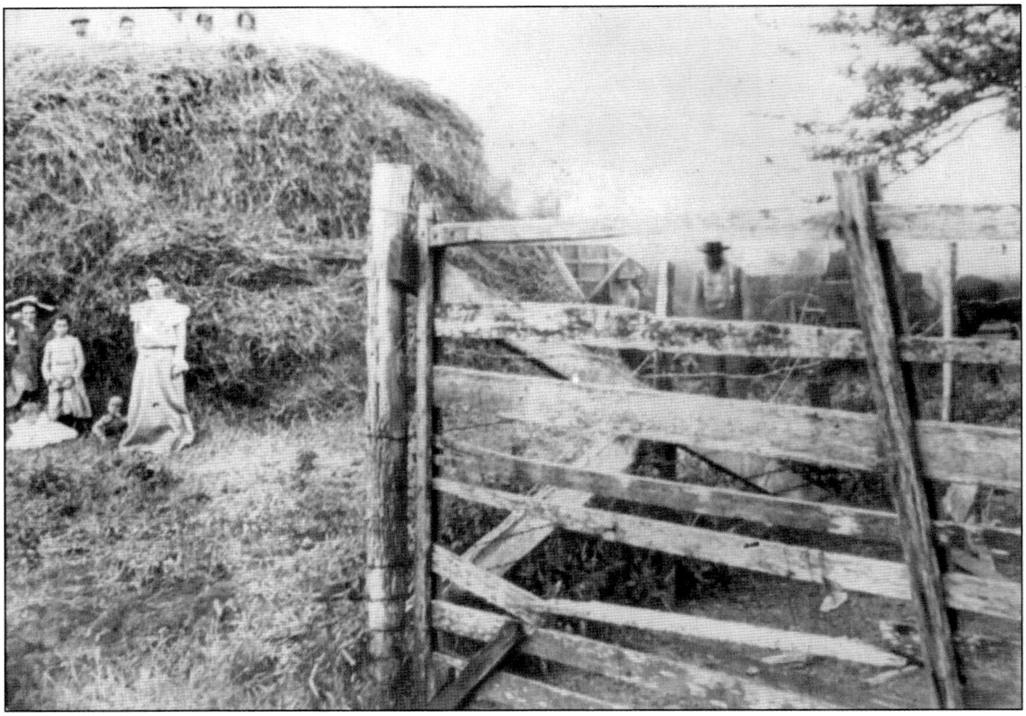

Hay balers were not invented until the 1850s. Farmers stacked their hay in big piles using pitchforks. Children loved to play in the haystacks. They could play hide-and-go-seek in the hay as well as make slides from the top to the bottom. Hay was the main feed source for the livestock during winter.

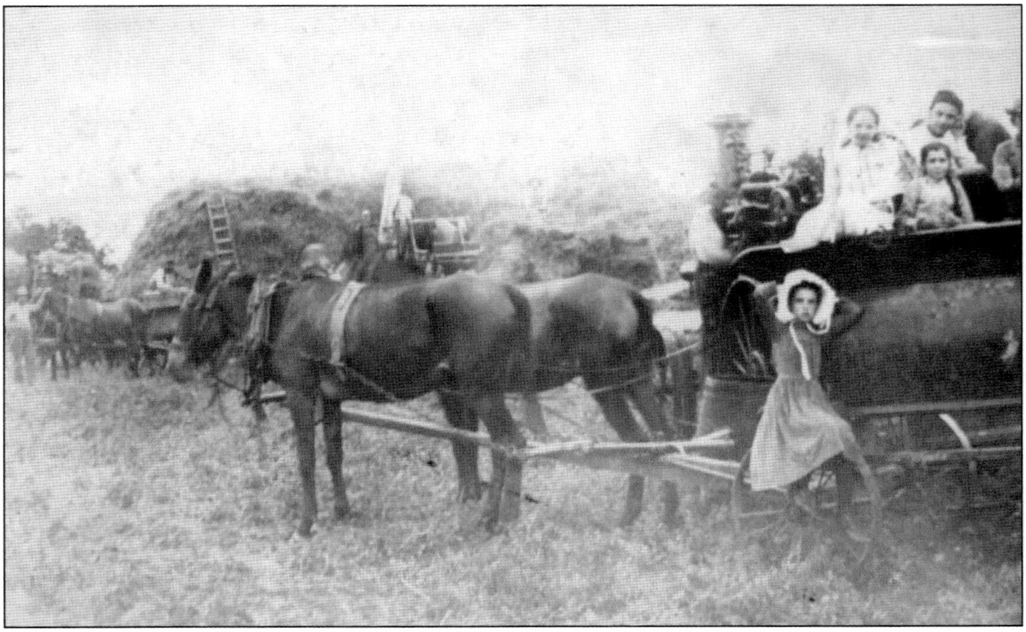

Another major resource for farmers was their children. The whole family was expected to help with the farming. Farm work was done with horse- or mule-drawn equipment during the 1850s and 1860s. Hay was an important crop for farm animals' survival. Farmers of all ages have dealt with drought, hail, freezes, and floods.

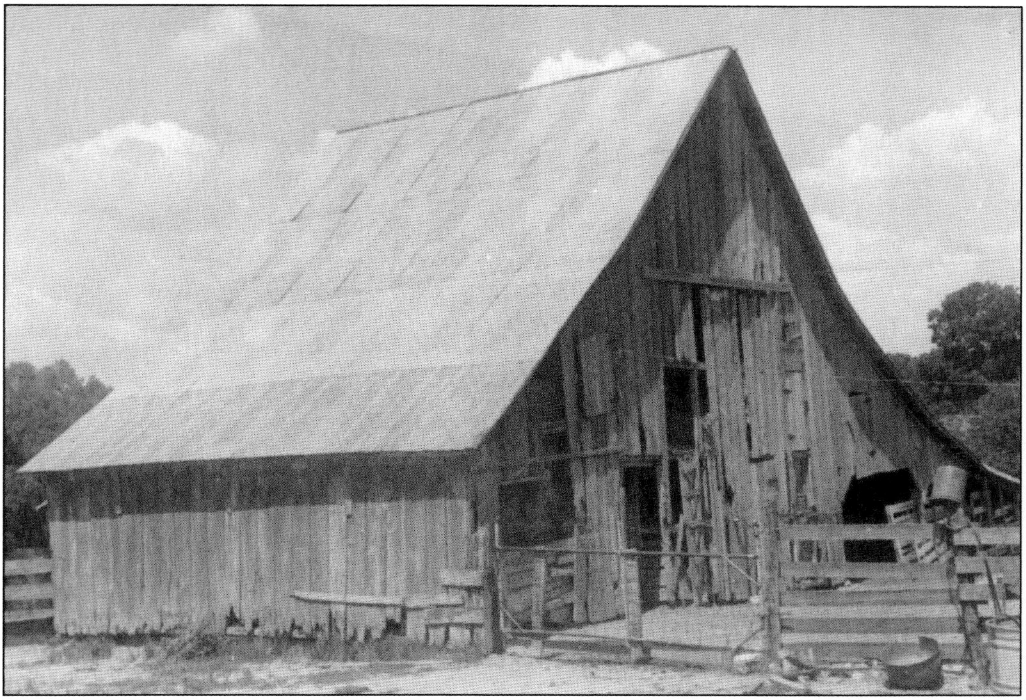

Jones Greene and Mary Ann Ellis Greene came to Lancaster from Illinois with her sister and brother-in-law, Ellen Melinda Ellis Perry and Middleton Perry, around 1844. These are the two families who brought the colt Steel Dust to Lancaster. He was led behind a wagon from Illinois to Texas. A descendant of the Greene family believes this barn was built about the time Steel Dust was on the farm. The actual photograph was made in 1971, making this barn 126 years old.

Early Texans were creative when they built barns. This barn on the Moffett Farm was built later than the barn above and shows a different style. Teams of horses or mules pulled wagons loaded with grain or hay to the second level to unload. Trap doors in the floor allowed feed to be dropped into the troughs below. (Courtesy of Carlton Moffett.)

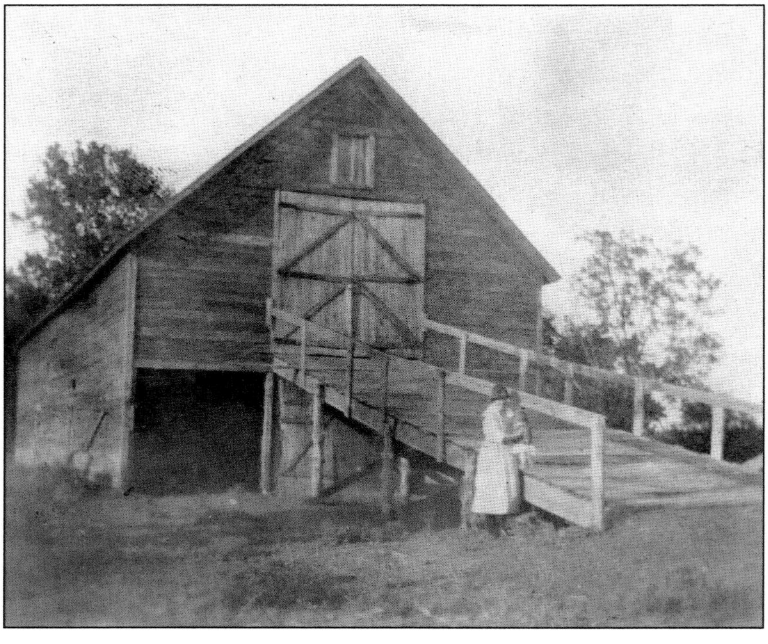

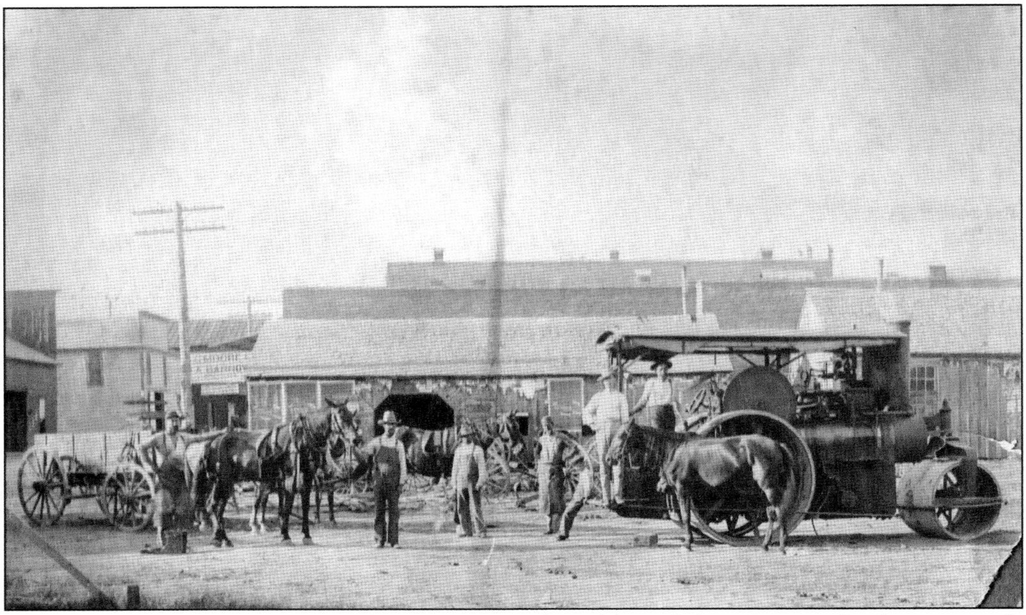

Shaping and connecting metal takes great strength and knowledge. Wagon wheels were inside a metal ring while harness and wagon connections all required welding. Other various metal objects had to be shaped by hand. Horseshoes were in great demand too. Jim Moore owned this blacksmith shop, which was essential to the citizens of Lancaster.

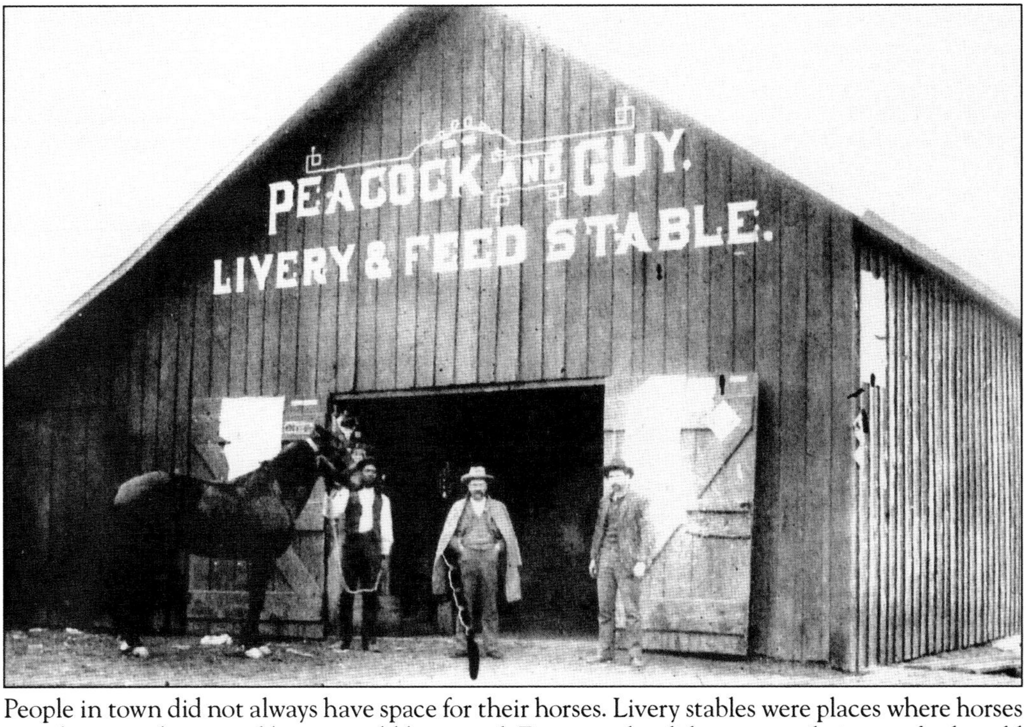

People in town did not always have space for their horses. Livery stables were places where horses were kept or a horse and buggy could be rented. Farmers who did not grow their own feed could purchase feed at the livery. Peacock and Guy Livery and Feed Stable was on the southeast corner of the square.

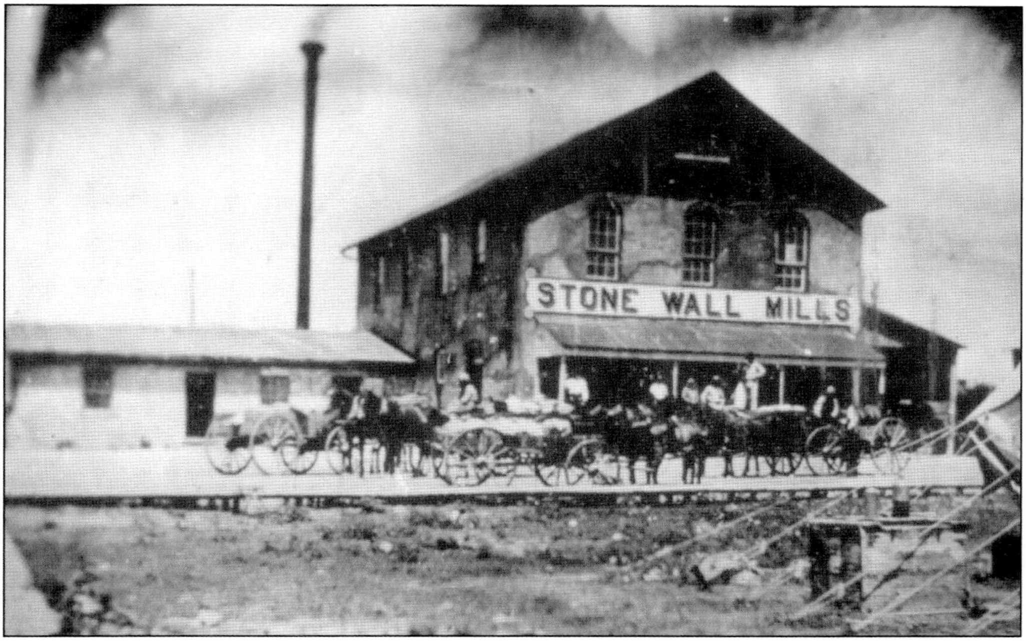

Grain grew well in the black lands around Lancaster. Samuel Keller had a grain mill early on. In 1873, W. R. Moffett and T. B. Nance built a modern steam mill in the 100 block of North Dallas Avenue that had the ability to grind 1,000 bushels of wheat in 24 hours. Lou White bought out the mill, and John Tom Ellis operated it.

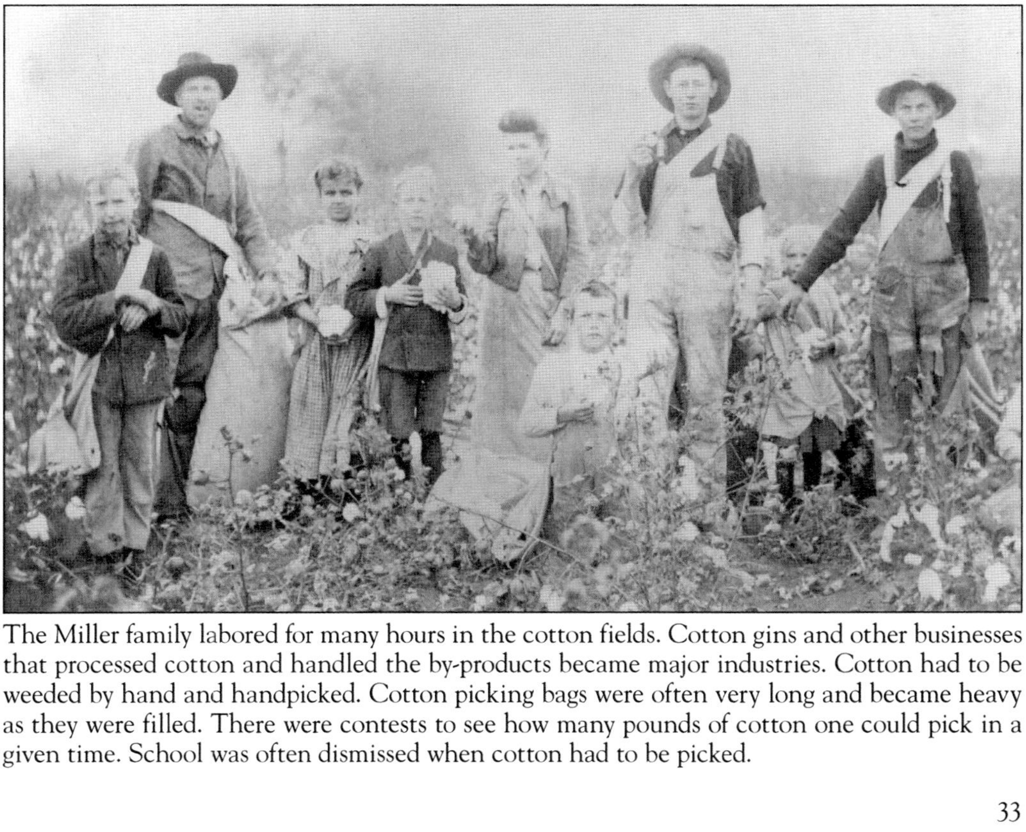
The Miller family labored for many hours in the cotton fields. Cotton gins and other businesses that processed cotton and handled the by-products became major industries. Cotton had to be weeded by hand and handpicked. Cotton picking bags were often very long and became heavy as they were filled. There were contests to see how many pounds of cotton one could pick in a given time. School was often dismissed when cotton had to be picked.

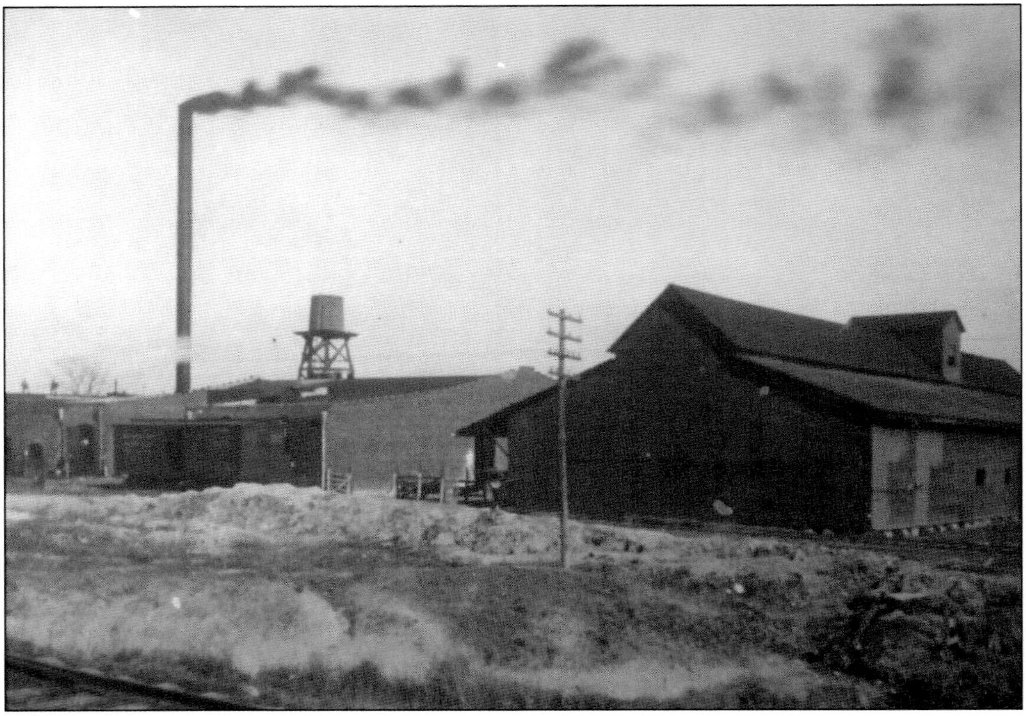

A cotton oil mill operated around 1901 east of the railroad tracks on Second Street. Since cotton was king and controlled Lancaster economy for many years, this mill was successful. The office of the Lancaster Cotton Mill was run by manager Alex Mitchell, seated below in the middle, with help from Earl Ellis and Bud Wilson, standing in the back.

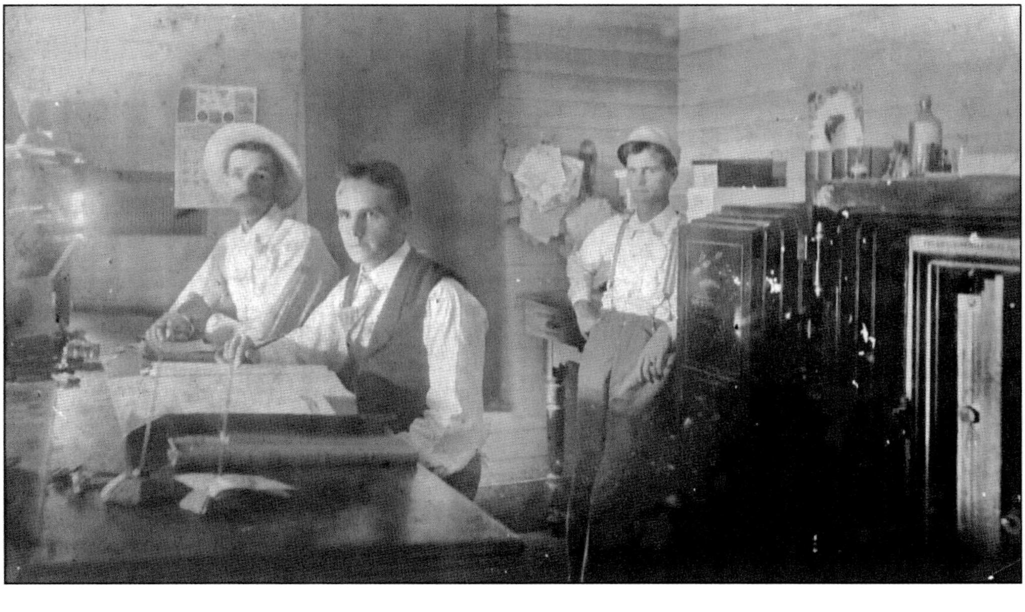

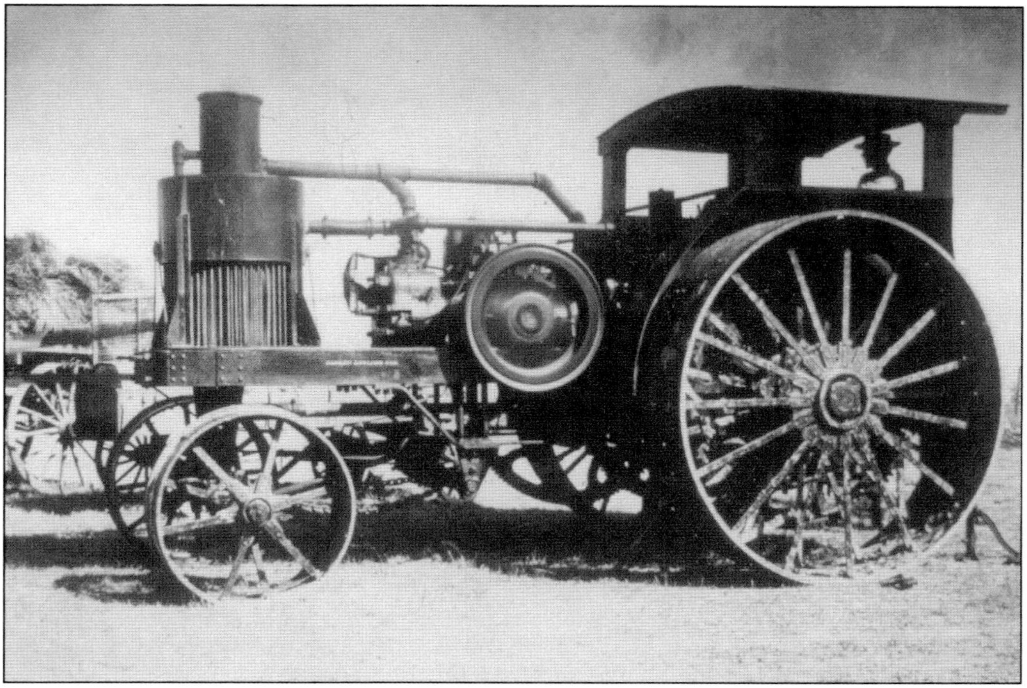

George Scott owned this steam driven tractor (above) around 1890. He lived in the Wheatland area but that area was included in Lancaster at the time. Below, on John Winniford's farm, Charlie Watts is operating the Winniford's steam tractor and thresher. This type of machinery made work easier, quicker, and more profitable.

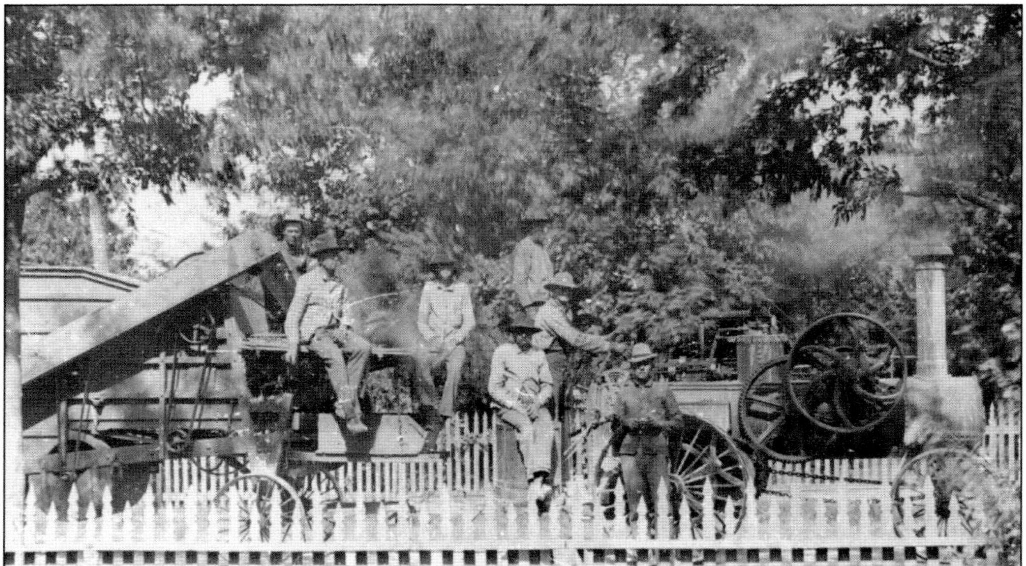

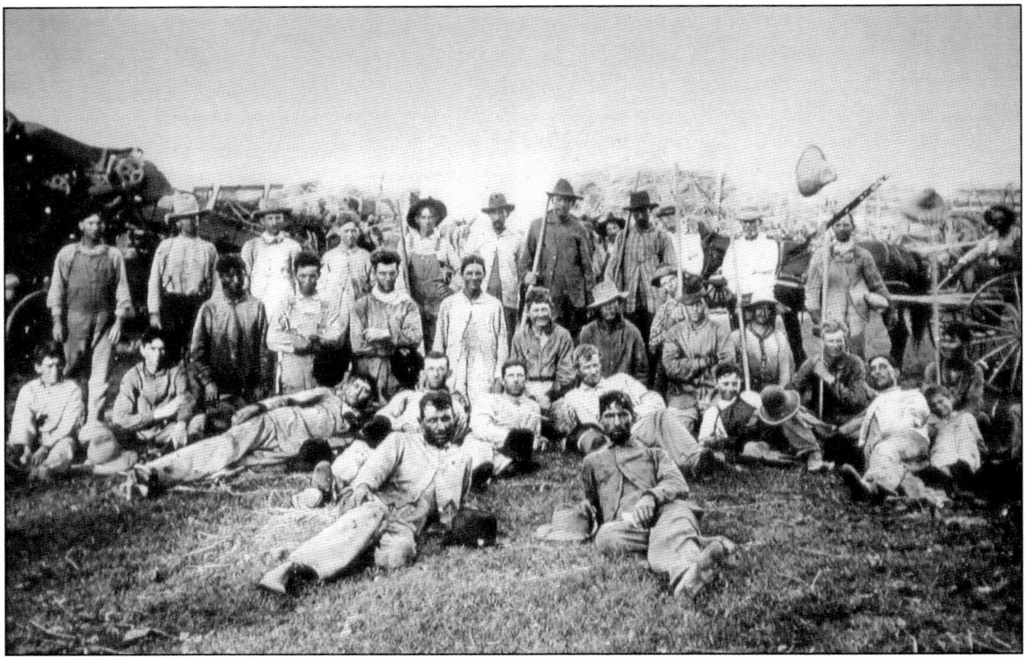

Around 1900, there were groups of men who traveled with their families to harvest crops. They had no homes of their own and accepted whatever shelter was offered. Farmers' wives fed the workers, and they received a small wage. When the crops were harvested, they traveled to another farm for work.

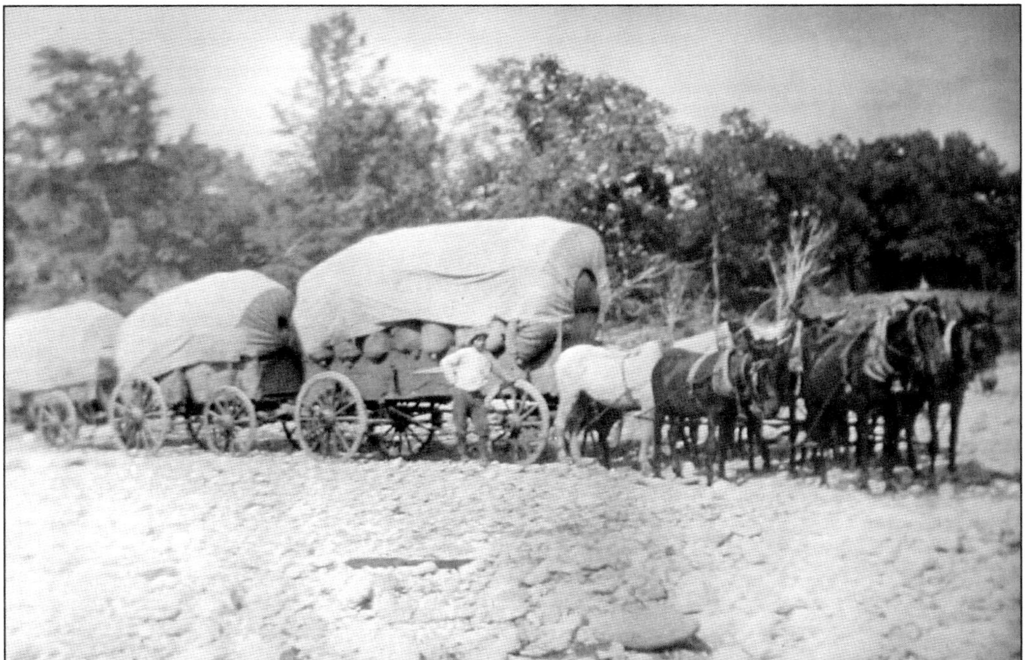

In the mid-1800s, goods from the coast or other waterways were brought to Lancaster and other cities by wagons. They exported cotton and flour that were produced in Lancaster to other buyers. Traveling the rough roads took weeks to receive orders and equally as long to sell products.

Four

Church Bells

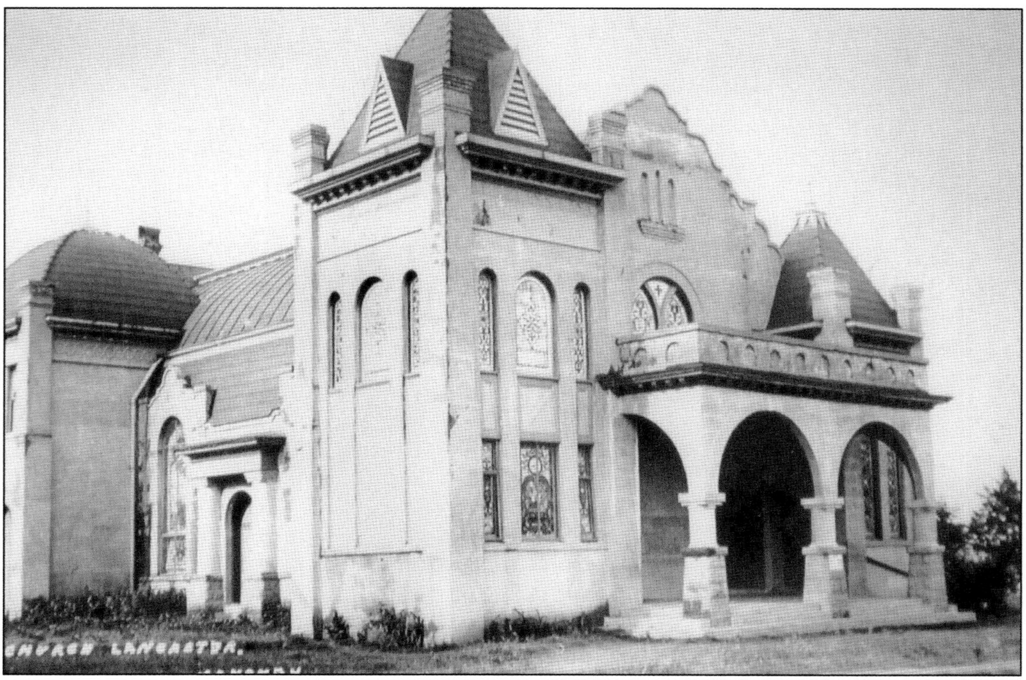

By 1901, Baptists had grown from their initial group of 14 to 1,200 members. The new building, completed in 1903, was debt free, had stained-glass windows, carpeted floor, a balcony, and a baptistery. The name was changed from Missionary Baptist to the First Baptist Church of Lancaster. (Courtesy of Mary Jane Colton.)

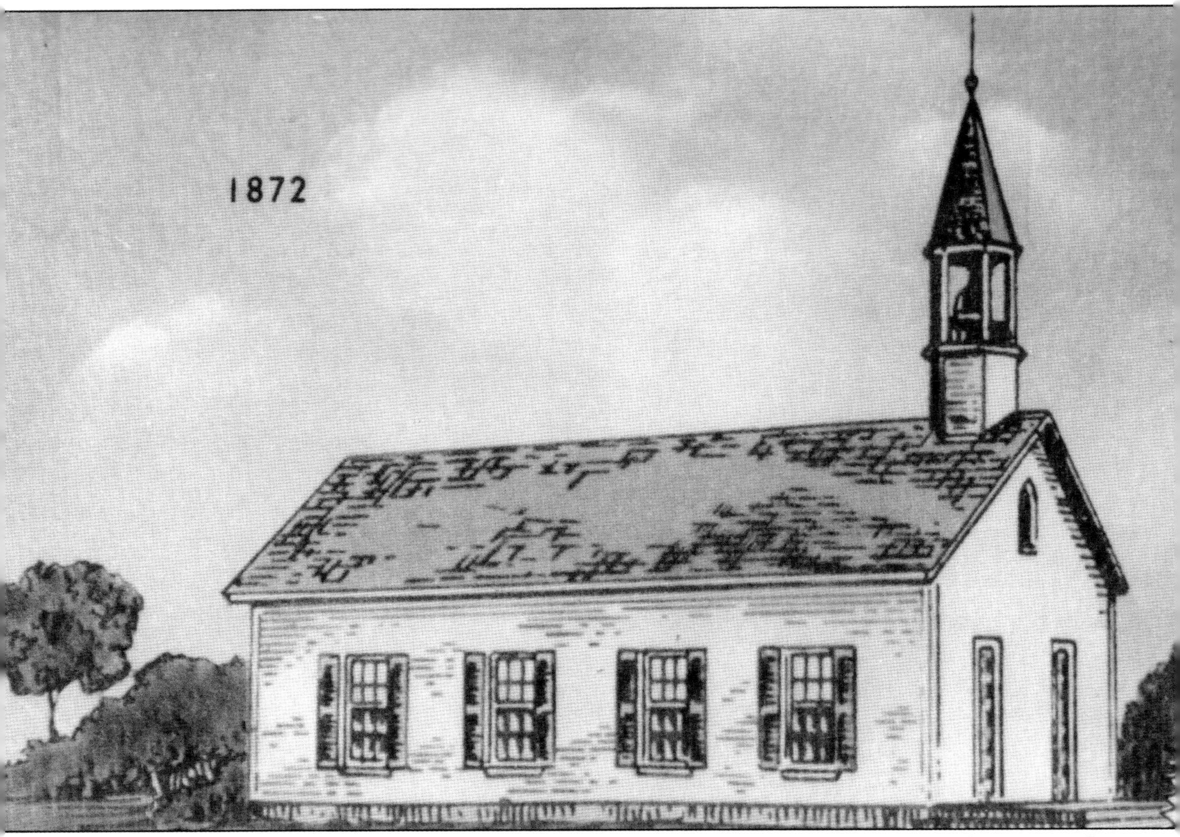

Before 1867, Baptists were unorganized and met in homes of members. Finally 14 charter members met to start the Missionary Baptist Church of Lancaster. In 1872, the group built a one-room frame building with a bell in the steeple at Second and State Streets. The original building was sold to the Black Baptist Church, but the bell from the steeple was moved to the new church.

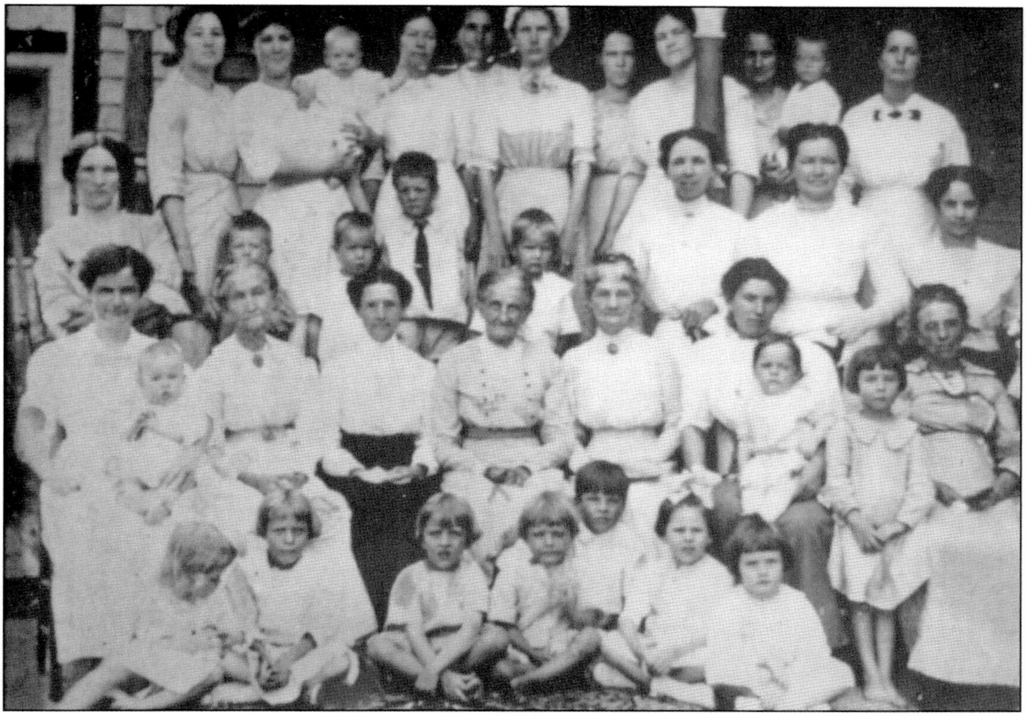

Methodist circuit riders were in Lancaster as early as 1855 holding church in the Masonic hall. In May 1868, Methodists were organized by Rev. Andrew Davis and the church became known as "Lancaster and Wesley Station." The first church was built on the west side of Hall's Branch but was sold. The funds were used to build the second church in 1886 on Cedar Street. In 1906, the church was formally named Lancaster Methodist Church.

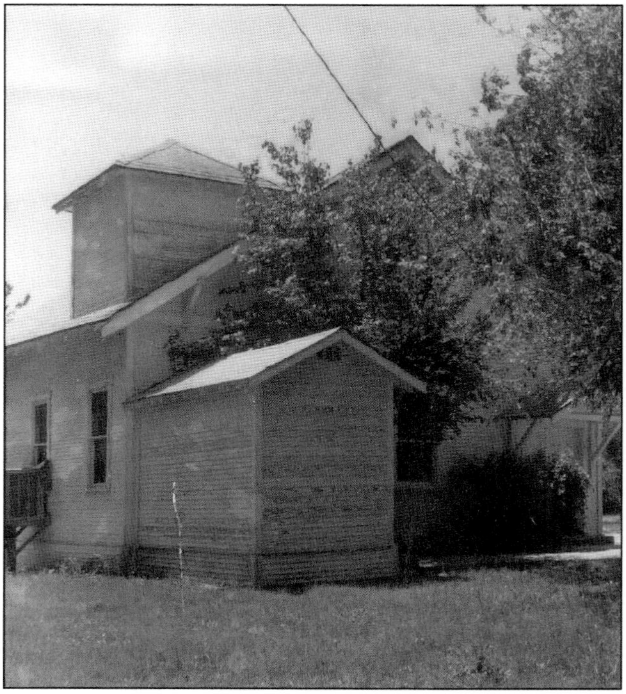

In the 1890s, Porter's Chapel United Methodist Church was organized in the home of the Porter family. This early church was located north of Third Street. Soon after it was built, Samuel Keller located his mill just east of the church building. Porter's Chapel later became Porter's Chapel Methodist Episcopal Church and was a cornerstone of the African American community in the 1920s.

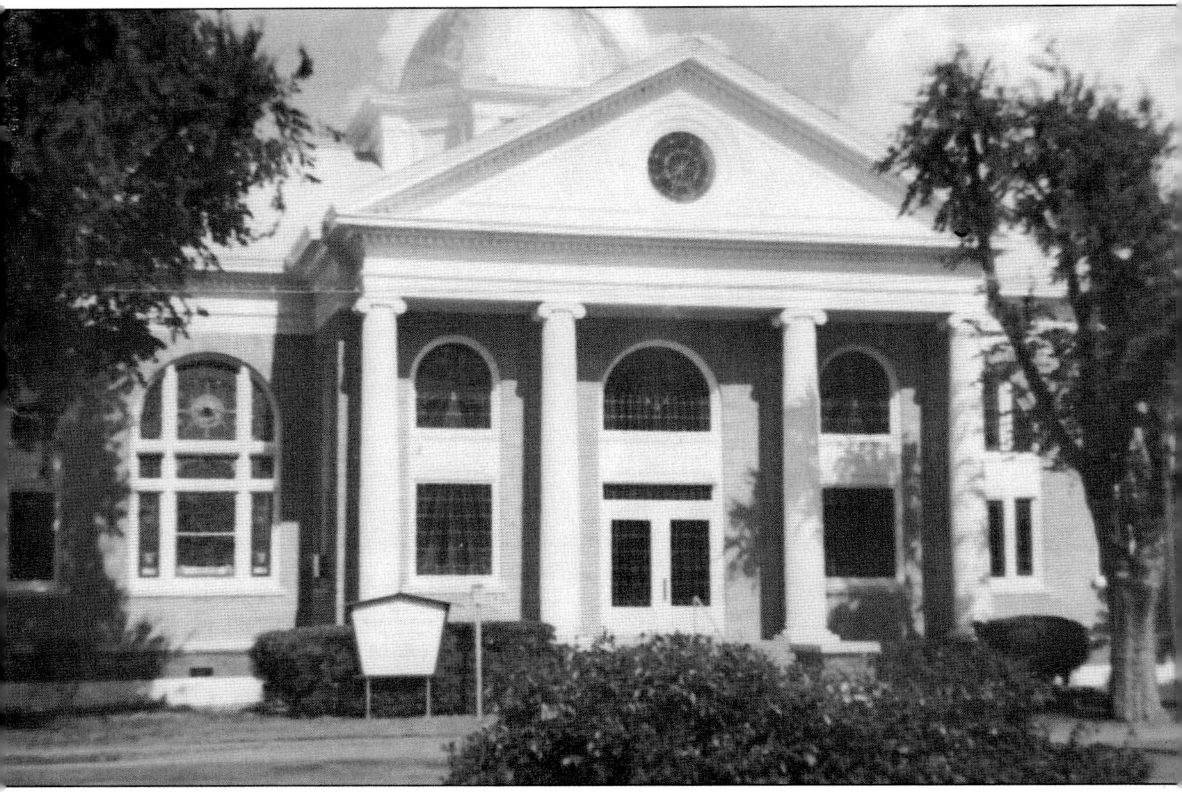

The First Presbyterian Church of Lancaster was organized on July 26, 1856, by Rev. Michael Dickson of Milford Central Presbytery. It was the second Presbyterian Church in Dallas County and was organized in the workshop of John Green, a cabinetmaker and primitive Baptist preacher. The charter members were Dr. H. J. and Anna Moffett, W. R. and Ellenore Moffett, Mr. and Mrs. John Harris, R. M. Harris, Emily Guy, and Elizabeth Grove. They put up their first building in 1884, and by 1906, they had 140 members. In 1912, their present church building was begun. (Courtesy of Carolyn Fulton.)

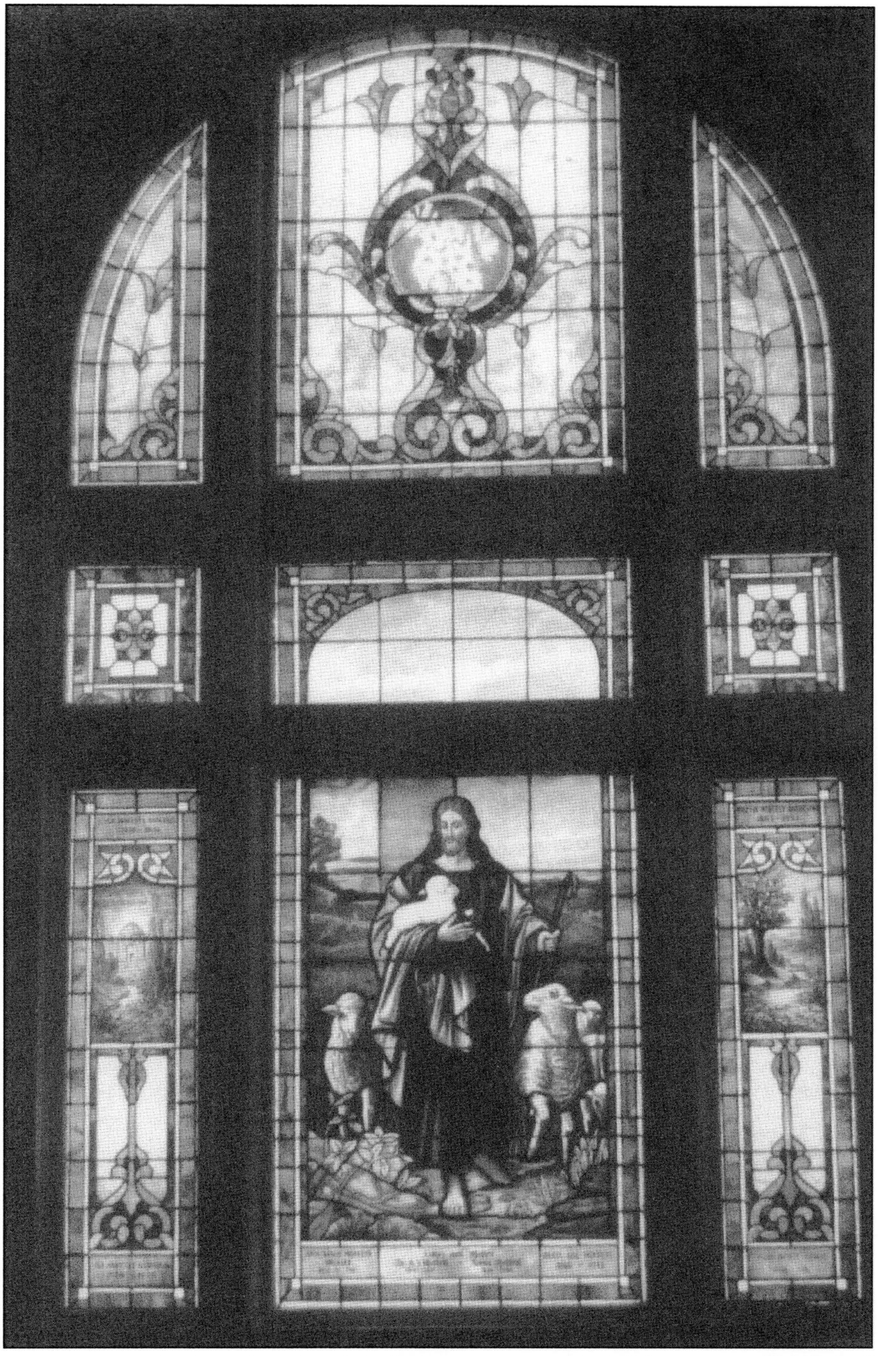

The first white-frame Presbyterian church building was erected in 1884 at a cost of $2,000. The land on which the church still stands was part of a 430-acre land grant from the State of Texas, given on May 3, 1855, to the heirs of Roderick Rawlins. The Ladies Aide Society raised the money for the church by hosting a fair and supper. The Presbyterian Church has gorgeous stained-glass windows given to the glory of God in memory of pioneer church members and former ministers by their families and friends. One of the early pastors was Dr. S. Addison McElroy, who oversaw the razing of the old wooden church and the building of the current one. (Courtesy of Carolyn Fulton.)

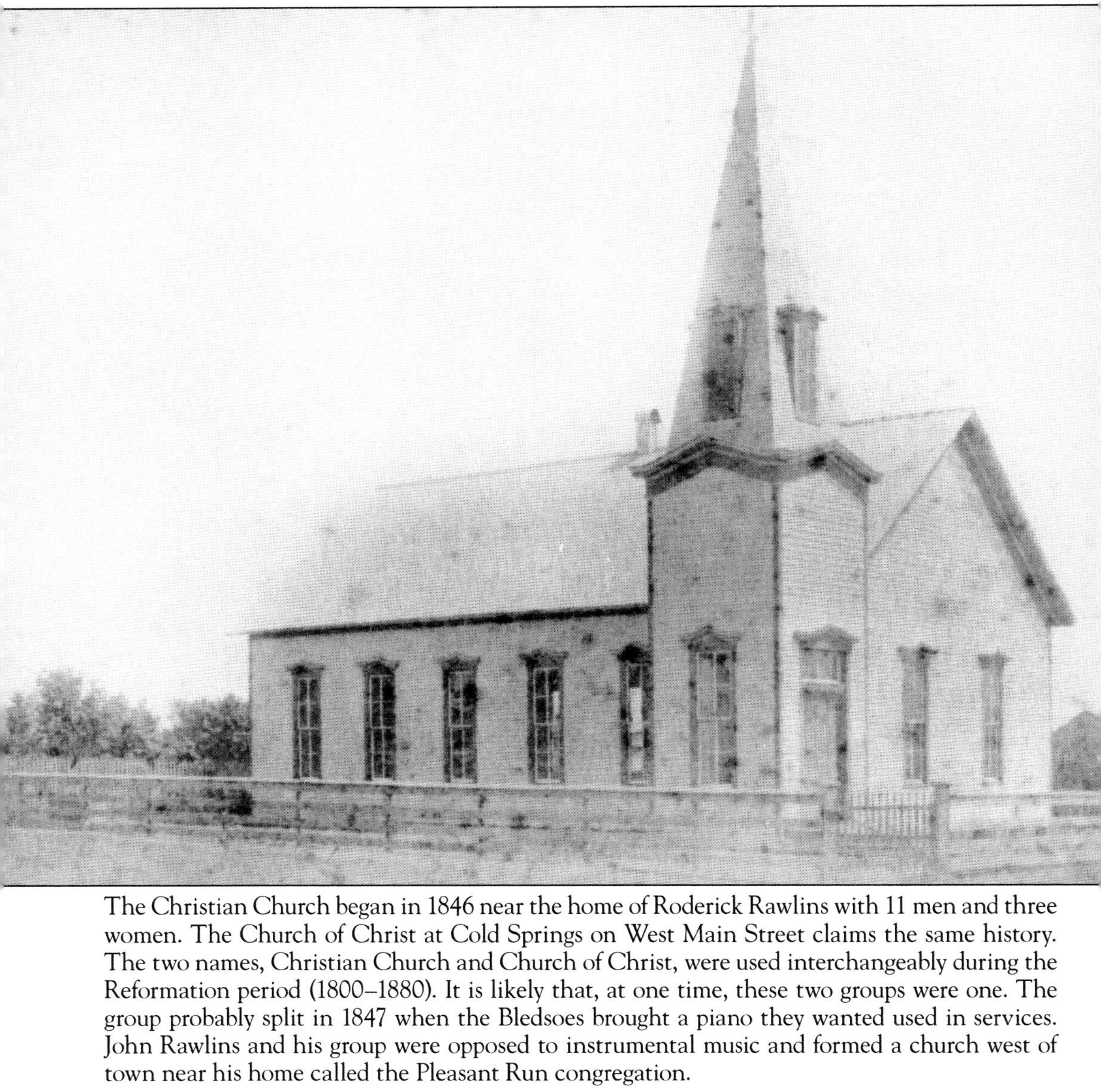

The Christian Church began in 1846 near the home of Roderick Rawlins with 11 men and three women. The Church of Christ at Cold Springs on West Main Street claims the same history. The two names, Christian Church and Church of Christ, were used interchangeably during the Reformation period (1800–1880). It is likely that, at one time, these two groups were one. The group probably split in 1847 when the Bledsoes brought a piano they wanted used in services. John Rawlins and his group were opposed to instrumental music and formed a church west of town near his home called the Pleasant Run congregation.

Five
HOME SWEET HOME

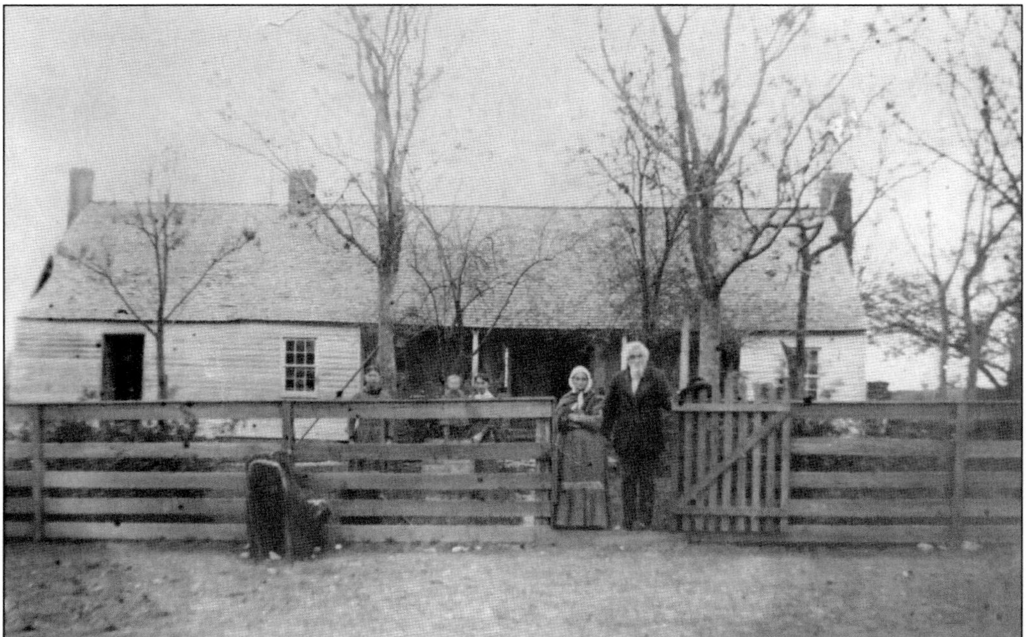

Thomas McKee and Mary Witt Ellis came in 1845 and completed this dogtrot cabin in 1846. It was the first clapboard house in Texas. From left to right are Emeline Ellis Taylor (1834–1929); Sade Cook, who was the housekeeper, holding her daughter Punch; Mary Witt Ellis (1803–1889); and Thomas McKee Ellis (1799–1890).

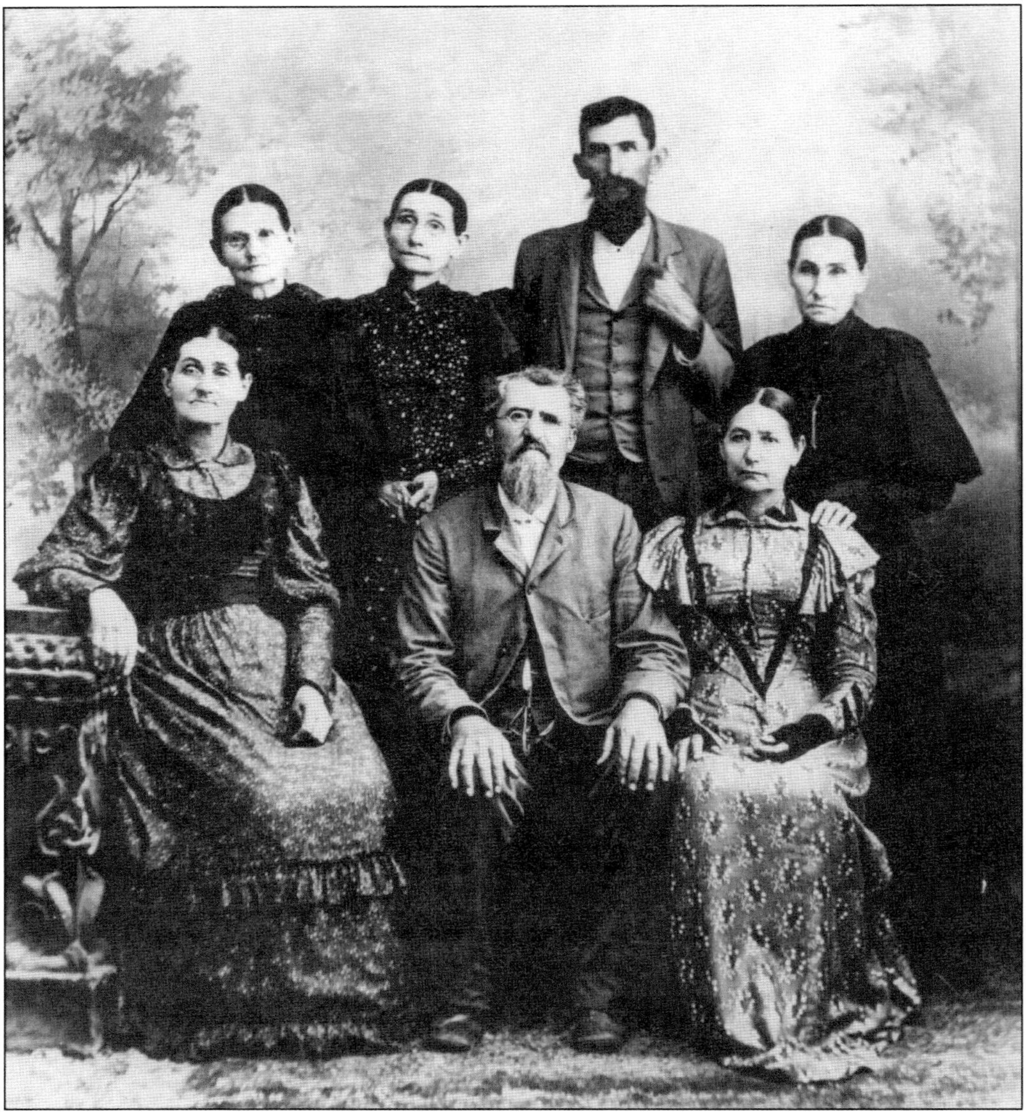

The Thomas McKee Ellis family arrived in Lancaster around 1845. Two of their children were married and already in Lancaster. They brought with them eight unmarried children. Most of these children married other settlers and stayed in Lancaster. Seven of their 11 children are shown here. From left to right are (seated) "Ann" Martha Angeline Smith Ramby, 1832–1920 (Mrs. Patrick Smith then Mrs. Tom Ramby); John Thomas Ellis, 1842–1929 (married Frances Stewart); and Harriet Emeline Taylor, 1834–1929 (Mrs. Calvin Thompson Taylor); (standing) Mary Greene, 1826–1916 (Mrs. Jones Greene); Lou F. White, 1844–1936 (Mrs. William Love White); James Henry Ellis, 1842-1929 (married Mary Elizabeth Rawlins); and "Carrie" Caroline Arilla Stevens (Mrs. William Shelton, Mrs. Alvin Bayless, Mrs. J. W. Stevens). For many years, early settlers could claim to be related to nearly everyone in Lancaster either by blood or through marriage.

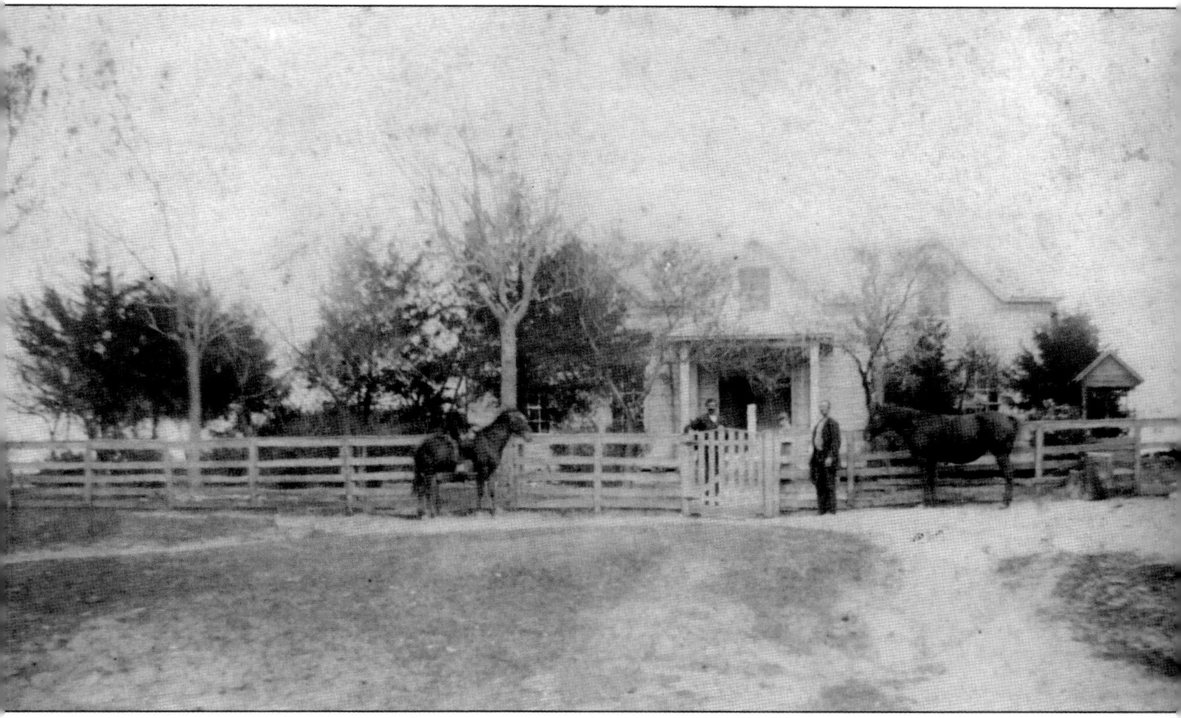

The son of elder Roderick Rawlins (1776–1848), Capt. R. A. Rawlins's home was started in 1857 with wood from trees along Ten Mile Creek. The siding and flooring came from a sawmill on the Trinity River that was 6 miles away. It had two main rooms, each 20 feet by 22 feet; one door to the south; one door to the north; four windows in the downstairs; and two windows upstairs. There was a porch on the south side and a tall chimney facing the State Highway-Texas 342. A lean-to on the east side had two rooms used for the kitchen and a spare bedroom. When R. A. Rawlins returned from the Civil War in 1865, his house was in shambles. He began to rebuild, using what was left and other available lumber. He completed the house in 1870. It is stilled owned by the Rawlins family today.

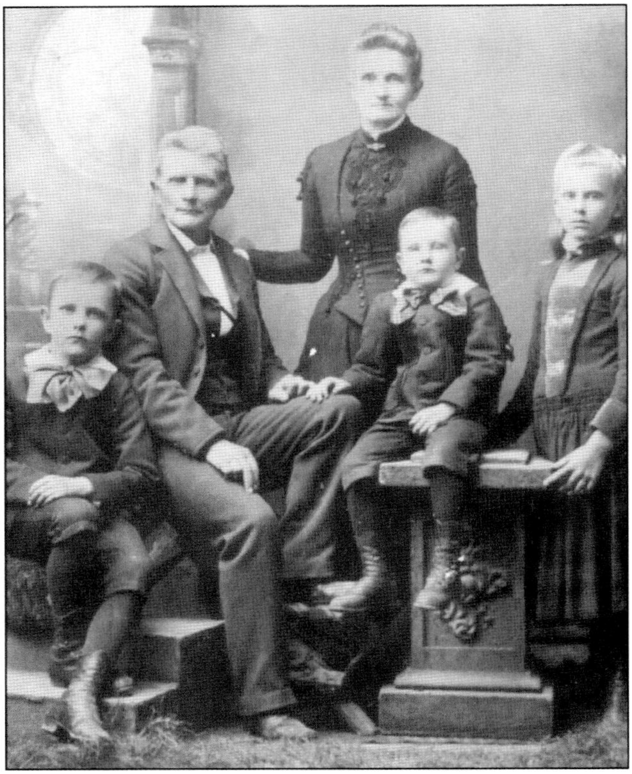

Francis Marion White (1828–1900) came to Lancaster in 1851 from White County, Tennessee. His first wife was Martha J. Gray, whom he married in 1853, and after her death in 1867, he married Mattie Trigg. He had four children with each wife. From left to right are Forrest White (1879–1902), F. M. White, Mattie Trigg White (1845–1920), Lester (b. 1883), and Maude White Rawlins (b. 1878). F. M. White taught school in the area around 1850, farmed for a while, opened a general merchandise store, and then returned to farming. His 1870 home was just two rooms. As business made money, he made the house bigger. By 1896, he added the second story. The house has had several owners, each having made some changes in the house, but it still stands on South Dallas Avenue.

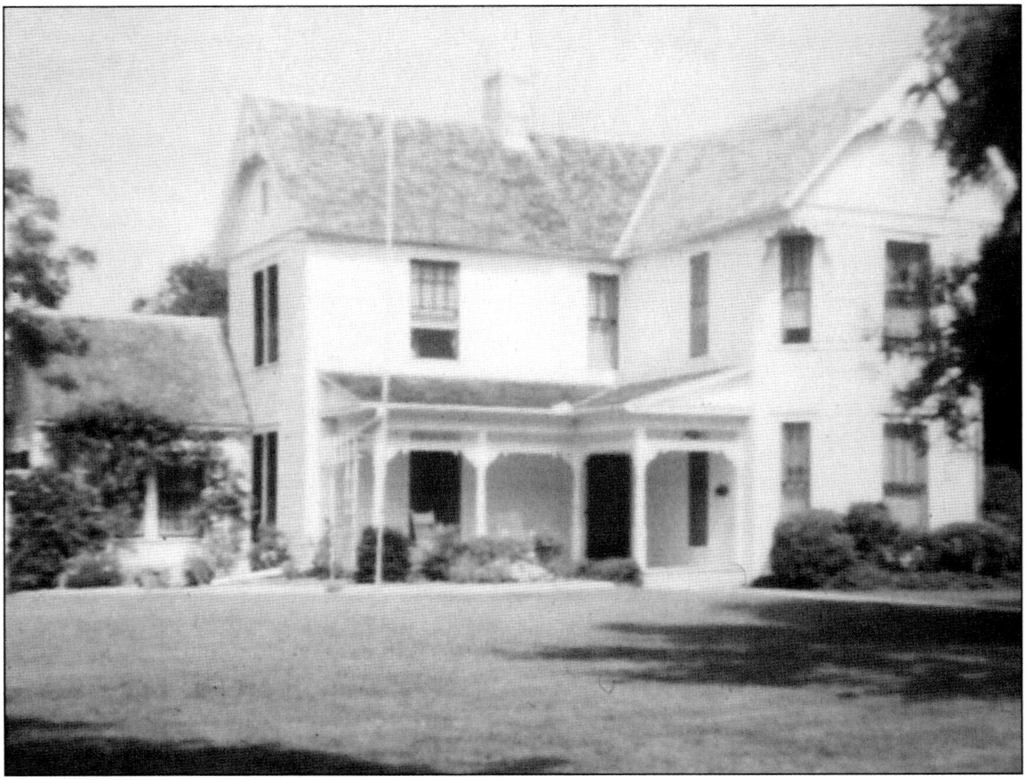

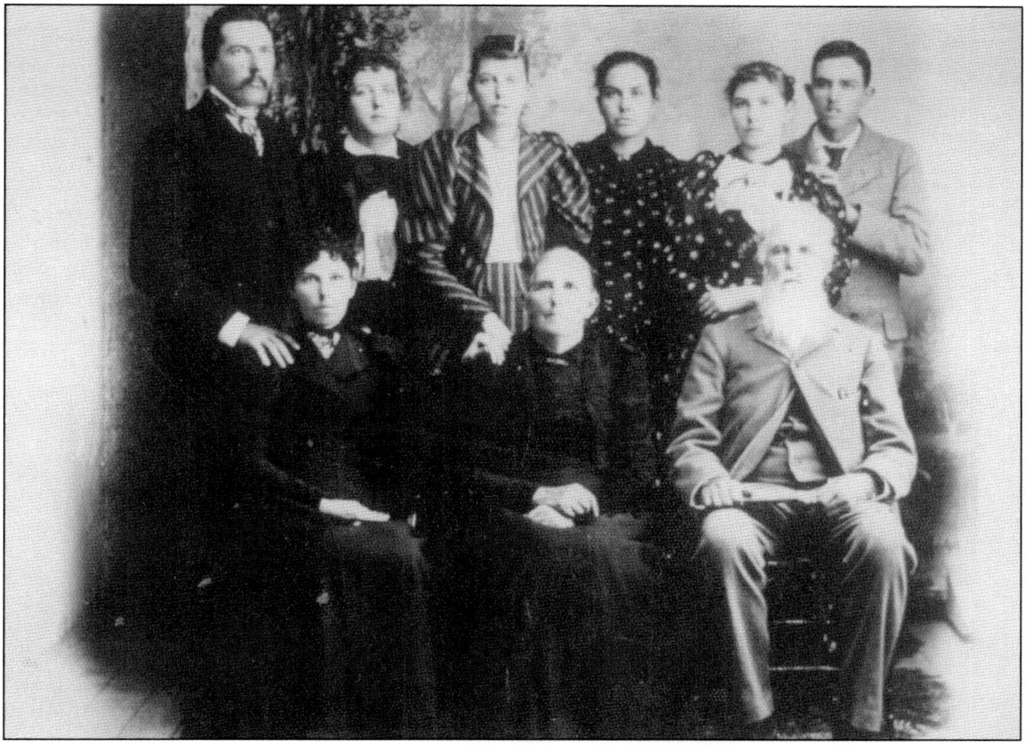

Thomas King Bernard (1825–1905) came to Tarrant County in 1847 from Adams County, Illinois. He was a saddle maker and farmer. His first wife was Mary Caroline Rawlins; he later married Mary Caroline Luck in 1862. The family are, from left to right, (seated) "Mollie" Mary Virginia Bernard Counts (b. 1863), Mary Caroline Luck Bernard, and Thomas King Bernard; (standing) Dr. John Bernard (b. 1865, doctor in DeSoto, Texas), Janette Bernard Cummings (b. 1866, Mrs. John Cummings), Eva Mondena Pogue (b. 1878, Mrs. Fred Pogue), Lucy Francis Bernard Bumpas (b. 1868, Mrs. Ira Bumpas), Celeste May Burns, (b. 1876, Mrs. Will Burns), and Jessie Virgil Bernard (b. 1864, DeSoto druggist until 1900).

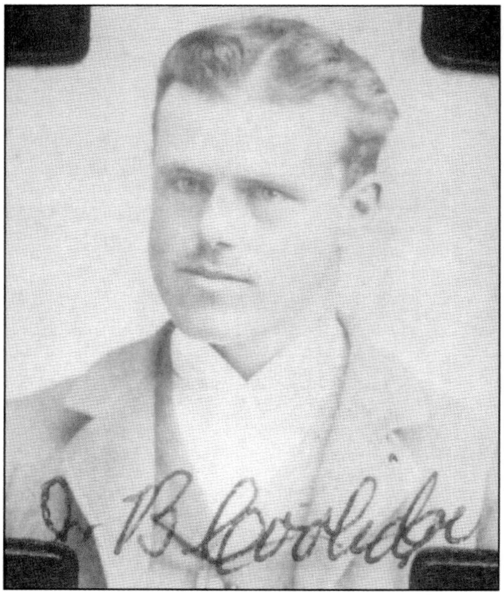

Joel Bigelow Coolidge was born in 1821 to Aaron Coolidge and Polly Bigelow. Joel's family was well known in Massachusetts. His grandfather Joseph Coolidge was the only person killed at the Battle of Lexington in 1775. His grandmother was related to John Adams. He married Mary White in 1859. She was the sister to William Love White and F. M. White of Lancaster.

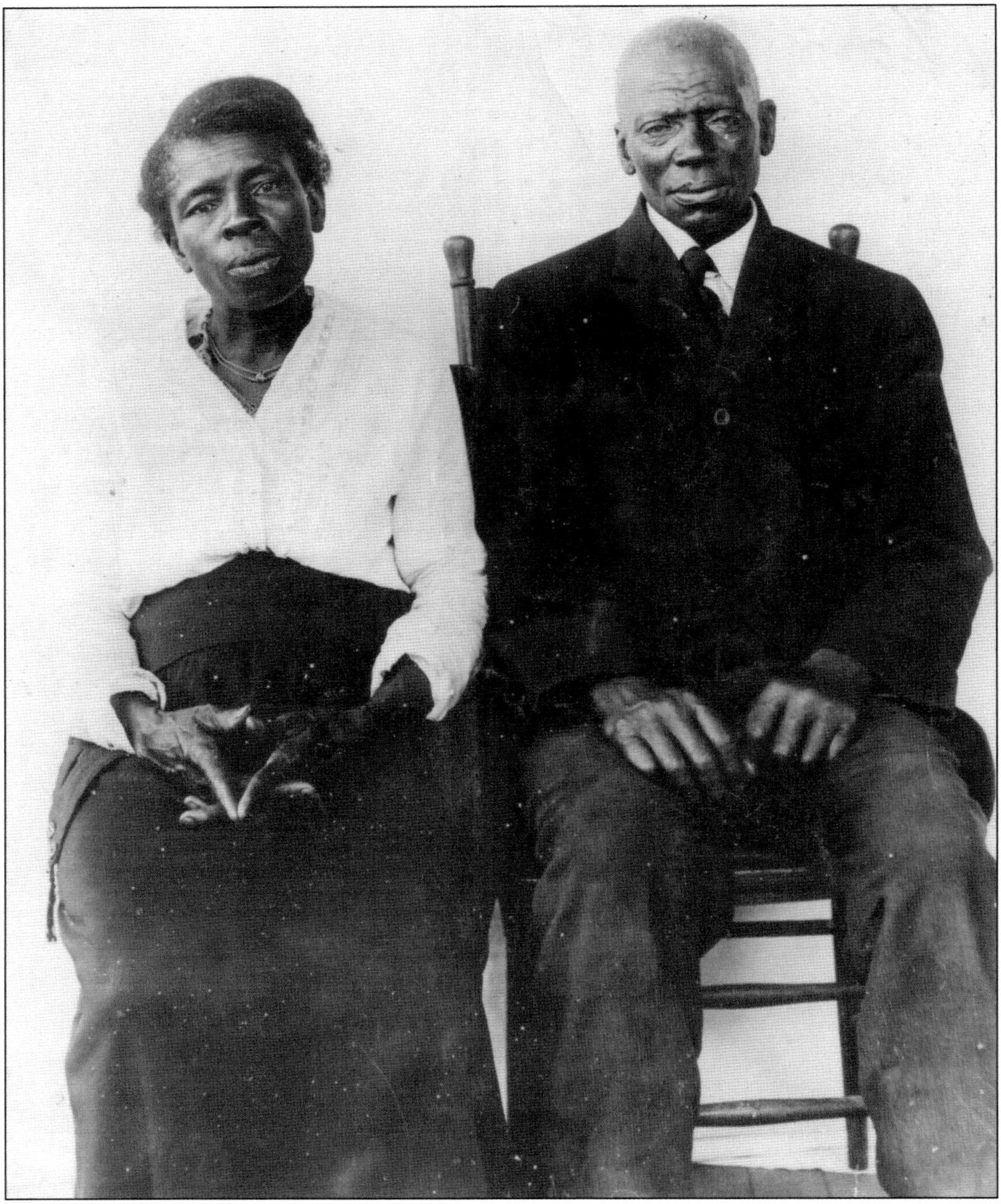

According to history books, Tom McKnight rode Steel Dust in the famous race with Mammoth in McKinney, Texas. Tom Ellis was to ride the horse but his staunch Baptist mother would not allow him. People from many places came to McKinney for the famous race. Ladies got hotel rooms, and men slept where they could find a place. Steel Dust won the race in McKinney. After the race, Lancaster citizens were full of joy while many empty pockets were found in McKinney. Steel Dust was famous for his quarter-mile races and is known as the father of the Quarter Horse breed. Much more can be found about him in history books and in the Quarter Horse Museum in Amarillo, Texas. However, it is unknown how or when Aaron McKnight, father of Tom, arrived in Texas.

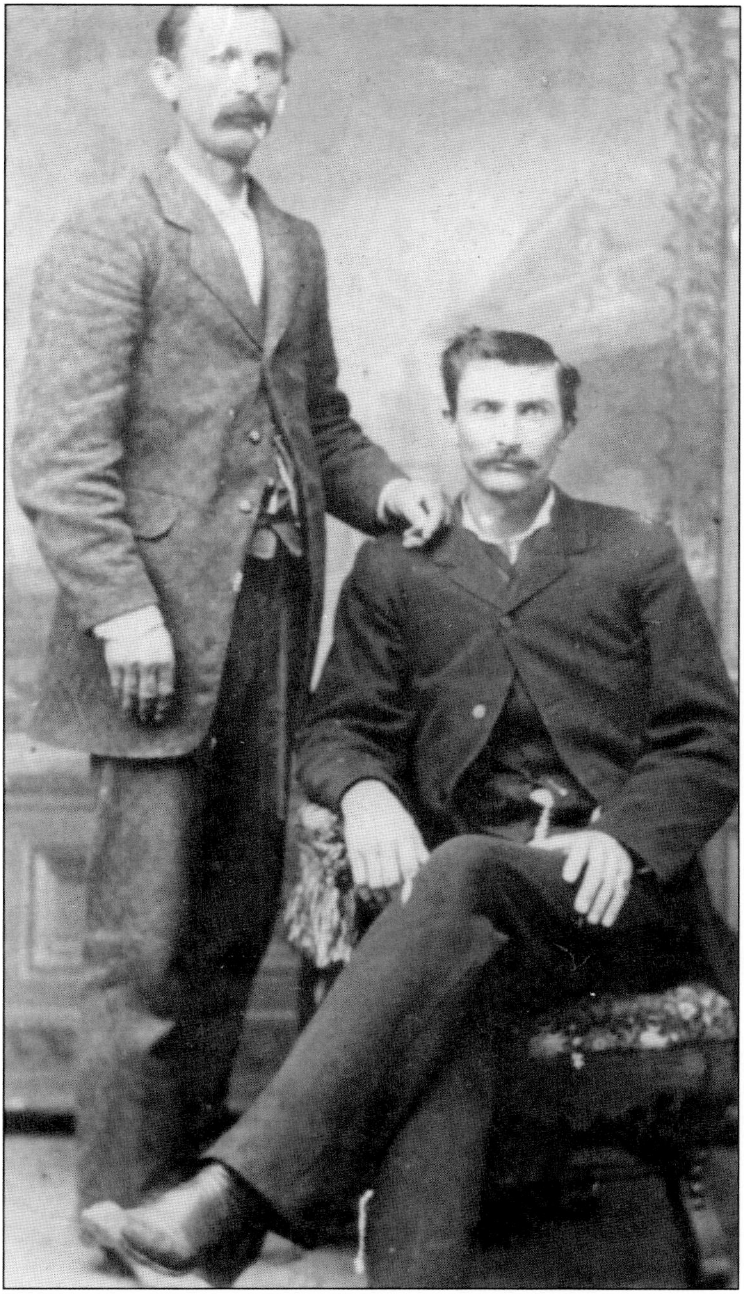

Pat Garrett, son of Col. John L. Garrett, came to Lancaster from Alabama in January 1869 at the age of 18. He is remembered as a gentleman and stood a soaring 6 feet, 4 inches tall. He worked for James B. Lowrey and became friends with Lowrey's son, Dudley. He is seated here with his friend, Dudley. Pat spent much of his spare time at the M. M. Miller Jr.'s store in Pleasant Run, Texas. He also courted Ida Hunter Lowrey, daughter of his boss, J. B. Lowrey. Everybody thought they would marry but Garrett left in 1876 when the object of his affections spurned his advances. Pat Garret ended up in New Mexico as the sheriff and is remembered by many as the man who killed "Billy the Kid." What would have happened to him if Ida had accepted his proposal?

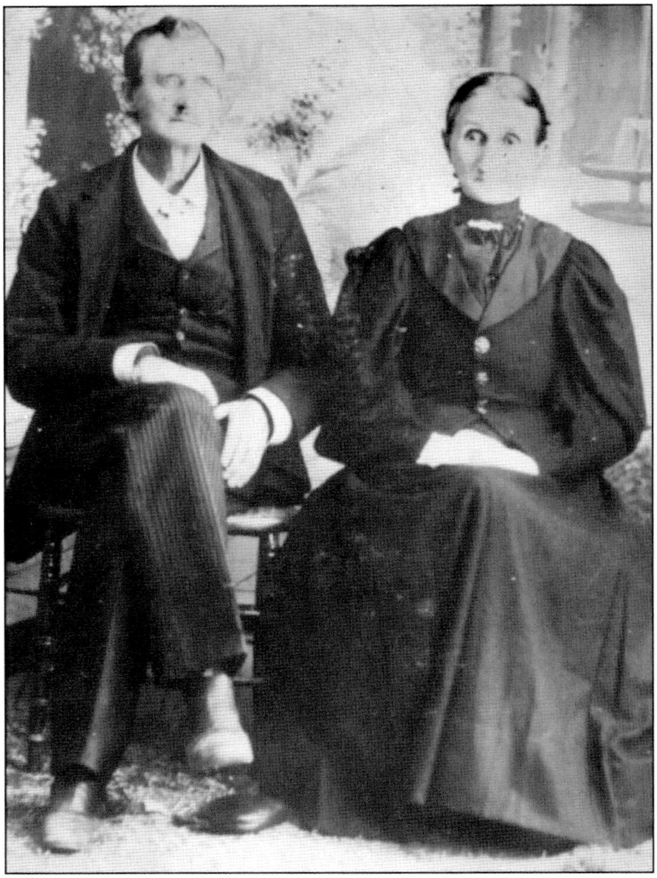

James B. Lowrey (1823–1906) and his wife, Elizabeth Hunter Lowrey, came from Sparta, Tennessee, to Texas in 1859. They had five children: Seth Carrick (b. 1848), Dudley, Nicholas Oldham (b. 1851), Henrietta, and Ida Hunter (b. 1846). He was a farmer and during the Civil War carried mail from Dallas to Waco by horseback. He later began to raise mules and on one of his drives became friends with future lawman Pat Garrett. He opened a mercantile business near the dry area of South Dallas County and sold liquor. The place was called the Cuckle Burr Patch. The Lowrey house shown below is that of Seth Lowrey. It was located on East Pleasant Run.

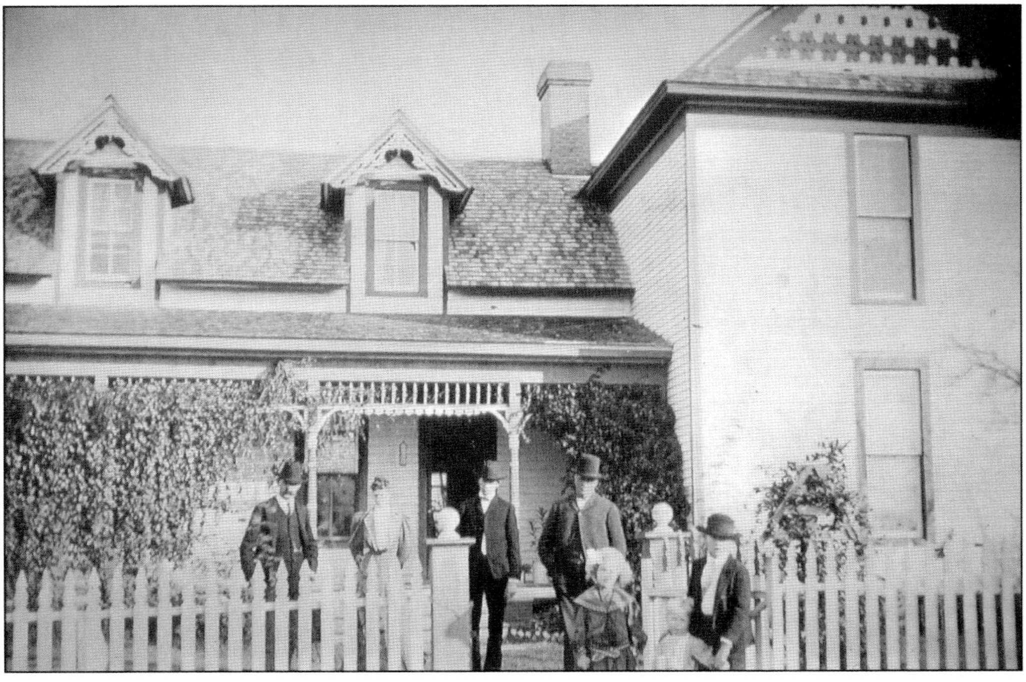

Mary Lou Creasy (b. 1902) was the daughter of Tommy Creasy and Asia Gillette and had one sibling, Ollie Creasy (b. 1906). She married James Wright. Mary Lou Creasy Wright worked for the schools for many years. Her stylish attire was typical of what the women of the day wore on Sundays.

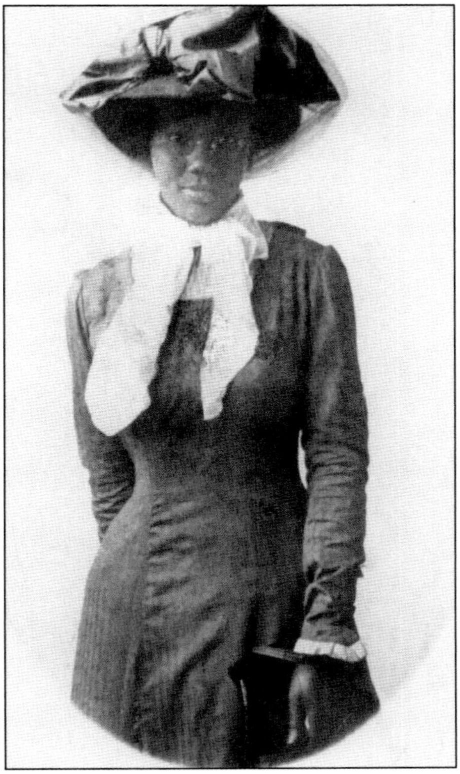

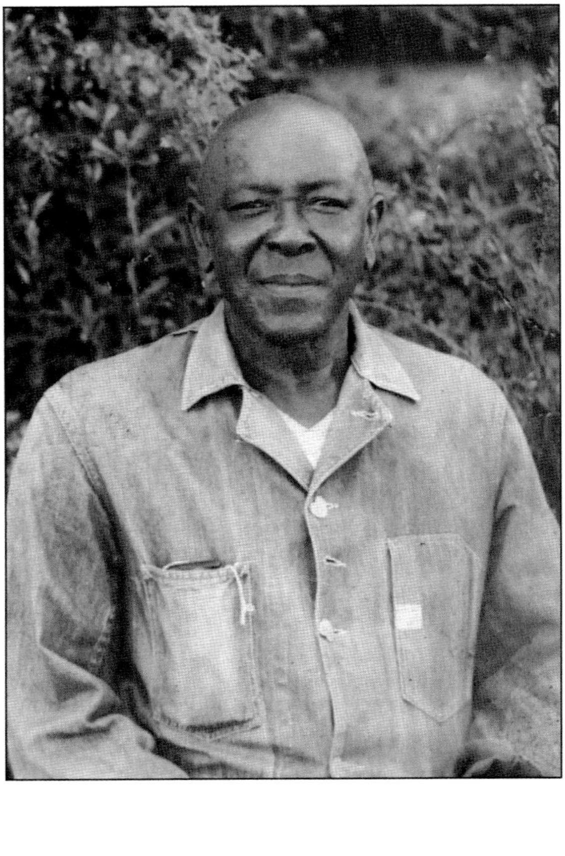

Tommy Creasy (b. 1880) was the son of Manuel and Louvina Creasy who came to Lancaster from Missouri prior to 1871. Tommy married Leslie Norman. After her death, he wed Asia Gillette. The children of Asia and Tommy were Charles Creasy (b. 1871), Lucy Creasy (b. 1873), Carrie Creasy (b. 1876), and Tommy Creasy. Tommy was a hardworking man who was held in high esteem by Lancaster citizens.

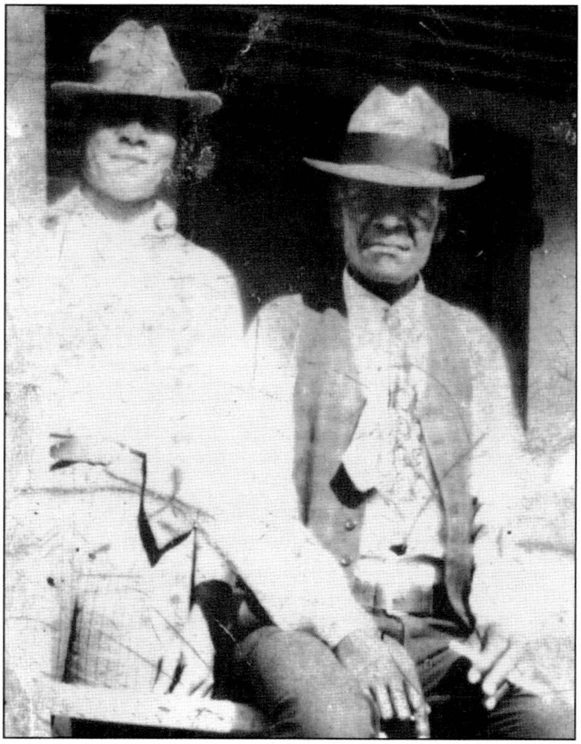

Ellis (left) and Carl (right) were sons of Mack and Mollie Stevenson. Mack was declared a free man in Waxahachie around 1866, moved to Lancaster, and purchased land near his mother, Kittie Stevenson (b. 1832, who had been freed earlier. Ellis raised hogs and rented small tracts of land on Telephone Road. He drove an old Allis Chambers tractor to cultivate cotton and corn. His old tractor only allowed him to plant one row at a time. Descendants still live on the land. (Courtesy of the Mack Stevenson family.)

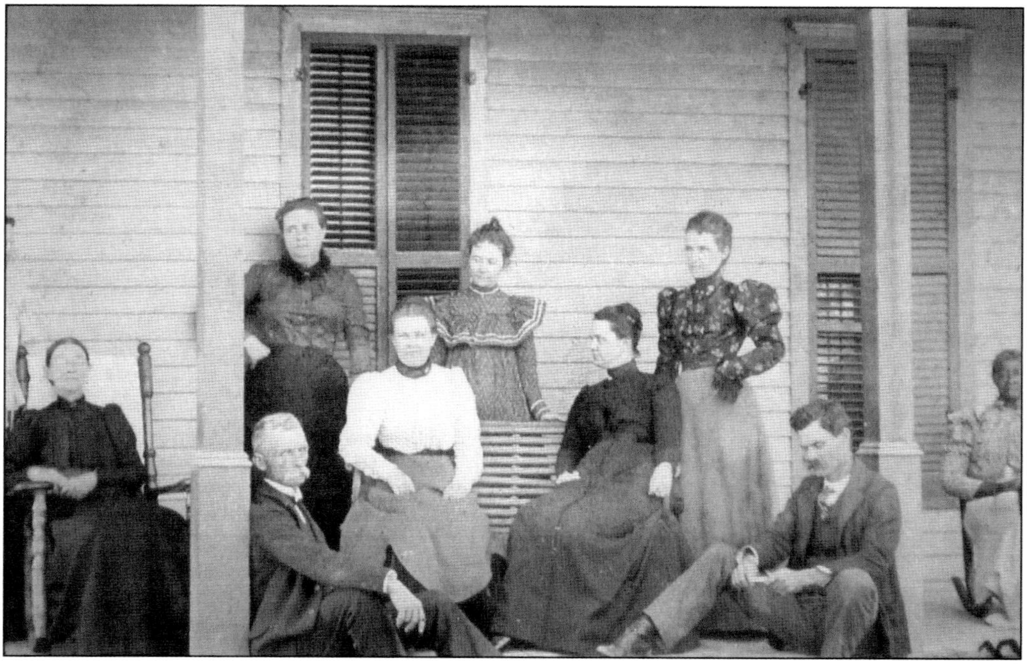

The Moffett family came to Lancaster around 1853 from Illinois. W. R. Moffett ran a stagecoach inn. The Moffett family's first home was on Fourth and Wilson Streets, and this picture was taken on the porch of the house. From left to right are (seated) Anna Moffett, B. R. Moffett, Ida Hammond, Ella Howell, Bob Moffett, and Aunt Lucy "Mammy;" (standing) Lula Beckley Moffett, Bertie Lee Moffett, and Mattie Anderson.

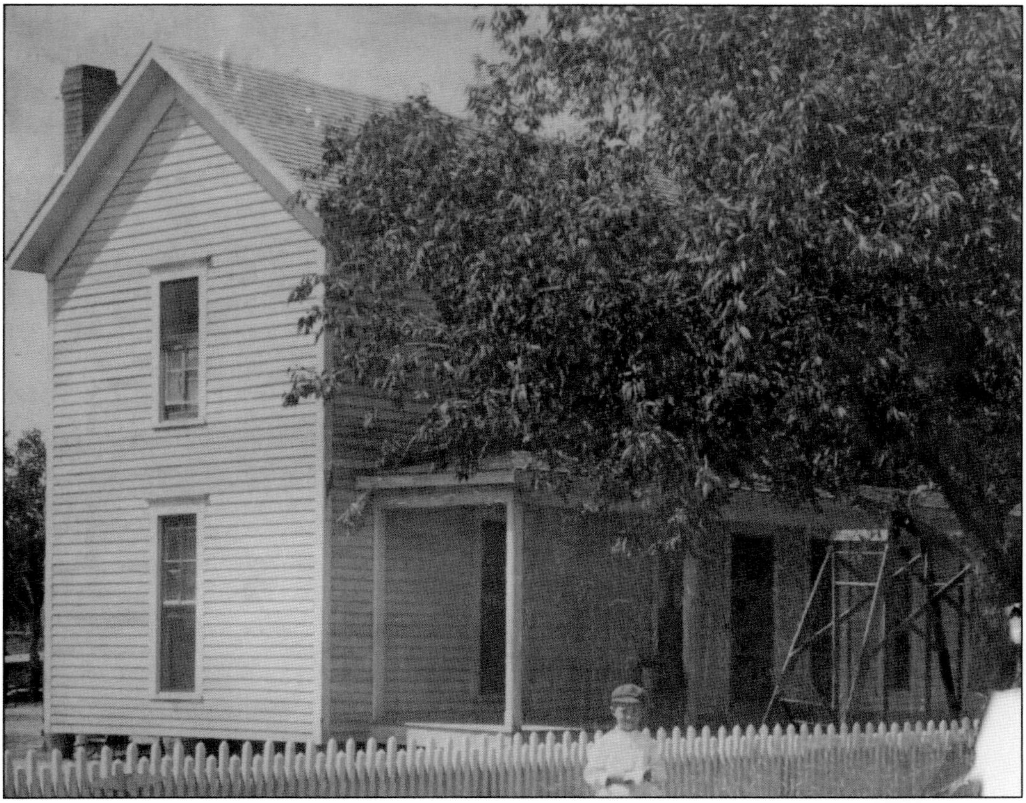

The Morton house was home to five generations of Mortons. Josiah Morton built this house around 1887, although he first came to Lancaster in 1867. He built the house himself with lumber brought from Shreveport, Louisiana. The house is an example of early Texas homes with a long porch and one central hall that runs from back to front. There are two rooms downstairs and four bedrooms upstairs. (Courtesy of Winn Morton.)

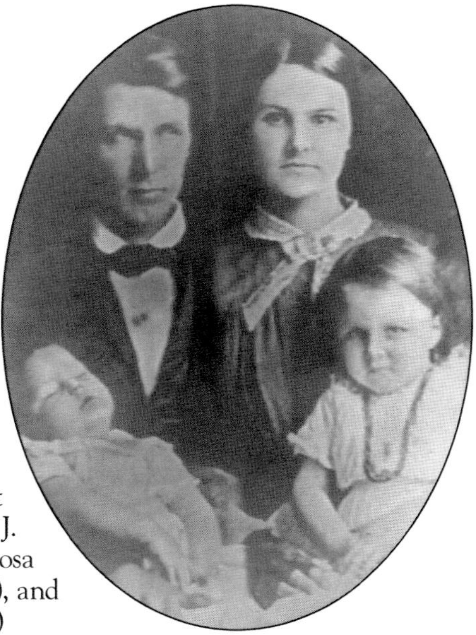

Josiah Morton (1823–1898) came to Lancaster after the Civil War. He served in the Confederacy in the 6th Texas Cavalry Battalion Company C from Tennessee. He was an accomplished woodworker from Smith County, Tennessee. In 1871, his wife, Jane Alexander, born 1824, died from tuberculosis. Josiah became a doctor of homeopathy. The family from left to right is Alva (1853–1933), Josiah, Jane, and Mary J. "Molly" Morton Wise (b. 1849). The family grew with Rosa Morton Lyon (b. 1856), Ella Morton George (b. 1862), and Emma Morton (b. 1859). (Courtesy of Winn Morton.)

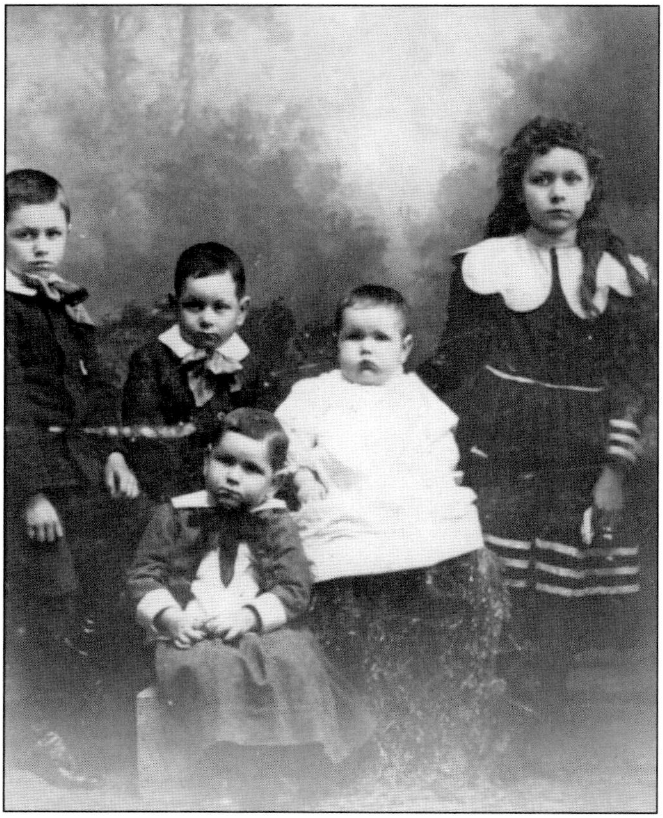

Alva H. Morton (1853–1933) came to Lancaster with his father, J. W. Morton, around 1867. Alva married Kate Griffin. Pictured here are their children, from left to right, Gayle (b. 1887), Joseph W. (b. 1889), Alva (b. 1893), Ressie Morton O'Neal (b. 1886), and Jack (b. 1891). Later they had Annie A. Morton (b. 1896) and Janie Lou Morton Vinson. Jack married Ethel Winniford. Several Mortons continued to live in the house after their father's death.

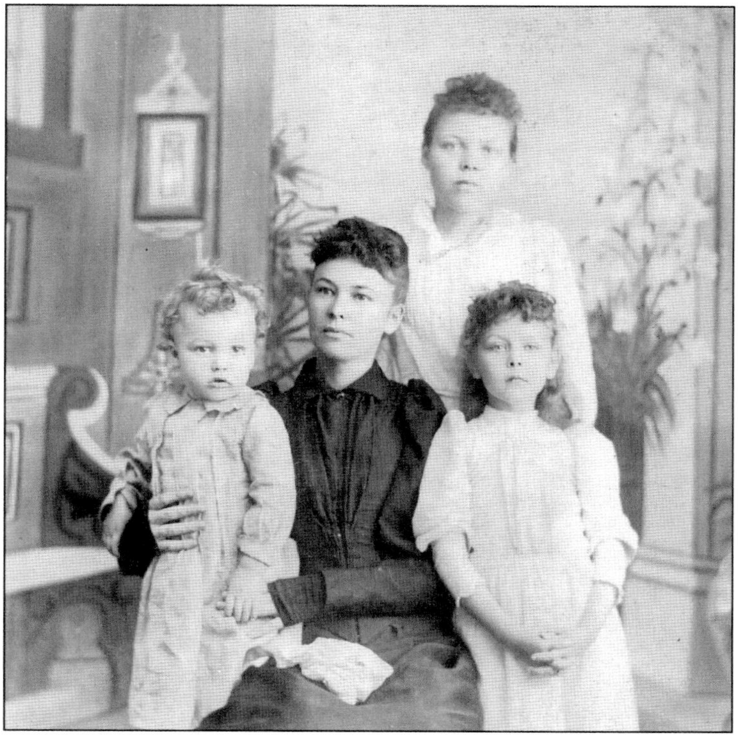

The Mortons, pictured around 1900 are, from left to right, Charles George (son of Ella Morton George), Emma Morton, Ressie Morton, and Elsa Wise (standing), daughter of Molly Morton Wise from Waxahachie. This images appears to have been taken in the First Presbyterian Church of Lancaster. The Mortons were active members, and their grandfather, Josiah, built a pulpit, which can still be seen the foyer. (Courtesy of Winn Morton.)

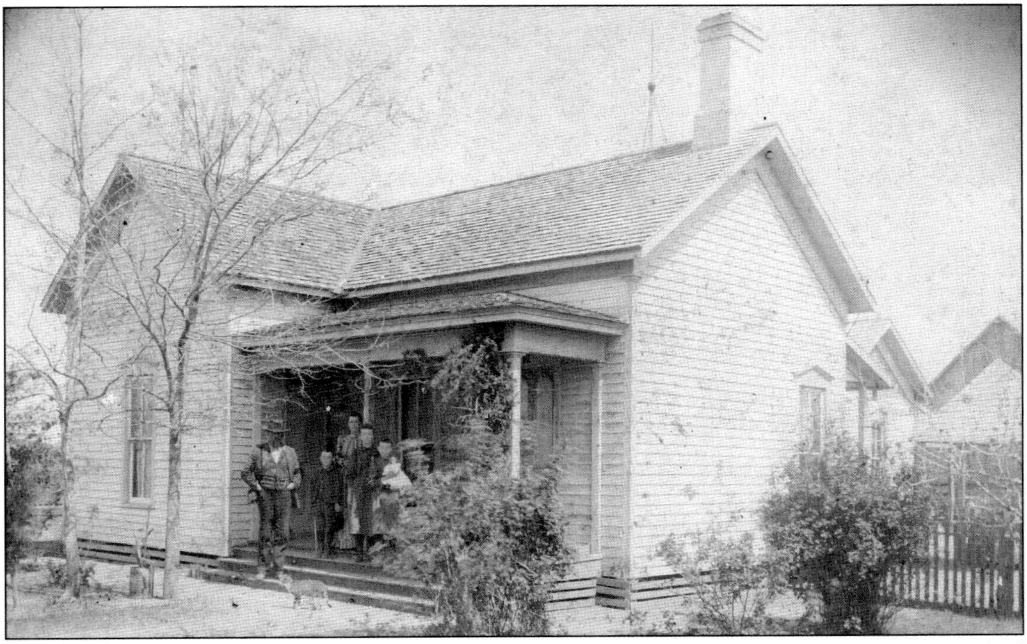

Dr. Thomas Little came to Lancaster from Sparta, Tennessee. His first wife, Flora Lowrey, died during childbirth in 1874. He married Flora's cousin, Ida Lowrey, in 1877; she was the woman Pat Garrett had courted. His first home was rather small. Shortly before his death, Little built this large house on the corner of Dallas Avenue and Fourth Street in 1887. This house features wrap porches, gingerbread trim, three fireplaces, and a turned stairway. The Little children were Elizabeth "Bessie" Hammond (Mrs. Larry Hammond), Lillian Lavender (Mrs. Clyde Lavender), and Clyde Elwood Little. The home still stands on the same corner of Dallas Avenue.

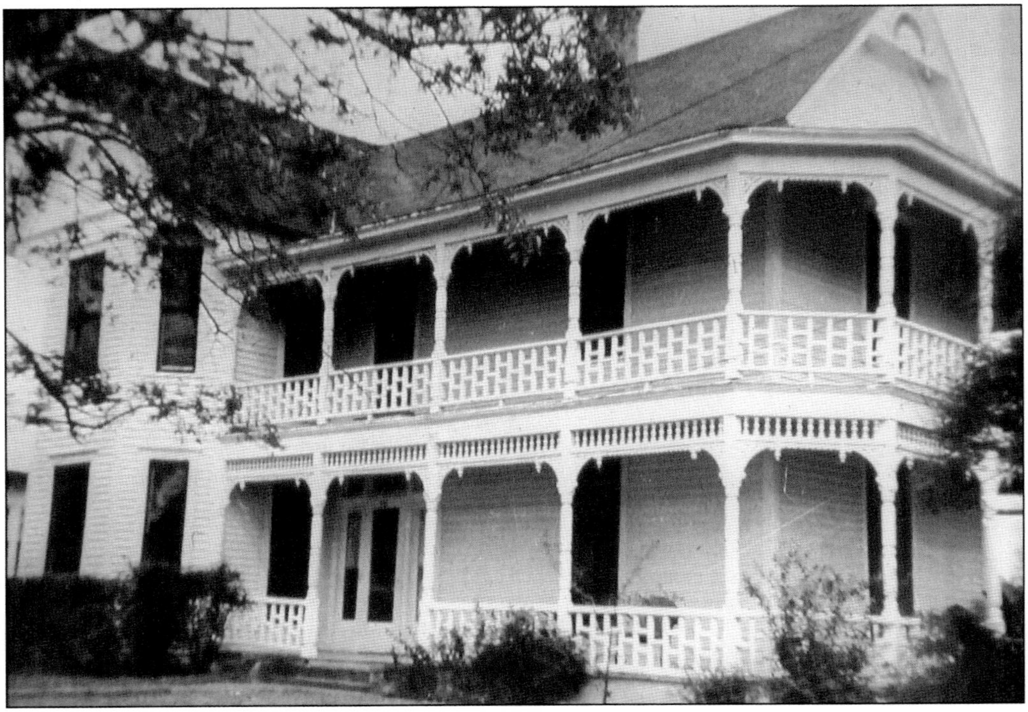

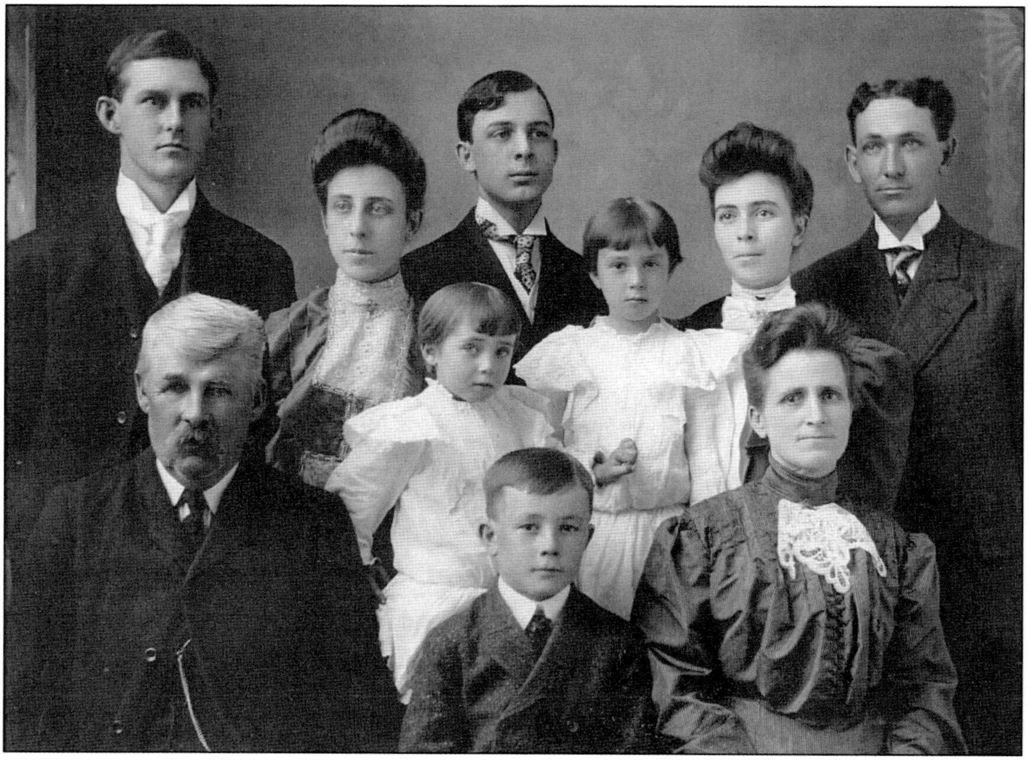

After Dr. Little's death in 1893, Ida Lowrey Little married Isaac Hamilton. Pictured here are, from left to right, (first row) Isaac "Ike" Hamilton (b. 1844), James Willard Hamilton (b. 1896), and Ida Lowrey Hamilton; (second row) Gladys and Kathleen Hammond; (third row) Clyde Lavender, Lillian Little Lavender (b. 1882), Clyde Little (b. 1884), Elizabeth L. "Bess" Little Hammond (b. 1881), and Harry Hammond. (Courtesy of Doris Hamilton Gibbons.)

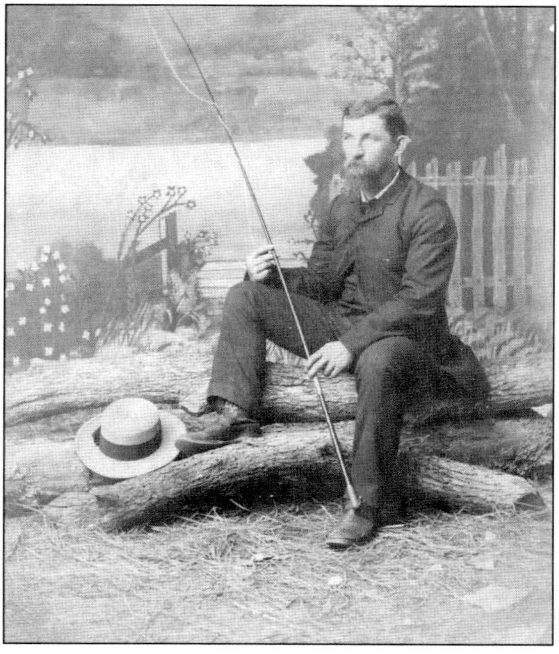

Willard Fisk (1849–1934) first came to Lancaster and worked as a teacher and a store clerk. He returned to Tennessee for his medical education then came back to Lancaster in 1884. He never married, instead putting his patients first. Being an expert cook, avid fisherman, and hunter, he was always busy. He raised watermelons on vacant lots and gave the fruit away. He was a frequent visitor at the Hamilton home.

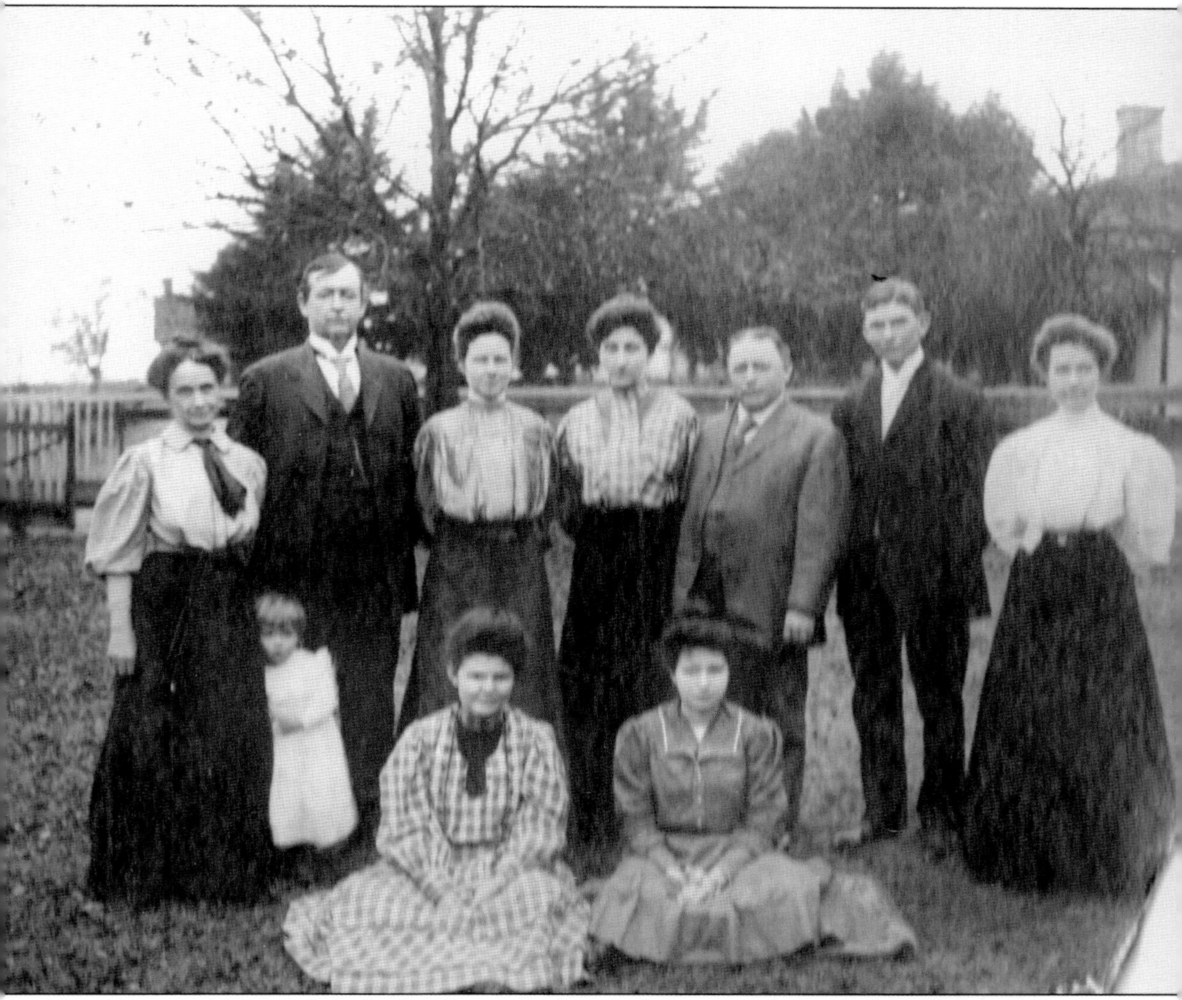

The Curtis and Meredith Parks families came from Indiana to settle in DeSoto, Texas, in the 1840s. Their father, George Parks, was a Revolutionary War soldier and his widowed mother, Kathryn, came with them. Curtis and Amelia Parks had nine children. One of their grandsons is Lancaster's Dr. George Parks, who married Nellie Campbell. He earned his medical degree in 1887 from the University of Tennessee in Memphis. The George Parks family includes, from left to right, (seated) Eddie Johnson Lacy (Mrs. Wortham Lacy) and Jennie Parks Orr (Mrs. Taylor Orr); (standing) Nellie Campbell Parks (1857–1951), Bess Parks Cordill, Dr. George T. Parks (1861–1917), Lina Parks, Mabel Murphy Batchler (Mrs. Will Batchler), Joe Guest, Will Batchler, Nannie Moffett Lavender (Mrs. Willis Lavender). (Courtesy of Carolyn Cordill Fulton.)

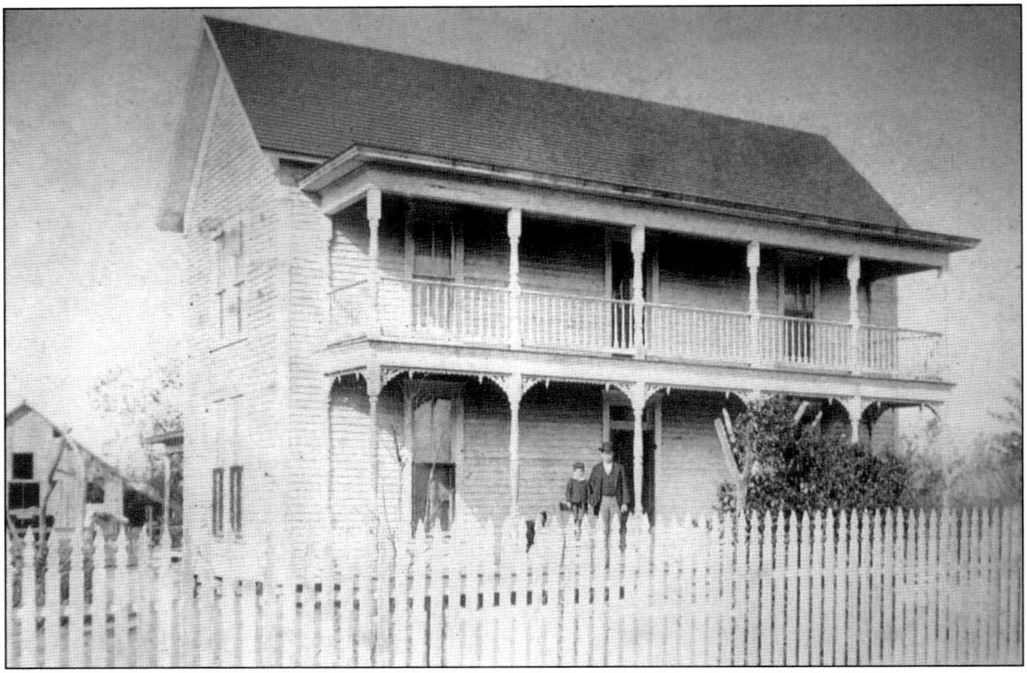

John Thomas Ellis built three homes but this was the first one, erected in 1870. At the time it was built, there was only one story that faced north on Cedar Street behind the First Methodist Church. He built the house for his soon-to-be wife, Fannie Stewart. They had four children: Earl Eugene (1874–1950), Benjamin Franklin (1875–1858), John Tom Jr. (1879–1920), and Edna Ellis Johnson Tuley (1883–1932). The house was sold in 1890 to John Scott, who added the second story.

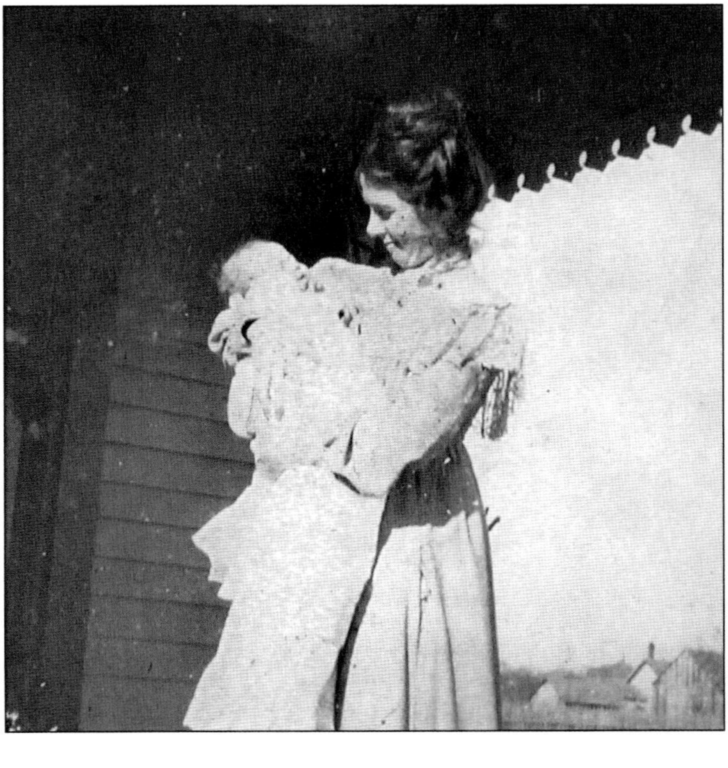

Frances C. Stewart (1849–1884) was born in Tennessee to David H. Stewart and Sarah C. Walker. Fannie is shown with her first-born child, Earl Ellis, around 1874. She married John Thomas Ellis in 1870. The house above was complete with furniture brought from St. Louis, shipped by water to Galveston, and brought overland to Lancaster. Pieces of this furniture are now in homes of their grandchildren.

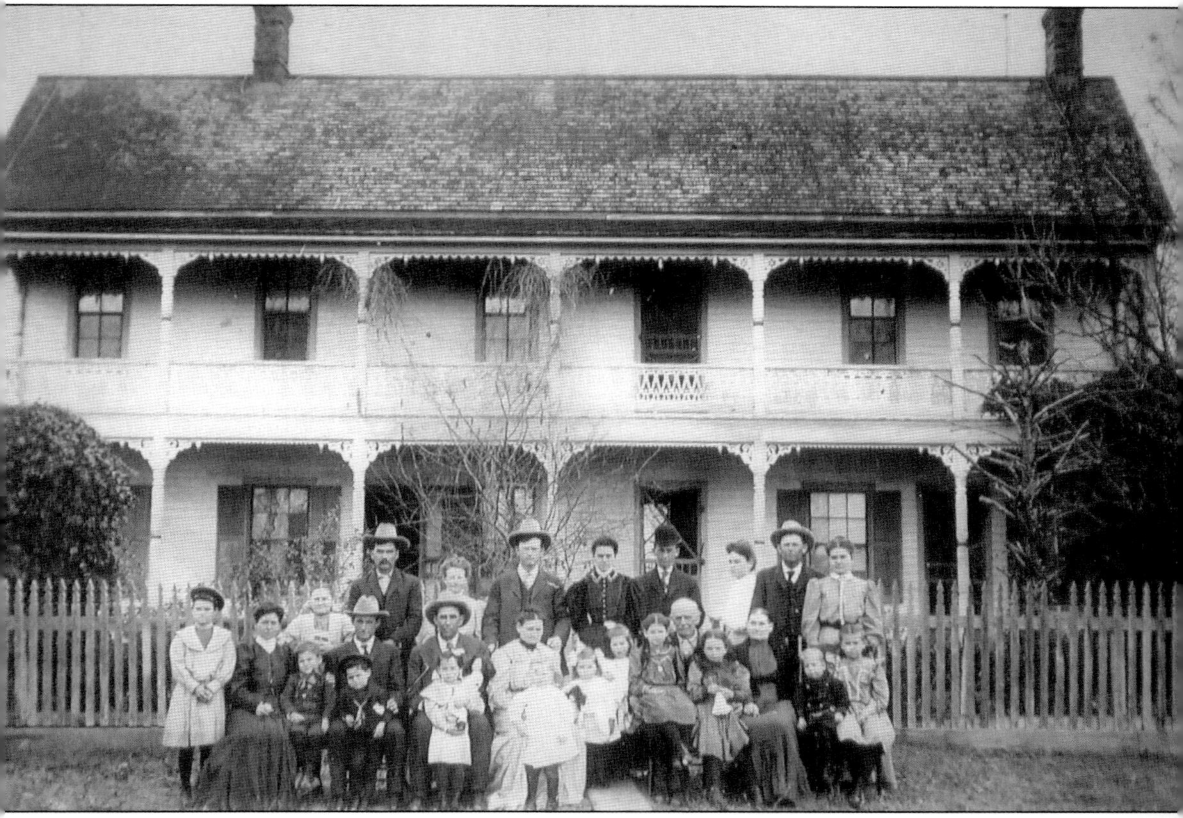

The Batchlers were in the Lancaster area around 1850, and this was their home near Bear Creek. Pictured are, from left to right, (two children standing in front) Ila Winniford and Ethel Winniford; (children in first row) Batchler Winniford, Roy Winniford, Mary Lou Batchler, J. B. Batchler, Marietta Jordan, Fay Jordan, Blanche Batchler, Dotty Batchler, Karl Jeffers, and Lela Munsey; (seated) Emma Winniford, John Winniford, Jim Batchler, Lou Batchler, Pappy Ramby, and Mother Ramby; (standing) John Batchler, Ida Batchler, Meno Jordan, Stella Jordan, Claude Batchler, Eva Batchler, Tom Jeffers, and Lilly Jeffers. Jack Batchler owned a horse named Shiloh, who raced Steel Dust. These races helped establish horses who ran a quarter of a mile race.

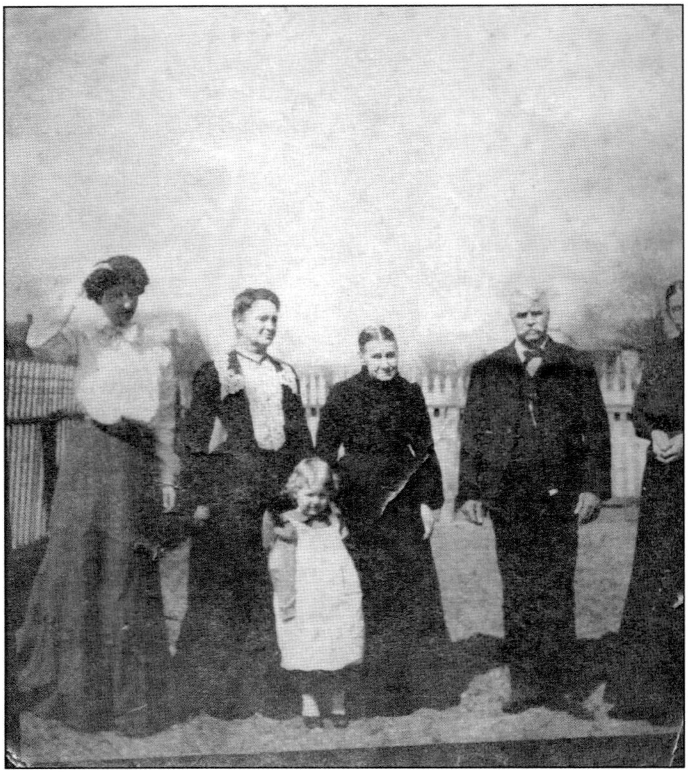

A gathering of some of the White family in 1904 included Pearl White, Sarah Scott Greene, Laura Gaston White, Mary White Coolidge (Mrs. Joel B. Coolidge), Scott Greene, and Lou F. White (Mrs. William L. White). The Greenes from Illinois were related to the Jones Greenes, son-in-law of Lou White, who lived in Lancaster.

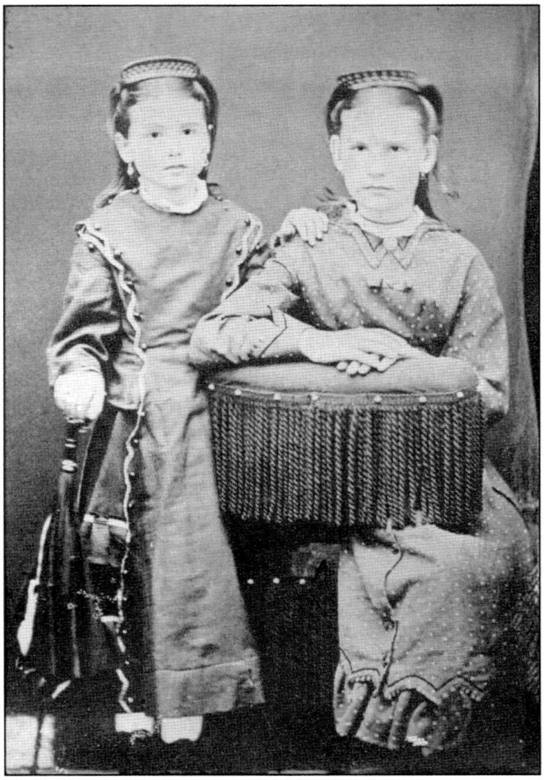

William Love White (1824–1881) married Louisa Frances Ellis (1842–1936) after his first wife died. These are two of their seven children. Minnie (Mary on early censuses) White (1868–1957) married William A. Strain, a local druggist. Addie (1863–1897) married Sam Randlett. Addie died from a poisonous spider bite.

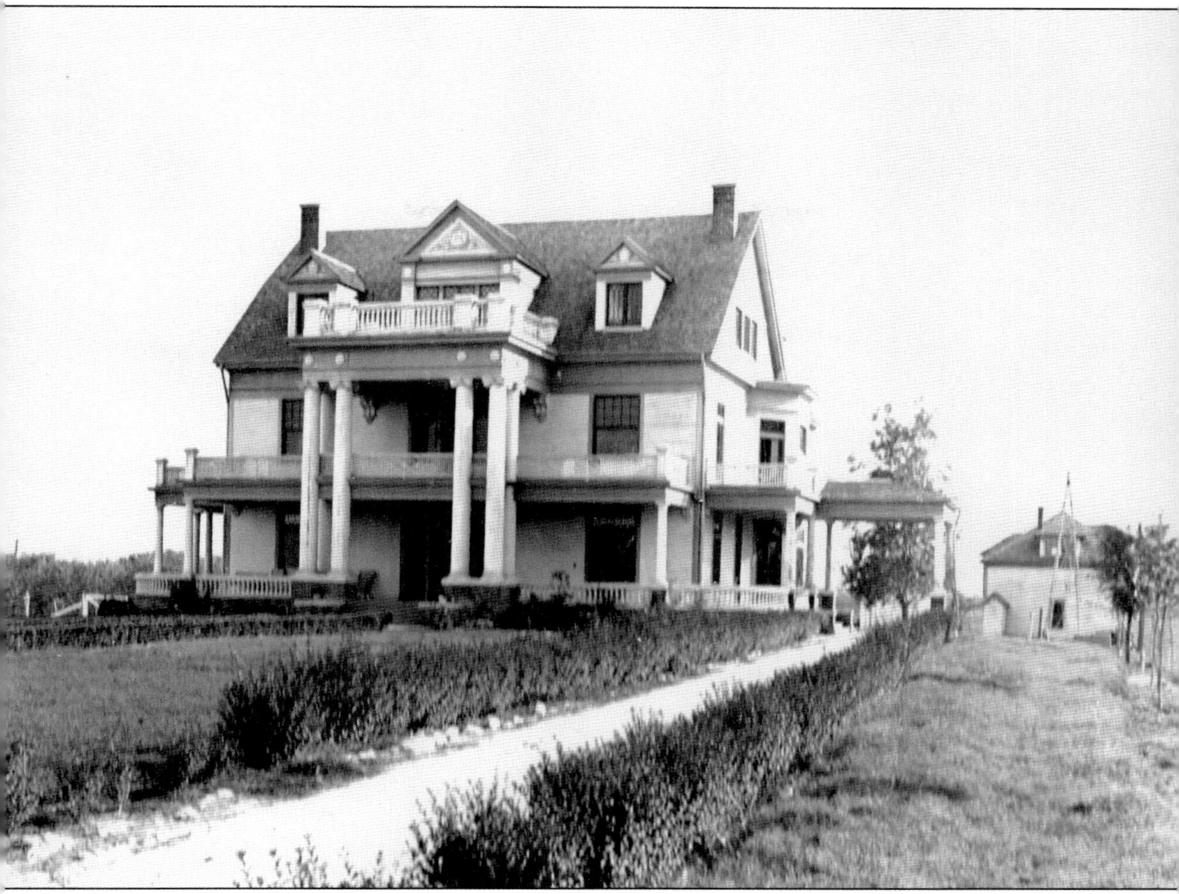

The White house was built in 1907 at the south end of South Centre Street facing toward the square. The house had three stories and a basement. On the first floor was a living room, a library, parlor, dining room, butler's pantry, kitchen, and a tile bathroom. The second floor had bedrooms, each of which opened onto a balcony. The top floor was a ballroom with a stage for a band. The house held many parties for various special occasions in Lancaster. The grandchildren called the ballroom on the top floor the gymnasium and often played there on rainy days.

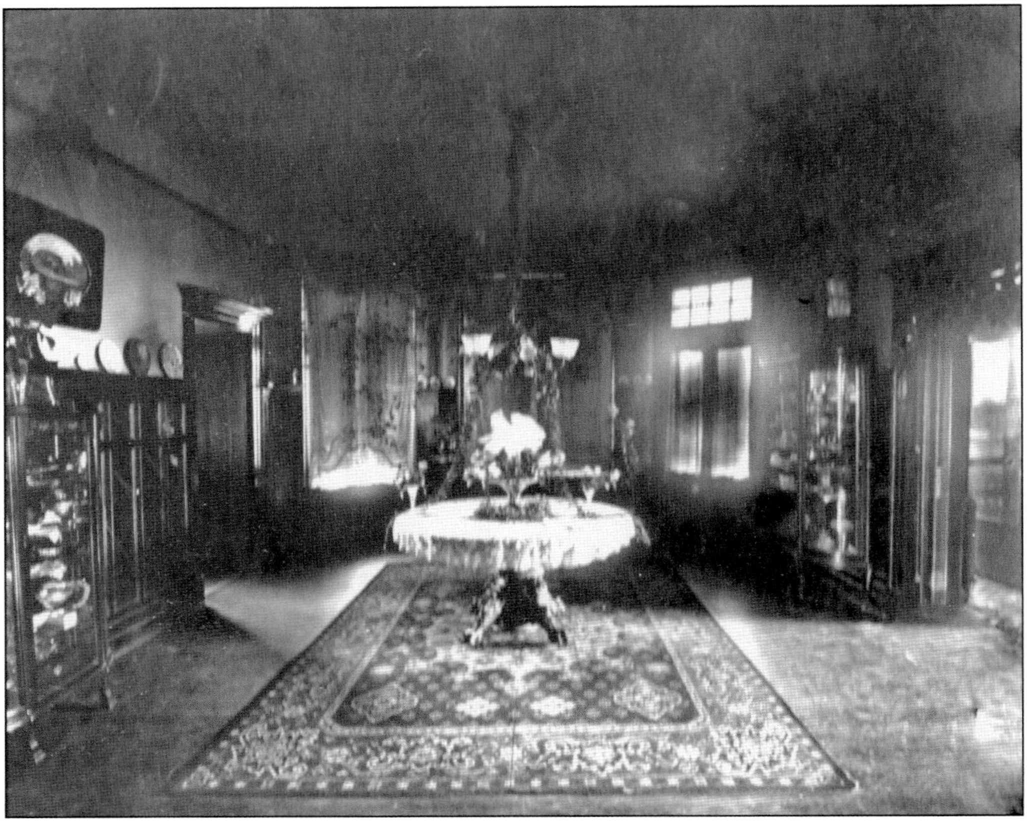

The dining room in the White house was for both family and formal meals. The setting shows the formality of the time. Wall colors were usually deep red because it was believed the color helped with digestion. The family gathered for meals in the dining room and were served by the house servants. Children were not allowed to talk at the table.

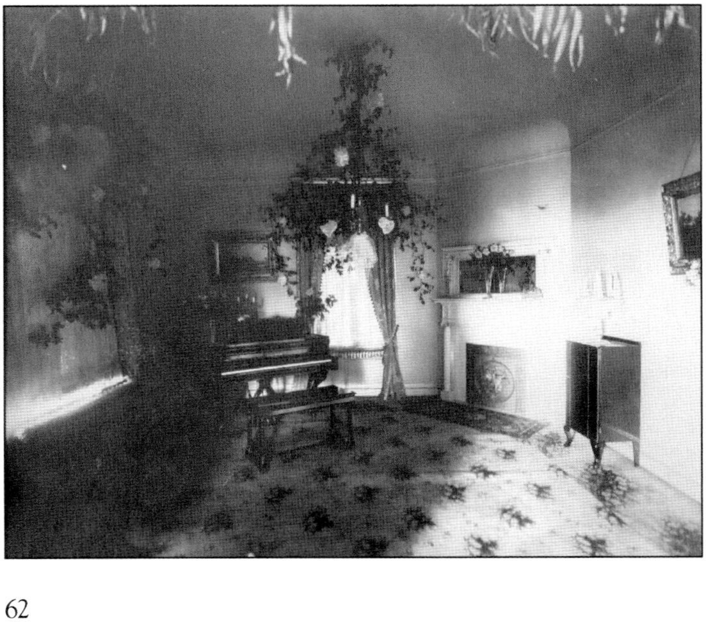

Young people of upper-class families were expected to train in music. They either played an instrument or sang. Programs in the town as well as family gatherings frequently had local talent perform. Rooms were spacious to allow for seating. Most of the children of Lou and William White either played an instrument or sang.

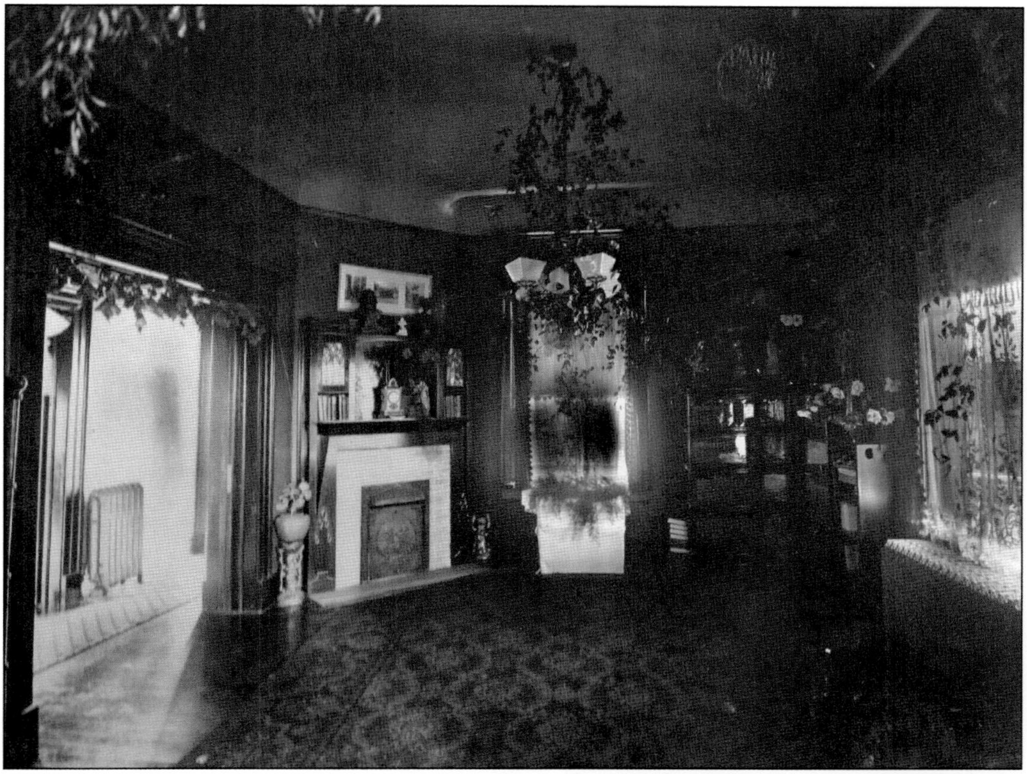

The library shows the value that early Lancaster citizens had in an education. All of the children of Lou White had some type of higher education. White allowed others to borrow her books. Later a borrowing library was set up on the second floor of the White Bank building, which was the beginning of the Lancaster Public Library. The White house was steam heated, as can be seen through the door.

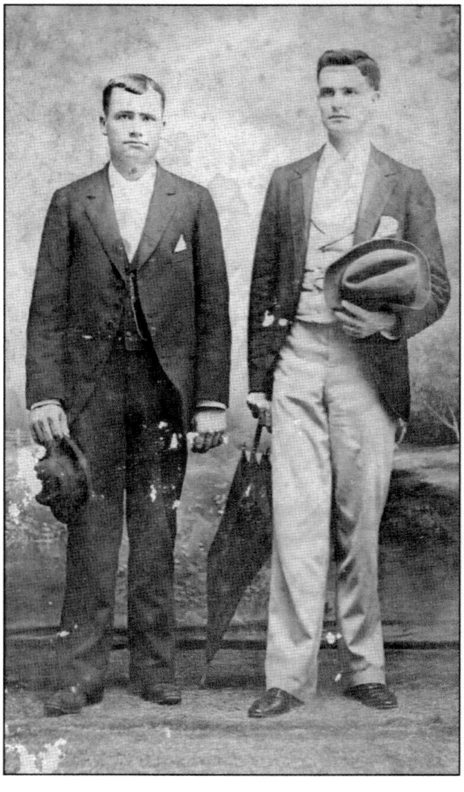

Hal Eugene White (1871–1931) and Karl White (1873–1949) were born to William Love White and Louisa F. Ellis White. They were both involved with the operation of the White Bank in 1898. Karl left the White Bank and became a very successful banker in Dallas. Hal White stayed with the White Bank until his death.

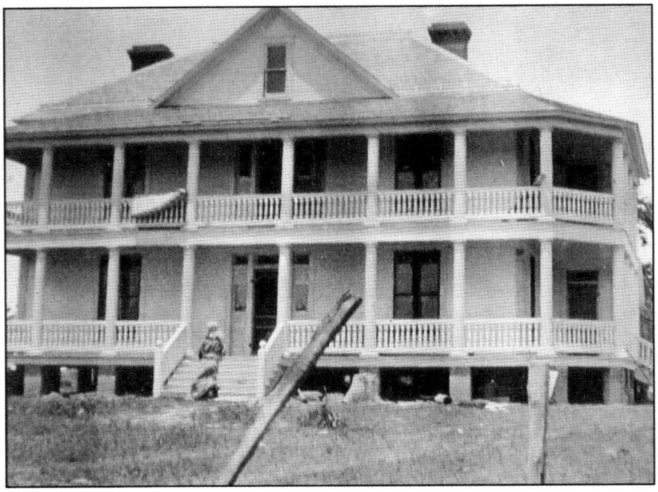

William Tolbert Lavender was the oldest child of William Lavender and Margaret Hall Little Lavender. He was born in 1843 and came to Texas in 1845 from Illinois. William T. Lavender built this house in 1905 on a hilltop on Ferris Road overlooking a valley below. The house had a central hall and double gallery porch across the front. Downstairs were five rooms with four fireplaces, a pantry, butler's pantry, and bathroom. Upstairs were four large bedrooms.

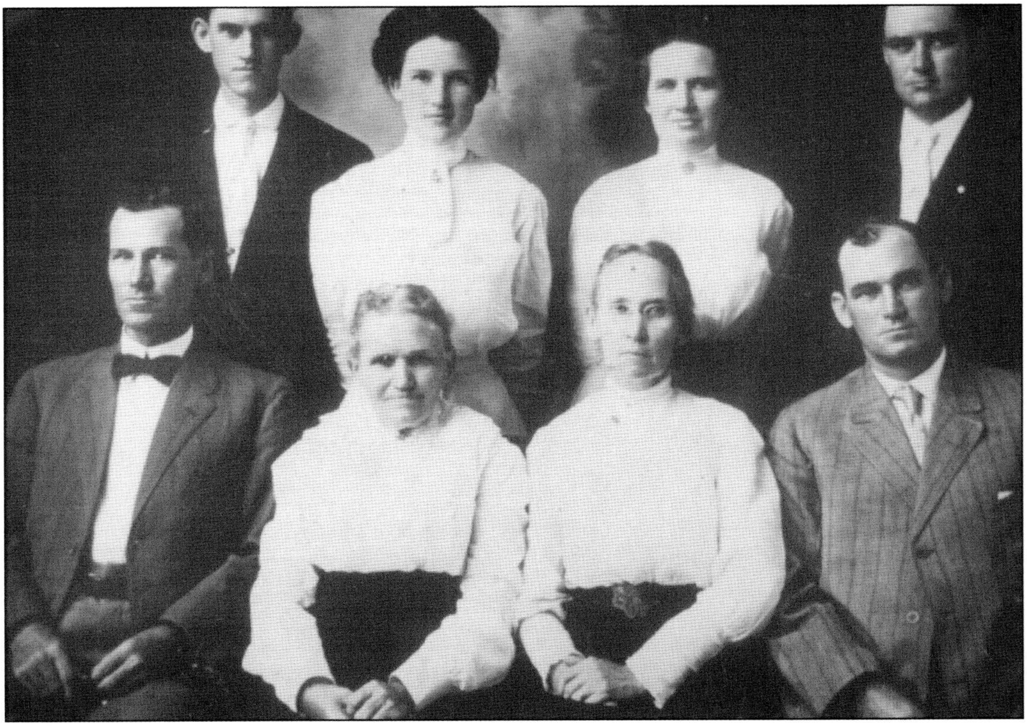

James Irvin Lavender (1833–1907) came to Texas in 1846 with his father, Archibald Lavender (1813–1864), and mother, Sarah Buffington (1811–1902). Irvin was a farmer and merchant. He served in the Confederate army, enlisting in 1862. Pictured are his wife and children. From left to right are (first row) Jim (James, 1871–1945), Lucy Rawlins Lavender (1845–1932), Ida Lavender Taylor (b. 1861), and Eber Lavender (1876–1963); (second row) Will Lavender (1886–1962), Adda Lavender Wills (1889–1971), Lydia Lavender Hospalle (b. 1873), and King Lavender (1882–1973).

Jasper Newton Fitzhugh (1857–1927) and his wife, Nannie Glenn (b. 1862), arrived in Lancaster after 1891 from Tennessee. The Fitzhughs were farmers in Lancaster with Stephen continuing in that occupation for 27 years. Pictured from left to right are (first row) Nell (b. 1898), Nettie (b. 1895), and Edna (b. 1889); (second row) Lester (b. 1892), Nannie, and Jasper; (third row) Audie (b. 1885) and Stephen (b. 1883).

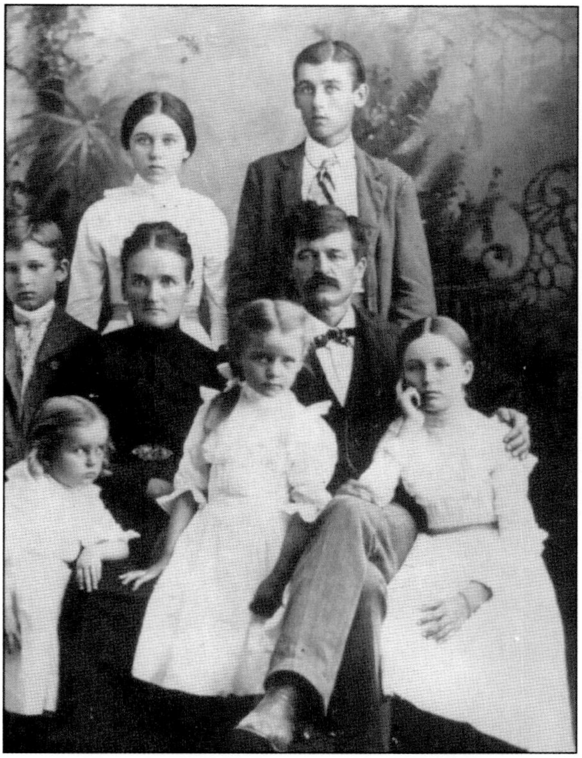

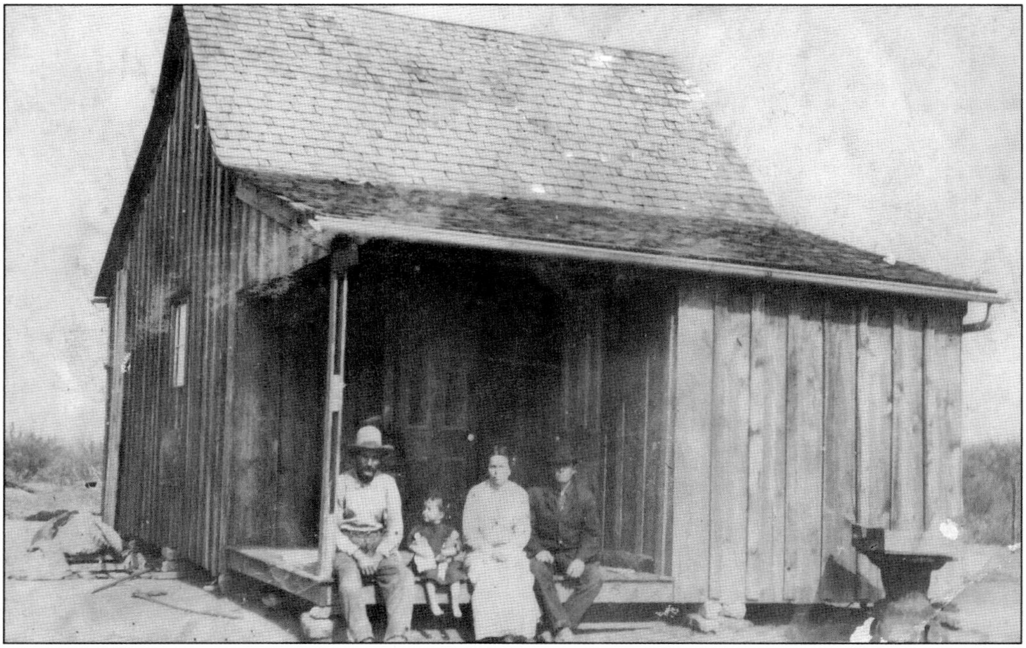

The Fitzhugh's farm was on Wintergreen Road. This is a typical early-settler's home in Lancaster. Usually there was a kitchen/family room and sleeping quarters. Much of the cooking was actually done outside. Washing was done in large iron pots over a fire to keep the water boiling. Most days, families were outside working the land. The Fitzhugh farm later became the home of Dizzy Dean, a professional baseball player.

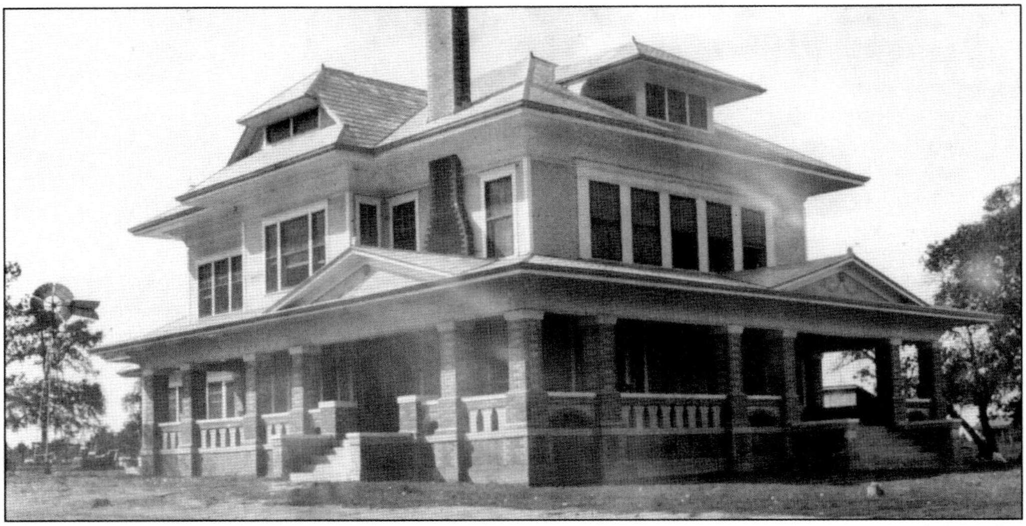

John Lewis Winniford (1870–1946) fell in love with Emma Lou Batchler (1875–1973), but the Batchlers sent Emma away to keep the two separated. Seventeen-year-old Emma and John soon hopped a freight train to Louisiana, though, and married in 1892. They returned home and settled down on the Winniford farm, where John eventually built this house designed by John's brother Andrew in 1913. The Prairie School–style house features a foursquare plan with large hipped roof, dormers, and distinctive multi-light windows. John and Emma had four children while living here: Ethel Ruth (1895–1977), Ila Estella (1897–1963), William Batchler (1900–1974), and Roy Edward (1902–1968). (Courtesy of Winn Morton.)

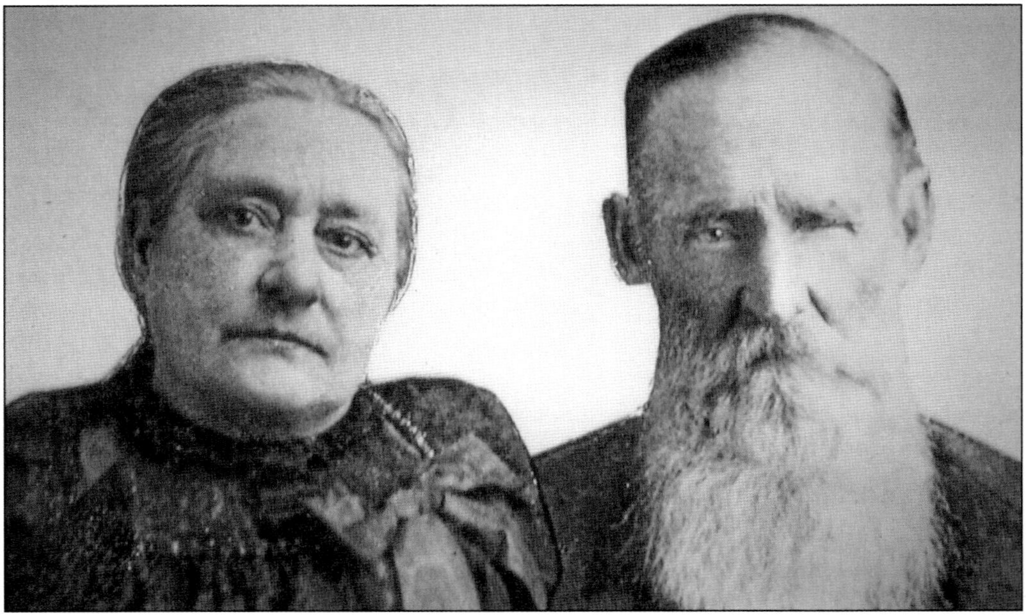

Three of the Winniford brothers went to California during the Gold Rush—William was 21 years old, Norvell was 26 years old, and David was 17 years old. They found gold and came home with more riches than when they left. After his first wife died and the Civil War started, William was conscripted into the Confederacy. He refused to fight for the South and fled to a camp in Trinity River bottoms known as Bois D'Arc Island. While there, he met Sarah Allen Lewis and later married her in 1865. They were married for 50 years. (Courtesy of Winn Morton.)

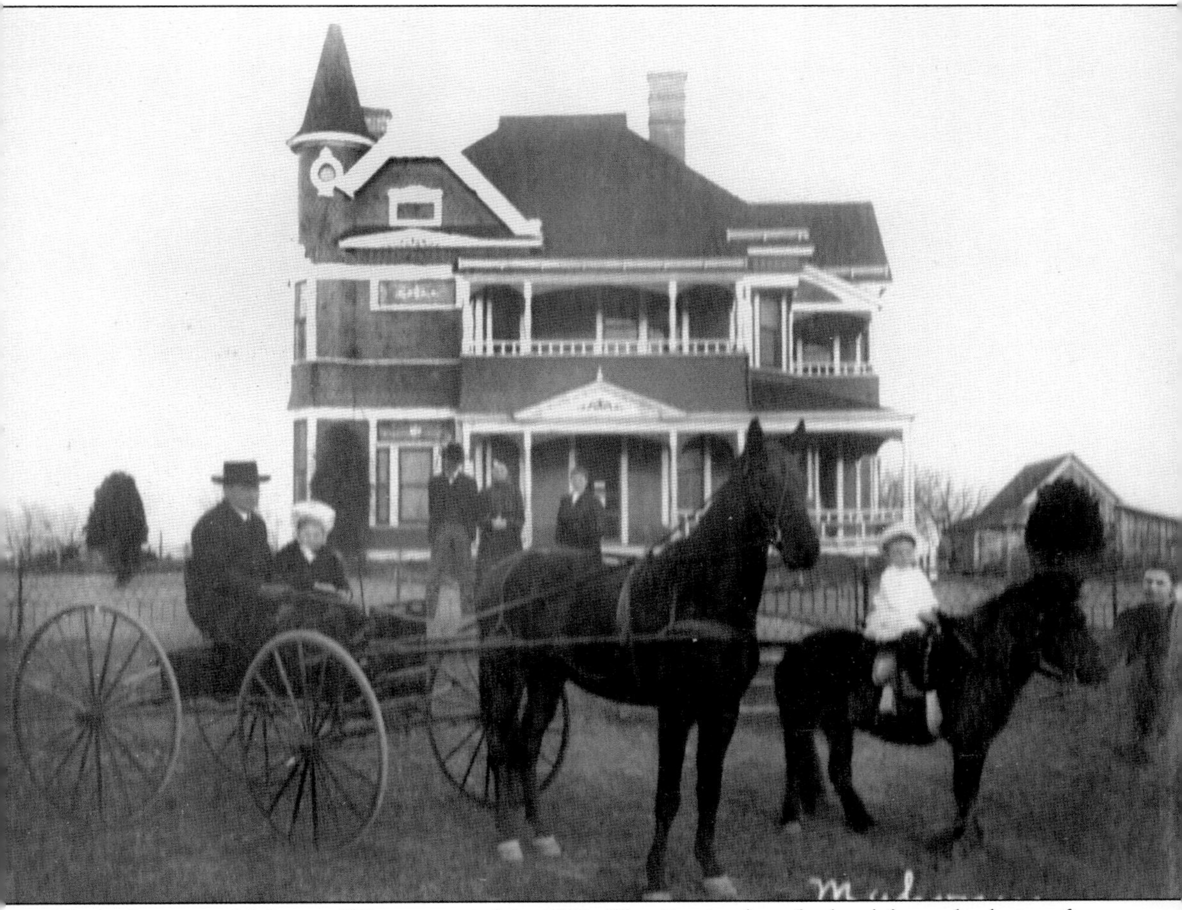

W. A. Strain and Minnie White married in 1892. The Strains bought land from the heirs of Minnie's grandparents, Thomas McKee and Mary "Polly" Ellis, to build their house and farm. Flander-Moad, two architects, were best known for designing county courthouses and churches in Texas. The Strain house is one of four homes known to be designed by these two architects. There are four fireplaces downstairs along with an entry hall, parlor, dining room, kitchen, and library. Upstairs is a family room, one family bedroom, a guest room, and a servants' room. The house and farm is on the National Register of Historic Places. Shown in the picture are, from left to right, Minnie Strain's brother Hal White; his daughter Laura; W. A.; Minnie; a friend, Mrs. Peck; and Arthur Strain on the pony being held by Mary Lou Strain.

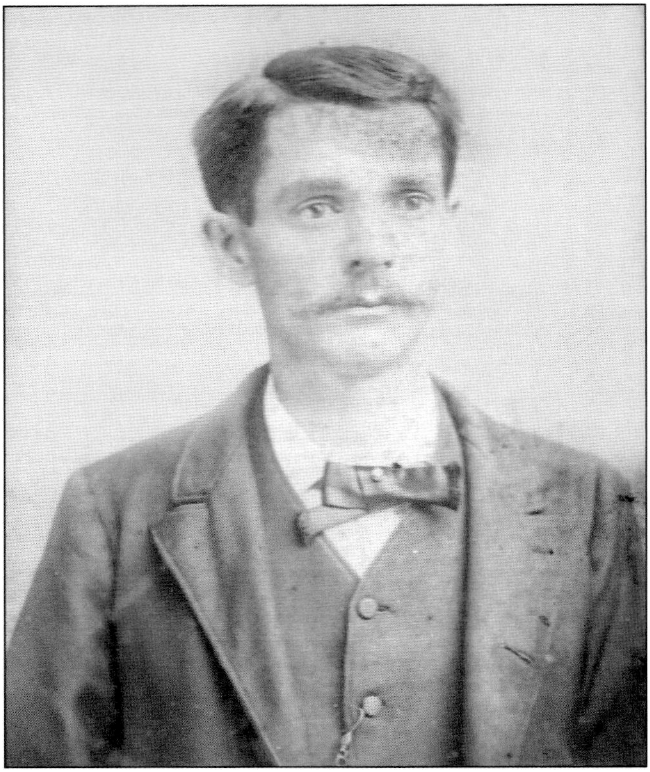

William "Strainer" Alexander Strain was born in Leesburg, Tennessee, in 1861 and came to Lancaster around 1882. He worked at the gin to earn his keep while he learned to become a pharmacist. He soon opened a drugstore in Lancaster and a second one in Waxahachie. He contracted tuberculosis and died in 1907 in Asheville, North Carolina. Minnie White married William Alexander Strain on July 7, 1892. This marriage took place after a very curt letter on July 2, 1892, to Minnie that said he (William) would not write again until her mother (Lou White) gave them permission to marry. They were married on July 5, 1892. The letter must have worked.

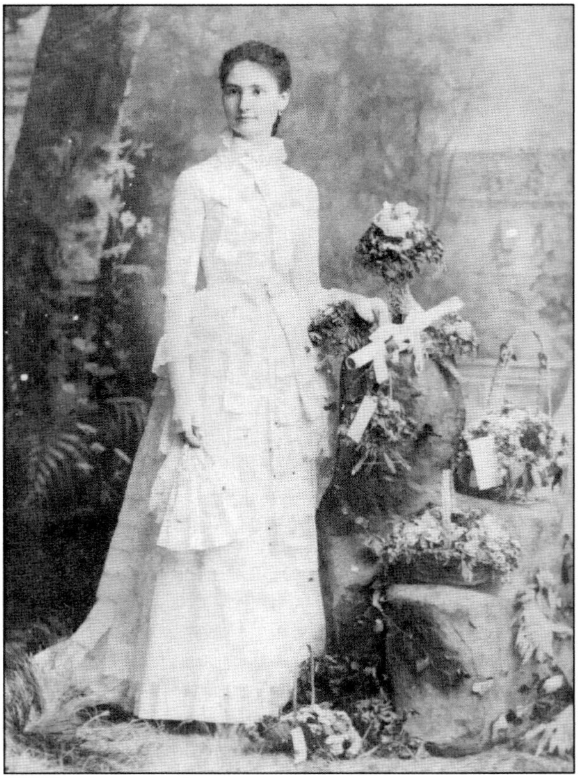

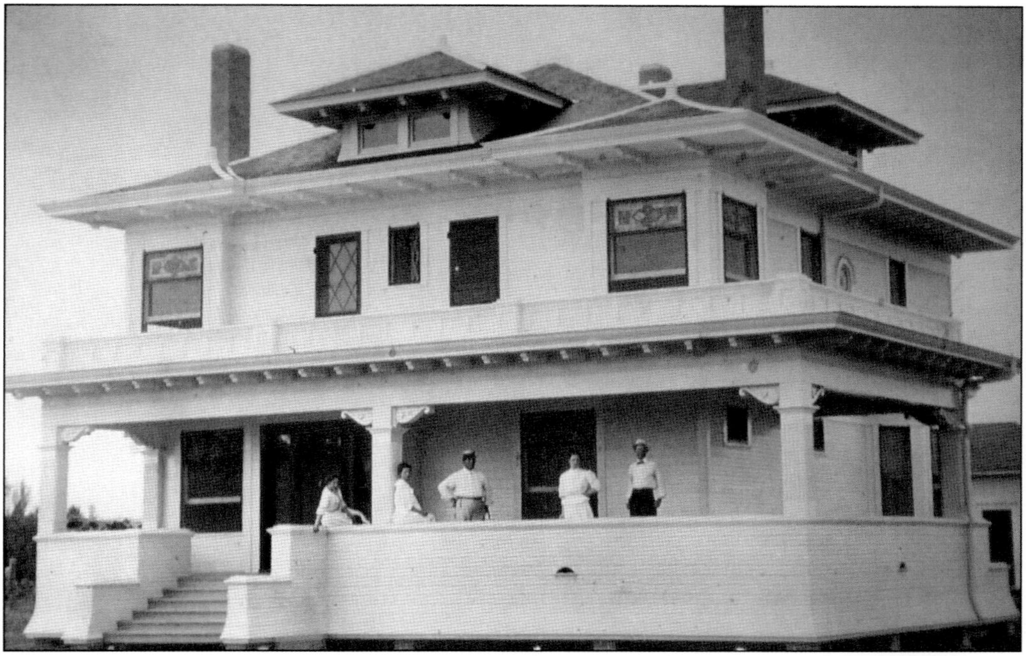

Fred J. Wilson (1870–1915) was born in Texas. Wilson married Roxanna Greene (1875) in 1894, and they had two children, Lucille (1906) and Frederick (1911). They built this house in 1907 on Seventh Street. It was a true Lancaster showcase with lots of stained glass.

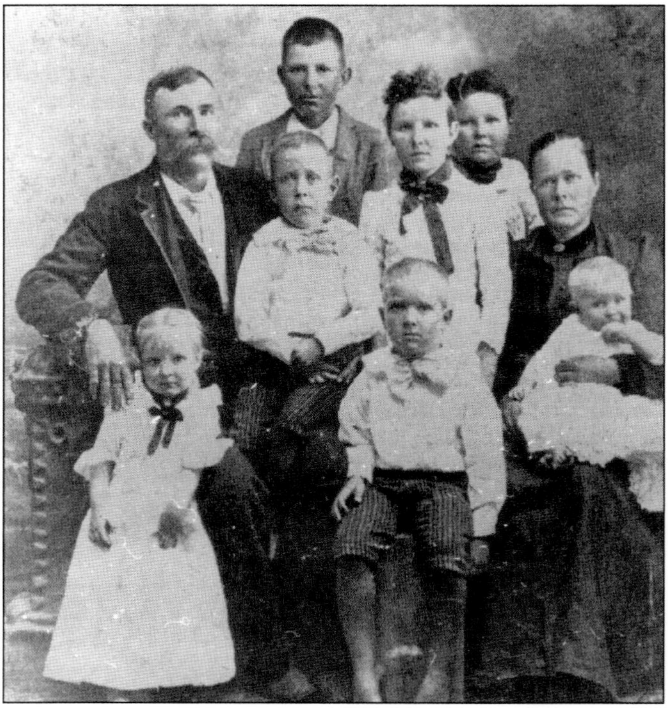

The Joseph Mabra family moved to the old Lavender place in 1876. They were mostly farmers but also worked other jobs. Pictured are, from left to right, (first row) Gussie Mabra Hightower (1891–1966) and seated is Frank M. Mabra (1889–1967); (second row) James Adkinson Mabra (1859–1928) holding Johnny Mabra (1887–1898), Maude Myrtle Mabra Keener (1883–1960), and Nancy Elizabeth Barger (1863–1938) holding Lena Mabra Brown (1896–1986); (third row) James Mabra (1881–1910) and Ada Lee Mabra Pennington (1885–1954). Born later were two sons Ed (1901–1963) and Mike Albert (1903–1989).

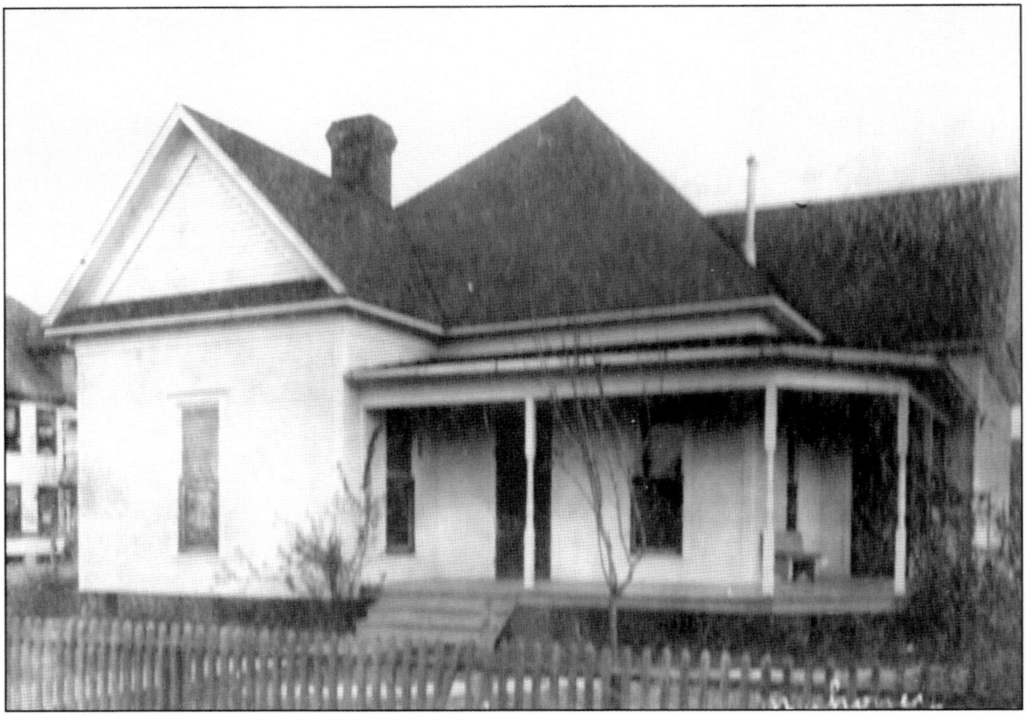

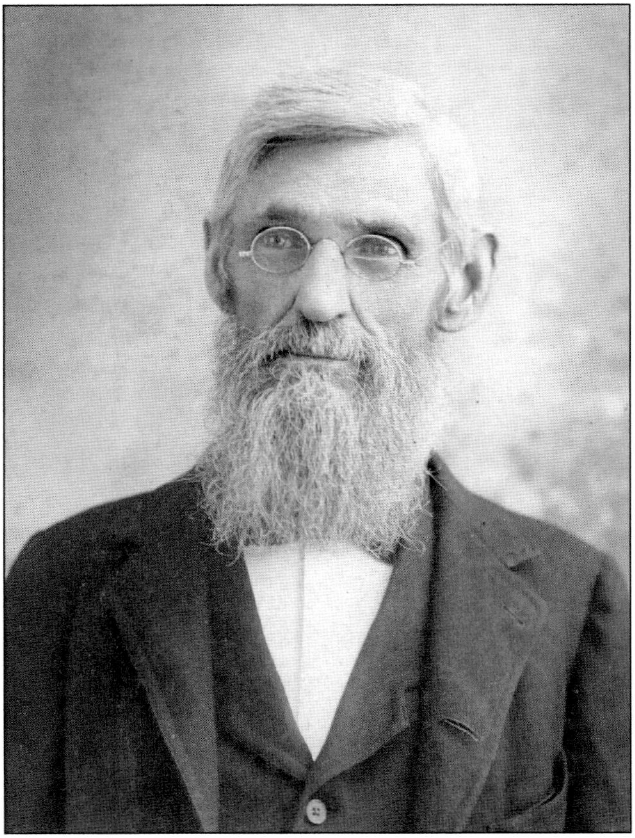

William Stephenson Strain (1833–1914) built this house in 1899 after the home he was renting burned to the ground with everything he owned. This one-story home had the same floor plan as his son's, W. A. Strain. W. S. Strain became a bookkeeper for the W. A. Strain Drug Store before he was appointed postmaster in 1898, remaining there until his death in 1914. Just to the right of the house is one of the buildings from Speer's College, which burned in 1912. The heat from the fire discolored the window glass, which can be seen even today. William Stephenson Strain was the son of William B. Strain and Mary Alice Stephenson of Washington County, Tennessee. His first marriage produced three children: W. A. Strain (1861–1907), Ruth Ella Strain (1856–1895), and Mary Alice Strain Lyon (1858–1911, Mrs. W. G. Lyon).

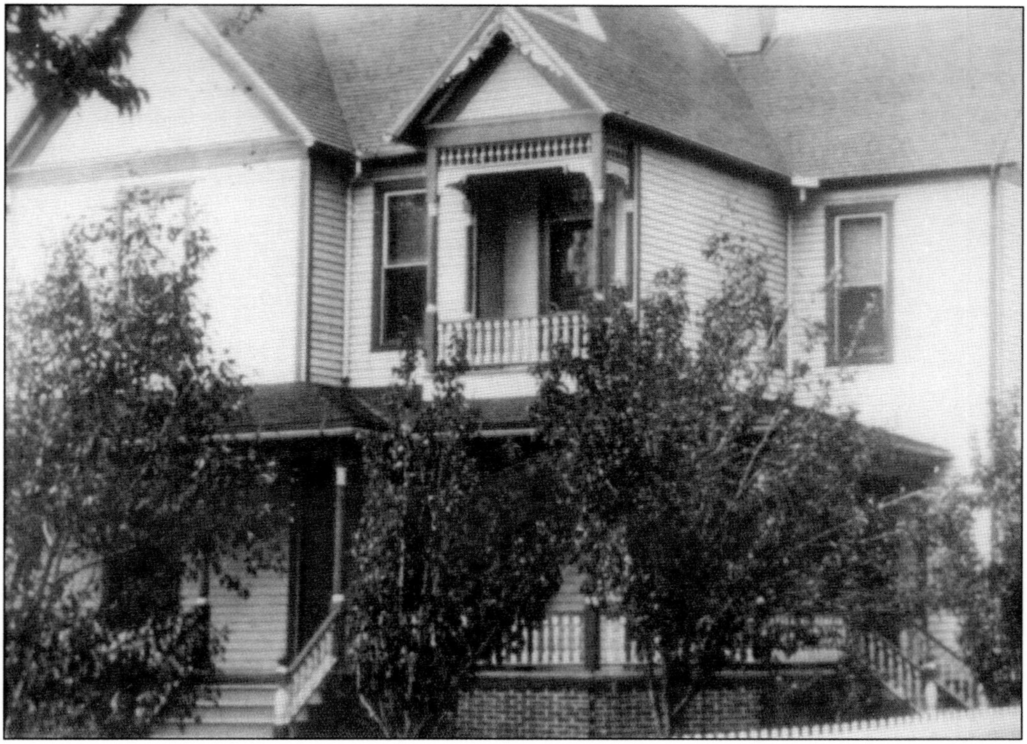

Thomas Jefferson Beesley (1836–1922) was born in Tennessee, married Martha Ann Jobe (1846–1925), and moved to Texas around 1874. T. J. served in the Confederate army under Gen. J. C. Johnson. Due to his service, he suffered severe hearing loss. They first lived in a log cabin near Rawlins Cemetery then in a house on State Street between Third and Fourth Streets. Finally the Beesleys moved into this house on Seventh and Jefferson Streets with their three younger sons. Beesley farmed nearby and his sons enjoyed catching crawdads in Keller Creek, which ran through their pasture.

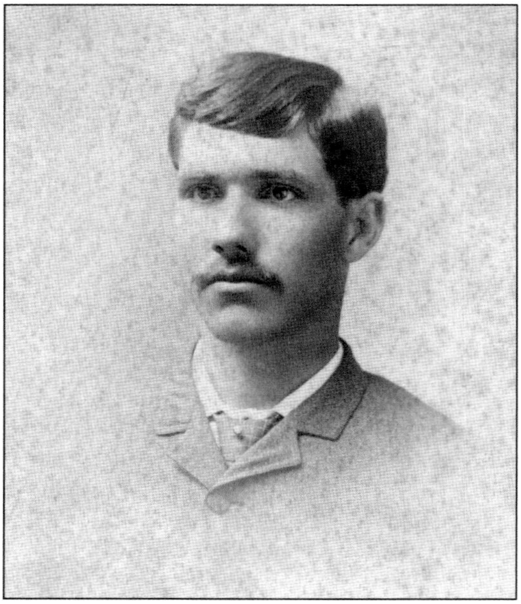

Walter Scott Beesley (1873–1952) was born in Tennessee and moved as an infant to Lancaster. He was the son of Thomas Jefferson Beesley. He graduated from Texas A&M University in 1892. In 1897, he married Annie Graham. Walter was a civil engineer, and Annie taught music. He is the father of Ann Beesley Lyon (Mrs. W. G. Lyon Jr.), Lottie Beesley, and Ben Beesley.

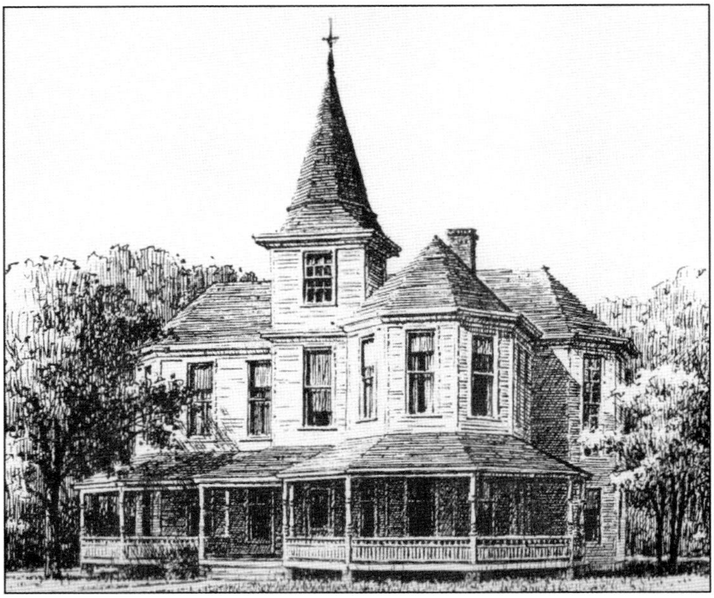

Sam Randlett came from Louisiana to Lancaster around 1886. He had been a plantation foreman and a sea captain. In 1887, he married Addie White, daughter of Louisa F. White. This house was finished around 1896, just before Addie's death from a poisonous spider bite. The house backs up to Dallas Avenue and faces Centre Street. This view is from the southeast side.

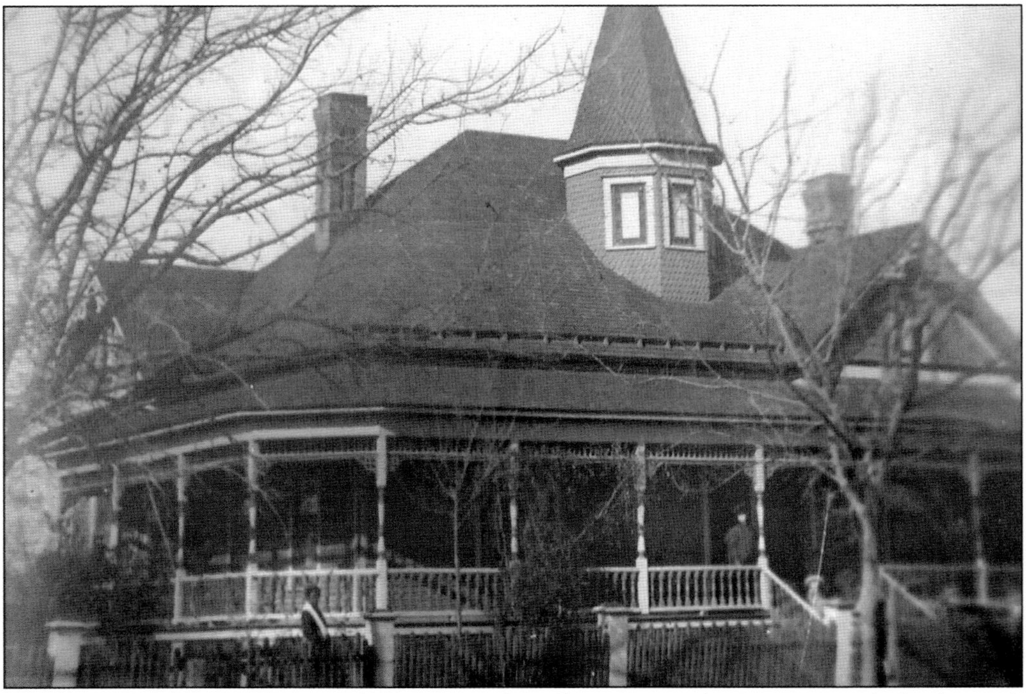

Wes Owens built this house around 1880 on South Dallas Avenue. The Owens owned a lumberyard. A storm destroyed the cupola, but the house still stands with much of its original hardware. The house is also known as the Moffett home and the Hunstable home. As Dallas Avenue has been rebuilt and raised several times, the house sits much lower to the ground now.

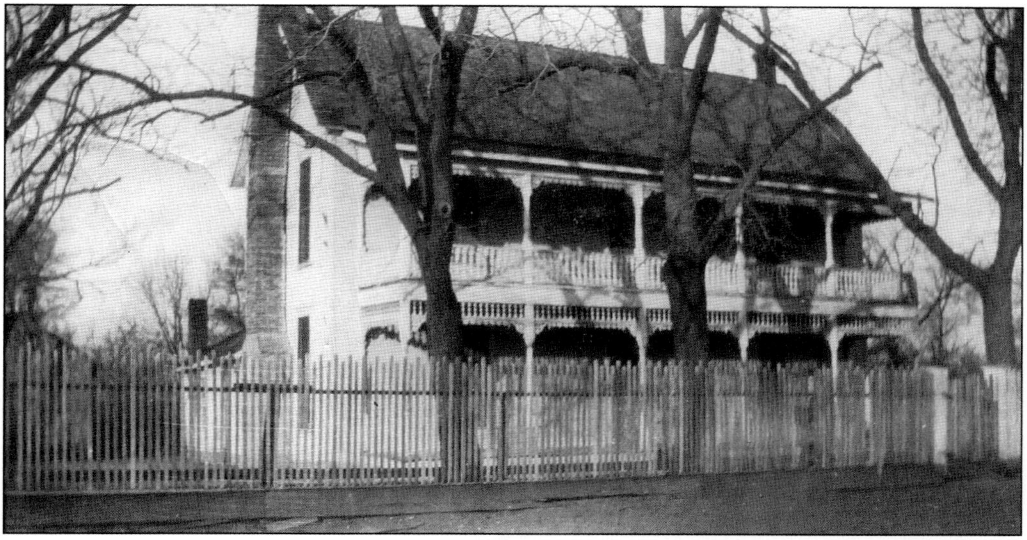

Calvin Taylor was born in Greene County, Illinois, and came to Dallas County around 1854. He married Harriet Emaline Ellis, daughter of Thomas McKee Ellis and Mary Witt Ellis in 1856. He entered the Confederate service in Capt. R. A. Rawlins's company but became ill and had to return home. His brother Perry took his place. Calvin died in Forrest, Mississippi, where he had gone to take his brother a replacement horse. The Taylor home burned in 1936 while the family of Fred Orr lived there. The Orr's young infant perished in the fire. The house was located just northwest of Deep Branch on West Main Street. (Courtesy of Mary Jane Orr Colton.)

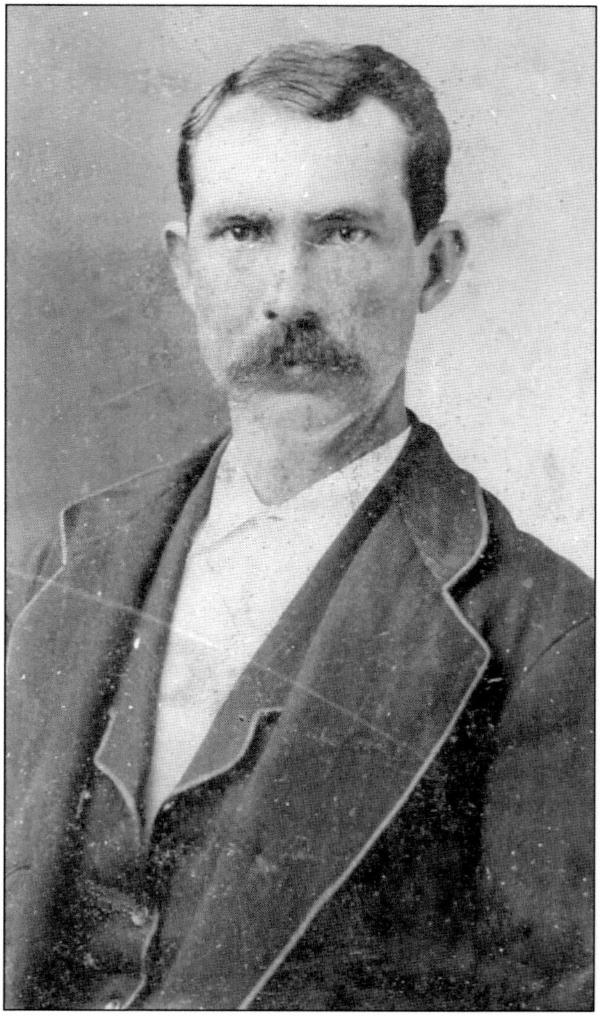

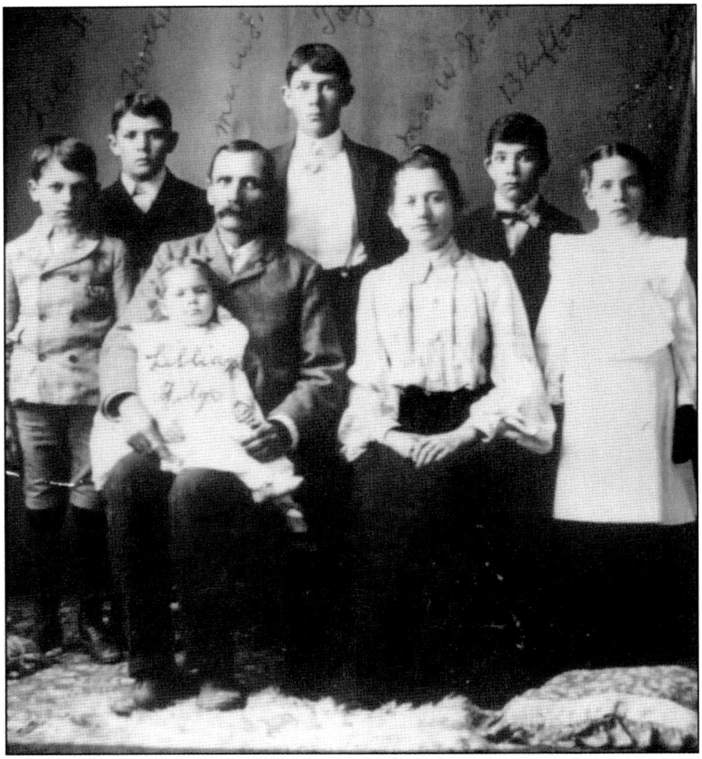

William Filgo (b. 1859) came to Lancaster about 1897 from Tupelo, Mississippi. He married Lena Price (b. 1888). The Filgo family has been longtime Lancaster farmers. Pictured from left to right are Lee Filgo (b. 1903), Holland Filgo (b. 1891), William James Filgo holding Lillian Filgo Orchard (b. 1901), Joseph Taylor Filgo (b. 1888), Lena Price Filgo, Blufford Filgo (b. 1890), and Mary Susan Filgo (b. 1895).

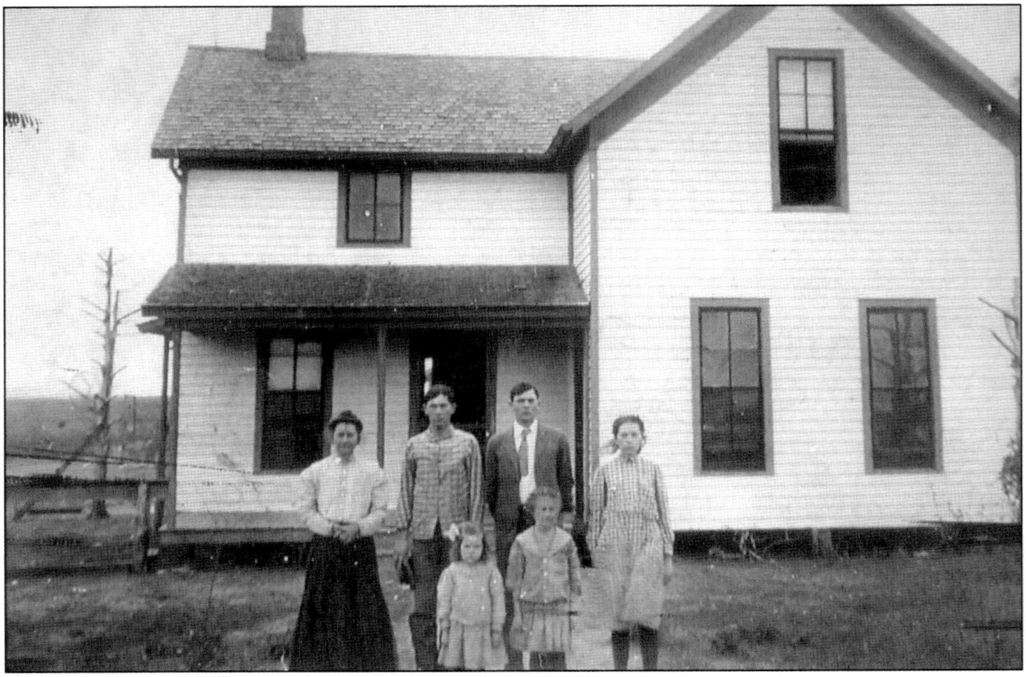

The Filgo family, standing in front of their house, included Lena Harrison Price Filgo (Mrs. William James Filgo), Taylor (b. 1888), Holland (b. 1891), Mary (b. 1895), Lillian (b. 1901), and Nellie (b. 1905) Filgo. William Filgo was active in the community and served on the Lancaster School Board. Lillian Filgo Orchard taught in Lancaster Schools for many years.

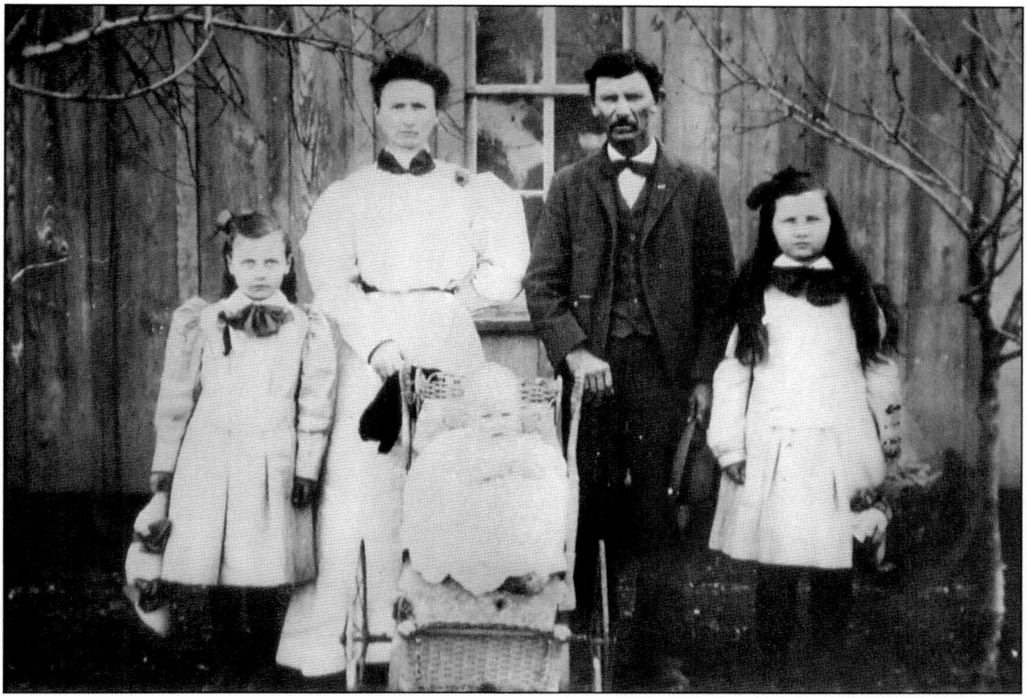

John Demarion Whaley (1860–1925) came to Lancaster in the 1880s from Cass County, Texas. He married Mary Lydia Long in 1890. Whaley operated a restaurant in the northwest corner of the square from 1918 to 1919, and then he ran a feed store on First Street. At the same time, he did a dairy run to supply merchants with ice cream and other goods. He also delivered coal and wood by wagon to local homes. Other jobs included delivering caskets and auctioneering. The family from left to right includes Mettie Emily Claudie (1900–1978), Mary, John, Myrtle Lee Whaley (1897–1910), and Leonard Vencile (b. 1905) in front. Six other children were born later.

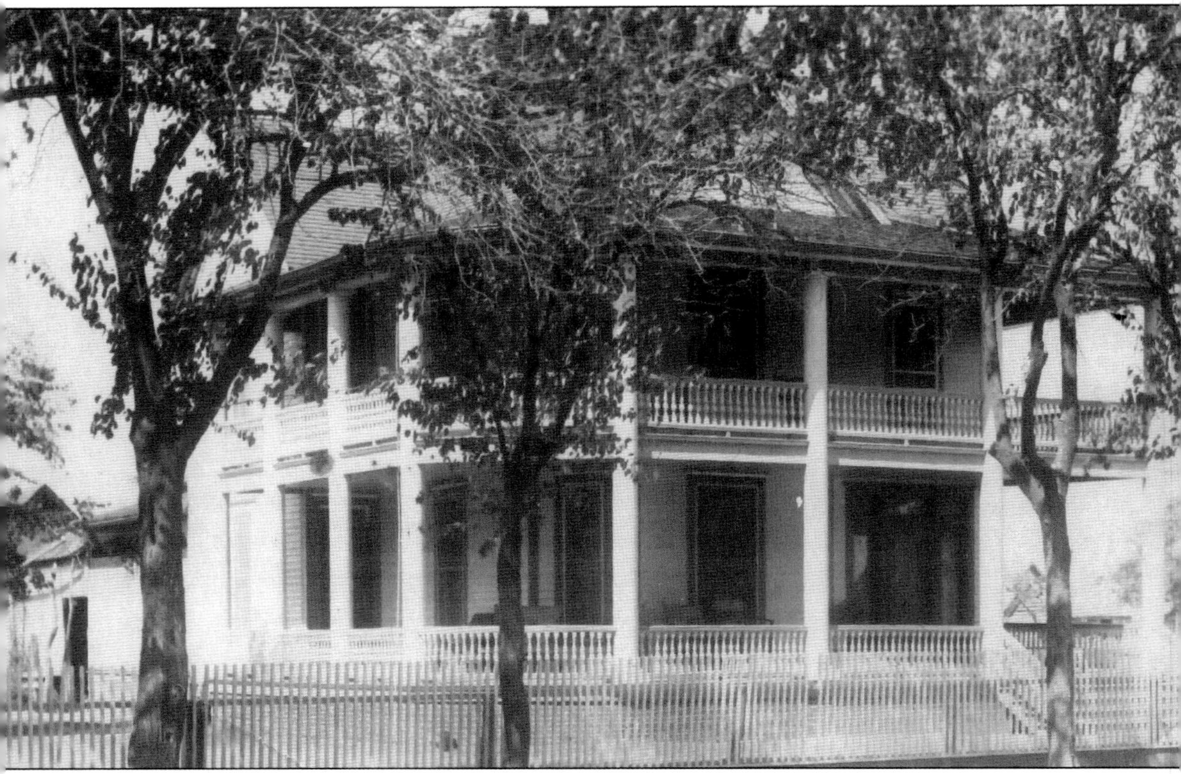

John Gibson (1833–1913) built this house around 1899 for his daughter, Ellen Gibson (b. 1874). Ellen was engaged to Charles Randolph Rea (1870–1924), who was considering a move from Lancaster. In order to keep Ellen in Lancaster, Gibson built this house as a wedding present on the condition that they stay in town. The couple wed in 1899. Rea was successful in business and the family was very wealthy but suddenly Rea died in his 50s. Rea's brother was executor and managed to pocket much of the wealth, leaving the family in tight financial needs. The Reas' daughter, Jeanette (b. 1900), married Cole Craig, a journalist, and moved to Massachusetts in 1924. Ellen promised Jeanette the house if she returned home. This was at great cost to her husband's career. The Craigs moved back though. Ellen Rea eventually moved back into the house, and the Craigs moved to Houston and did not return to Lancaster. (Courtesy of Carolyn Miller.)

Six

Life in Early Lancaster

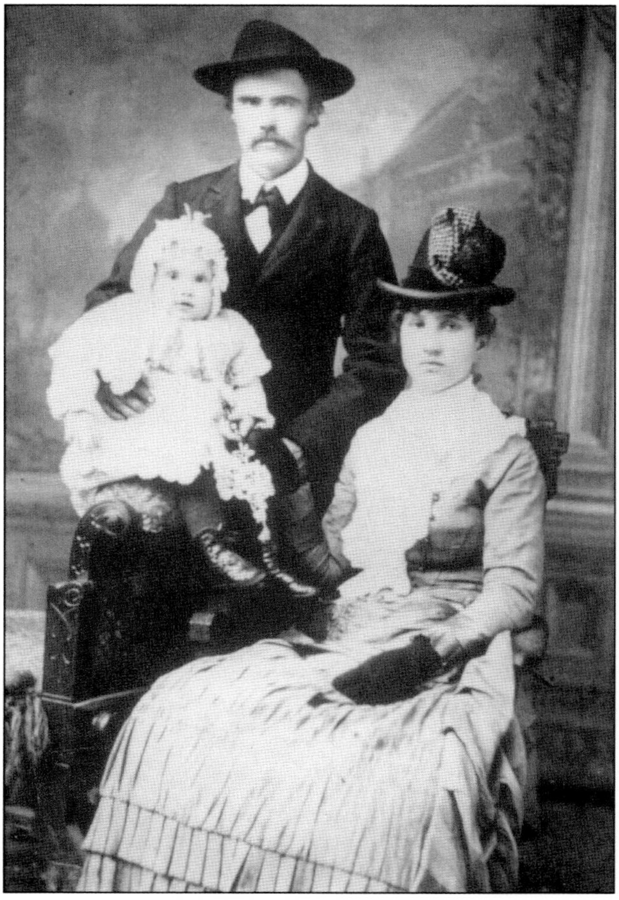

Charles Murphey and his wife, Mary Frances, with their daughter Phoebe Murphey Edwards were very involved in Lancaster. Charlie Murphey, a former Texas Ranger, owned a blacksmith shop and was active in the Independent Order of Odd Fellows. They lived in the 660 block of North Dallas Avenue.

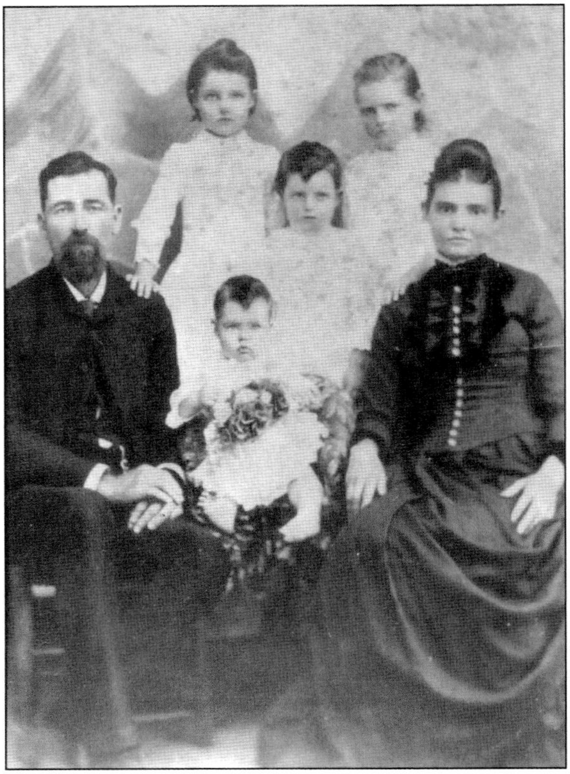

John William Curry (1753–1922) came to Dallas County about 1870 from Virginia. He worked at the cotton gin and later farmed. He married Lucy Angeline Greene (1856–1919). Curry served on the school board, was a Mason, a member of the Independent Order of Odd Fellows, and a deacon in the Baptist church. Pictured are from left to right, (seated) J. W. Curry (1853–1921), Lucille Curry (1856–1919), and Lucy Angeline Greene (b. 1919); (standing) Jesse M. Curry (b. 1880), Alpha Bill, Lenice (b. 1885), and Baby Lucile (b. 1888).

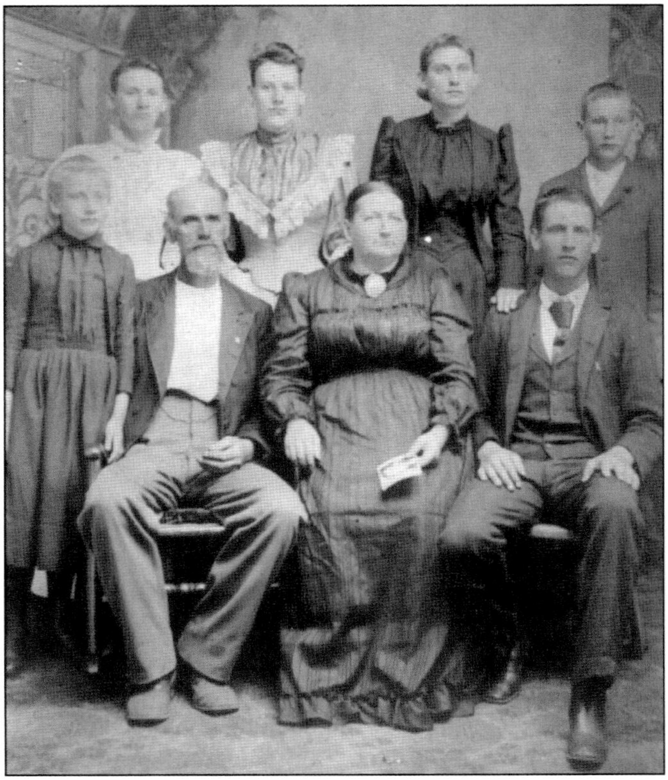

Pictured is the Hugh Lowrey family. From left to right are (first row) Minnie Lowrey (b. 1884), Hugh L. Lowrey (b. 1842), Malinda Gracey Lowrey (b. 1840), and Montgomery Lowrey (b. 1867); (second row) Kittie Lowrey (b. 1871), Harriet Lowrey (b. 1878), Maggie (b. 1876), and Hugh Lowrey Jr. (b. 1879). Hugh Lowrey served in the 13th Tennessee Cavalry from White County, Tennessee, during the Civil War. He was captured in 1863. The Lowreys were farmers in Lancaster.

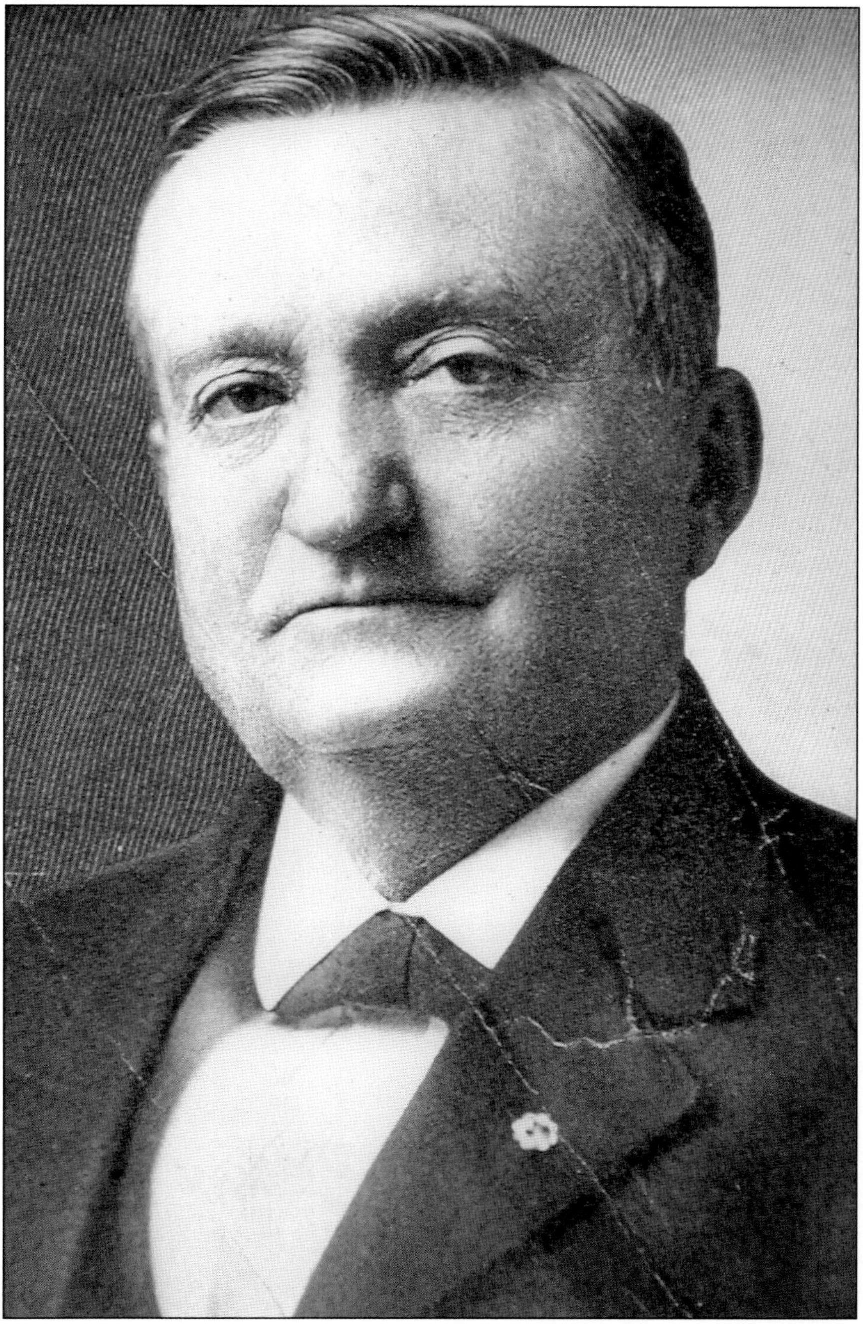

Rene Paul Henry was born in France in 1850, the son of Joseph Paul Henry and Florence Adelaide Dehoque. Joseph Henry was an engraver. When the family came to America in 1855, Joseph had a job as an engraver in New York, but in a few months, the Henrys joined a group heading to Houston, Texas. They finally settled in La Reunion, near Dallas, where the Henry family tried farming. When the Civil War started, Joseph's skills were needed at the gun factory in Lancaster. Rene Paul (R. P.) was a very industrious young man and earned money in a variety of ways. He soon purchased the stock of Ellis and White's mercantile business. In 1889, he opened a private bank in Lancaster and also had banks in Ferris, Dallas, and Galveston.

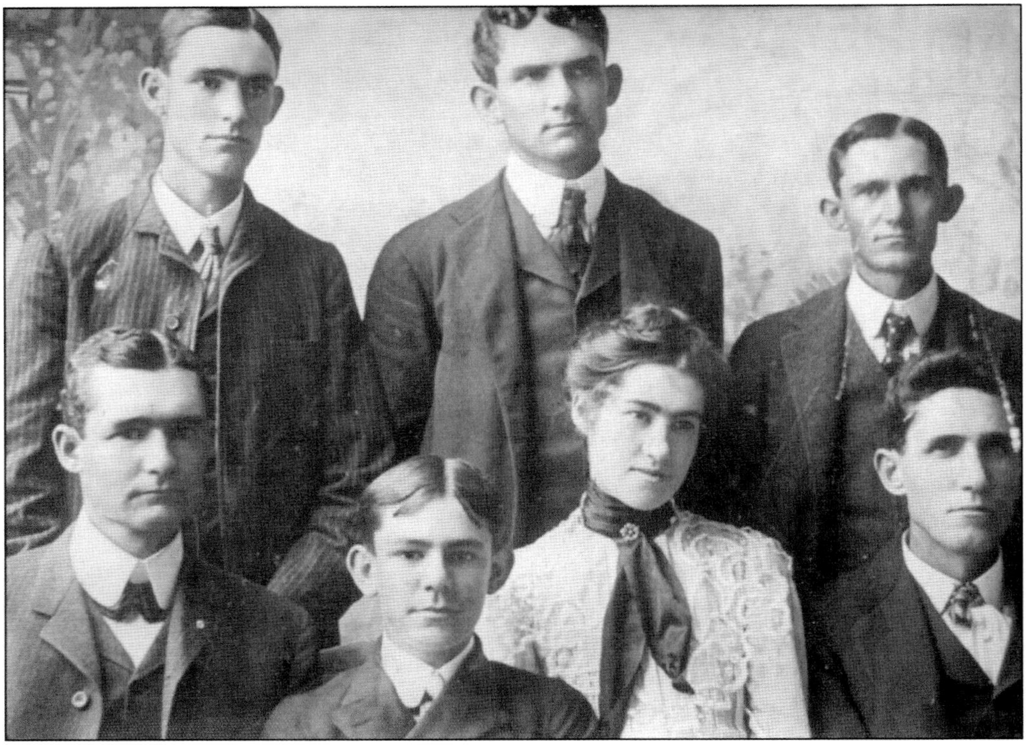

James Henry Ellis came to Lancaster around 1845 with his parents, Thomas McKee Ellis and Mary Witt Ellis. He married Mary Elizabeth Rawlins, daughter of Pleasant King Rawlins, in 1867. Their children are, from left to right, (seated) Ross Ellis (b. 1873), Henry A. Ellis (b. 1887), Ethel Ellis Scott (b. 1883), and John Henry Ellis (b. 1870); (standing) King Ellis (b. 1882), William Rawlins Ellis (b. 1879), and Tuck Leslie Ellis (b. 1877).

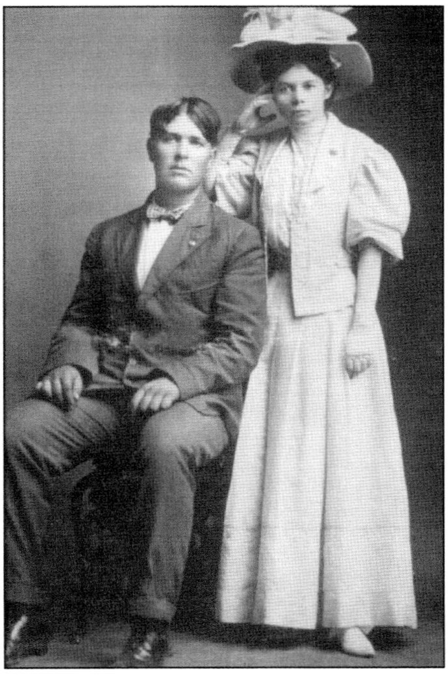

Frank M. Mabra (1889–1967) and Lily Mae Cheshier (1890–1916) married in October 1908. Frank was the son of James Adkinson Mabra and Nancy Elizabeth Barger. Lily was the daughter of James Henry Cheshier and Susan Jennie Arthur. They are both buried in Rawlins Cemetery in Lancaster, Texas. The Mabras were farmers north of Lancaster.

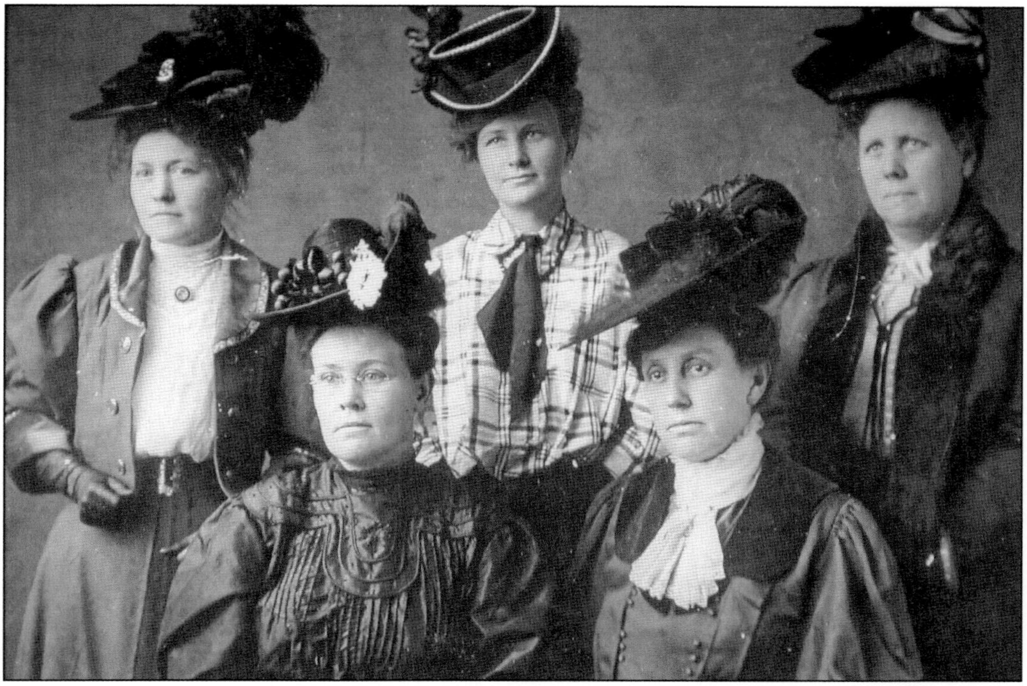

Many women could afford housekeepers, which gave them time to socialize with other ladies during the day. These friends are, from left to right, (seated) Ida Moffett Hammond and Maude Nicholson Smith; (standing) Janie Lavender, Ella Moffett Howell, and Annie Graham Beesley.

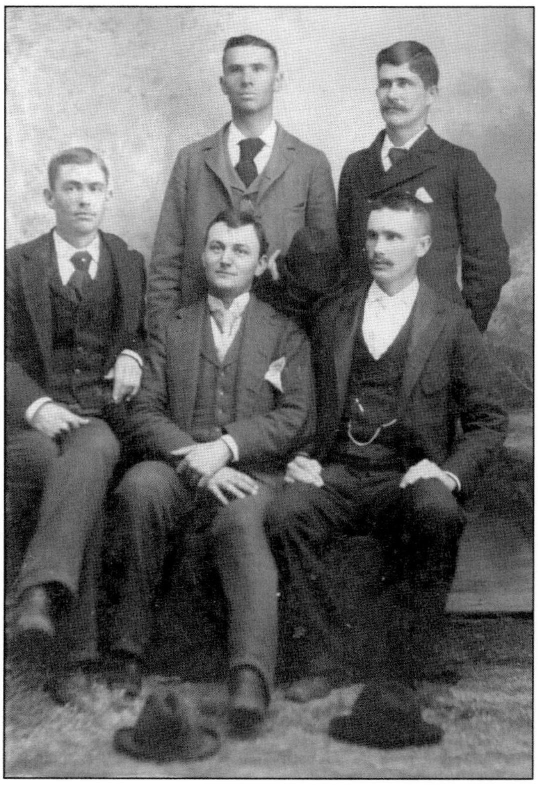

Young gentlemen of the period dressed in suit and ties unless they were working in the fields. Pictured here are, from left to right, (seated) two unidentified and Will L. White; (standing) Tom McCarty and Walter Beesley. This picture was taken in Ennis, Texas, so the two unidentified men may be from Ennis.

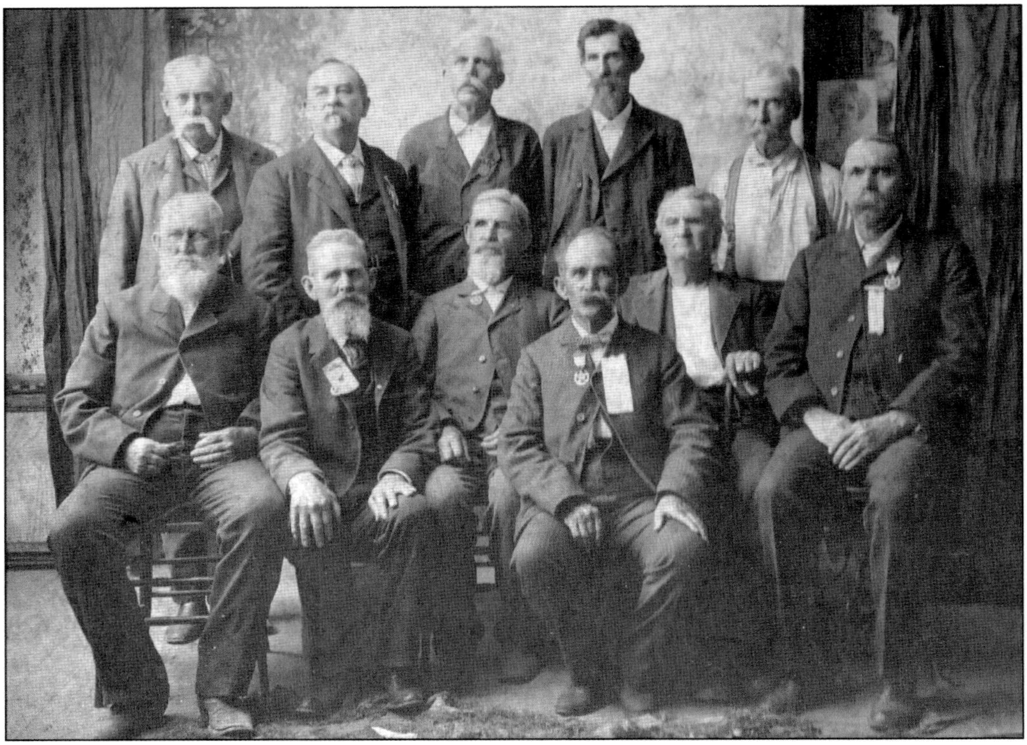

Many citizens of Lancaster fought for the Confederacy. In this photograph are some of the veterans from the war. From left to right are (seated) Irvin Lavender, F. M. White, two unidentified, John Thomas Ellis, and unidentified; (standing) James Lowrey, two unidentified, James Henry Ellis, and Frank Batchler. The Texas Cavalry, Company F and Company I were made up of many Lancasterites. Most of the horses for the cavalry were sired from the line of Steel Dust.

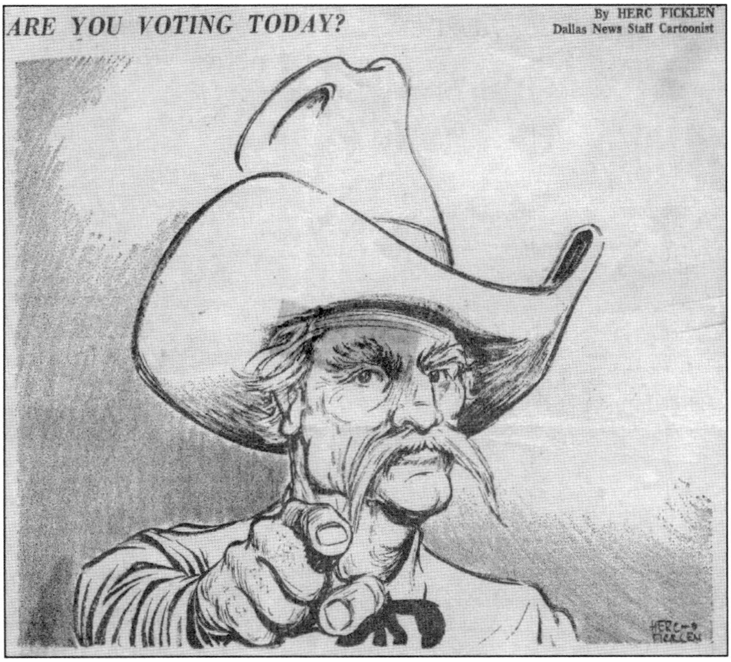

James A. Boyd (1851–1939) was the model that *Dallas Morning News* cartoonist John Knott used for his "Old Man Texas." Jimmy Boyd was the postmaster in Lancaster during the Cleveland administration (1893–1897) but is remembered most for the 1910 Model T Ford he drove until his death in 1939.

Seven
Reading, Writing, and Arithmetic

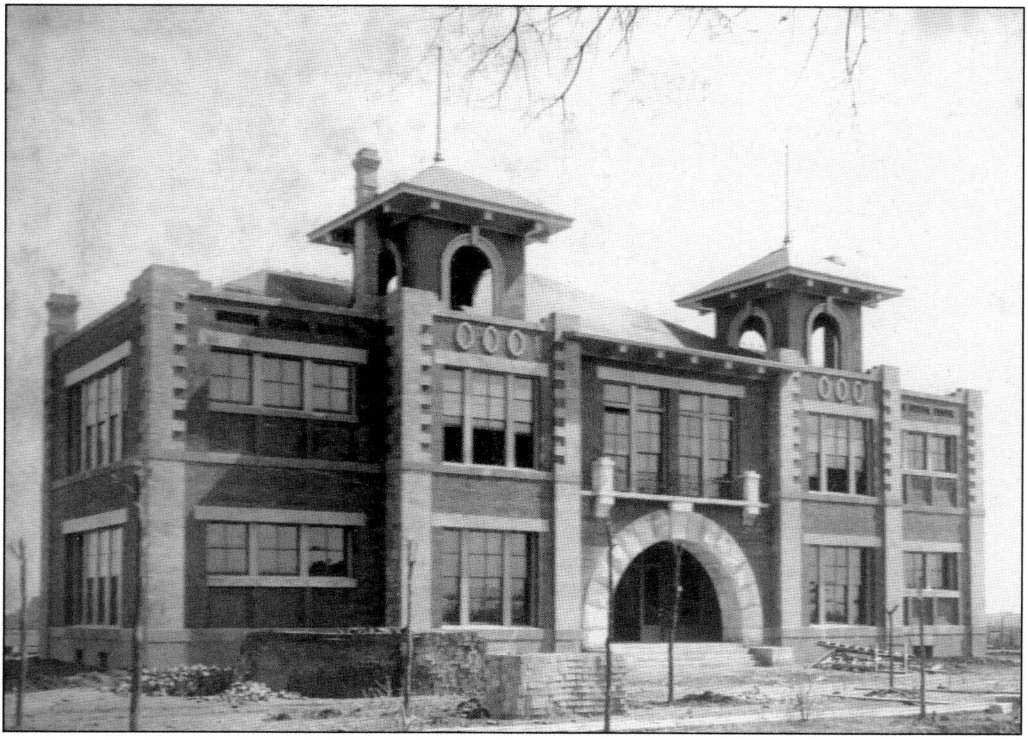

Lancaster became one of the first Texas Independent School Districts in 1905 and voted for a $15,000 bond to build a new school. The William L. White School was located on South Centre Avenue. The building was torn down around 1979.

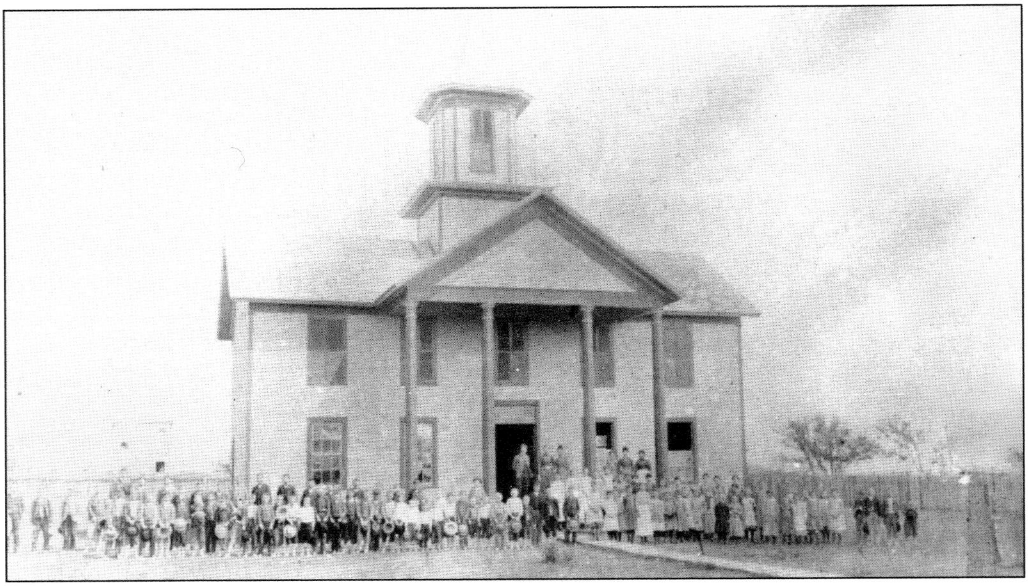

In 1868, Professor Clowney was in charge of the school being taught in the Masonic hall. Georgia Rogers ("Miss Georgia" Rawlins) joined Professor Reagor in 1873. In March 1874, the Masonic hall was moved to the lot where the First Baptist Church of Lancaster now stands in order to have more room. The citizens of Lancaster raised money to add a long wing on the north side of the building, which added four rooms. By 1891, the school was overcrowded and changes had to be made.

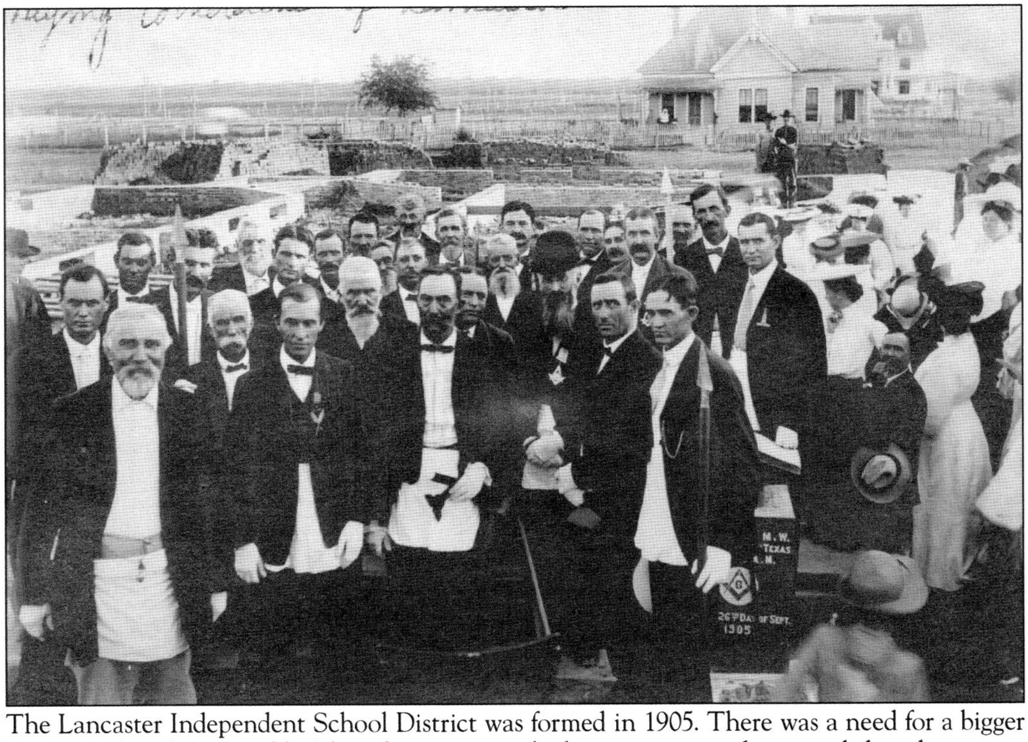

The Lancaster Independent School District was formed in 1905. There was a need for a bigger school, so bonds were sold. After plans were made, however, it was discovered that the cost to complete the structure would be $4,000. Will White made up the difference and to honor him, the school was named after his father, William Love White.

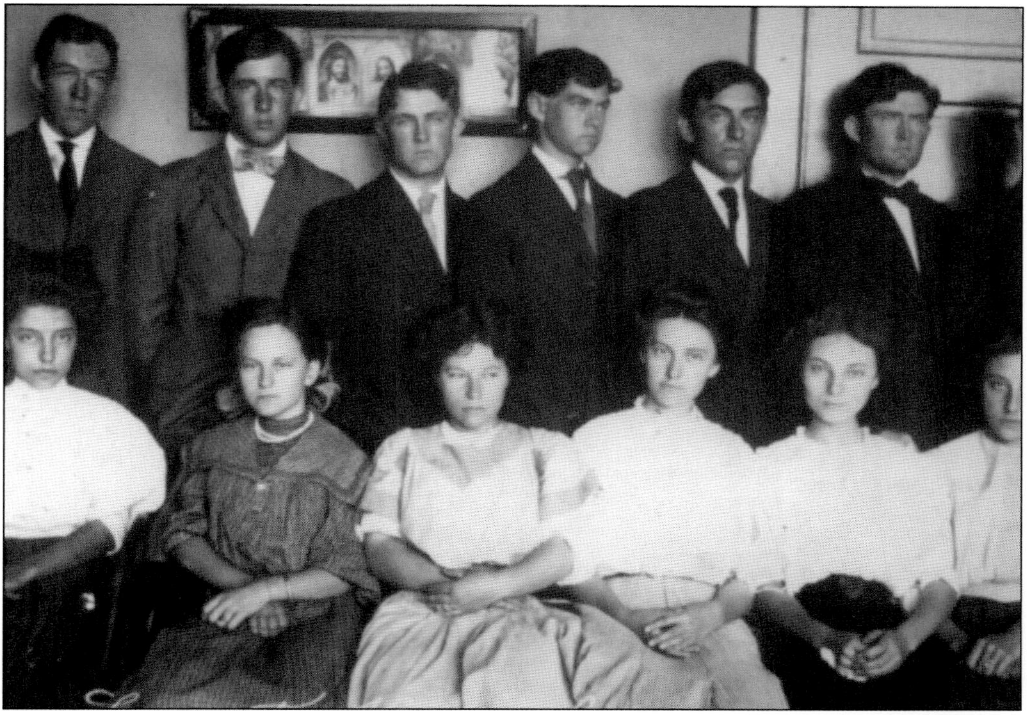

The class of 1908 missed part of the year due to an injunction against the school for illegal collection of taxes. Due to this injunction, the school closed on March 5, 1908, until a new election could be held. Female graduates that year were Ida Hood, Mattie Maurine Miller, Maggie Lou Gloves, Kathleen Stuart, Lucille Taylor, Hattie Bass, and Florence Louise Miller. The young men were Velpeau C. Denton, Woody L. Ferguson, D. D. Davis, Chester Davis, Ben W. Parks, Arthur Rumfelt, Leslie Simmons, and Henry Grady.

The William L. White School had been open only five years when this class graduated in 1911. The class was, from left to right, Ethel Winniford, Betty Vaughn, Stella Wilson, Frank Hull, Jack Griffin Morton, Layton Turney, Willie Turk, and Mary Lou Strain. Missing were Edna Graham and Will Glasscock.

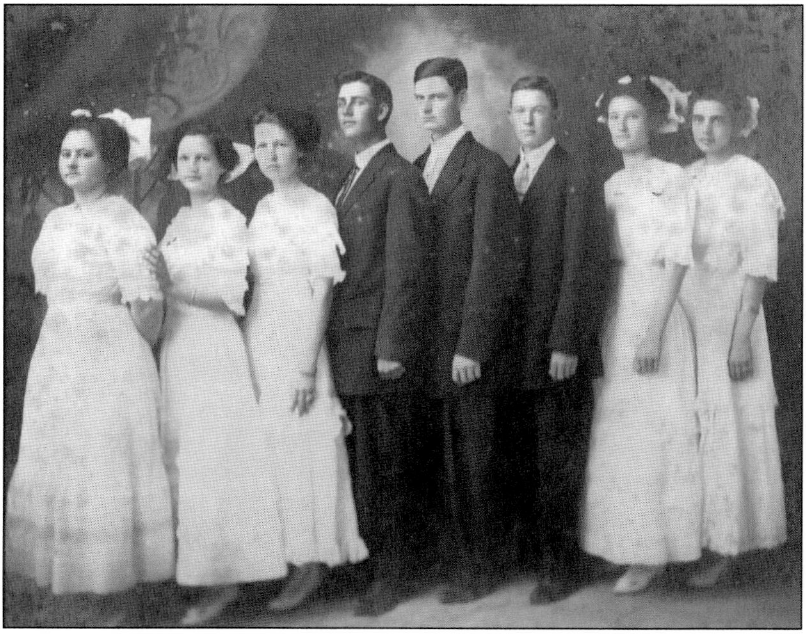

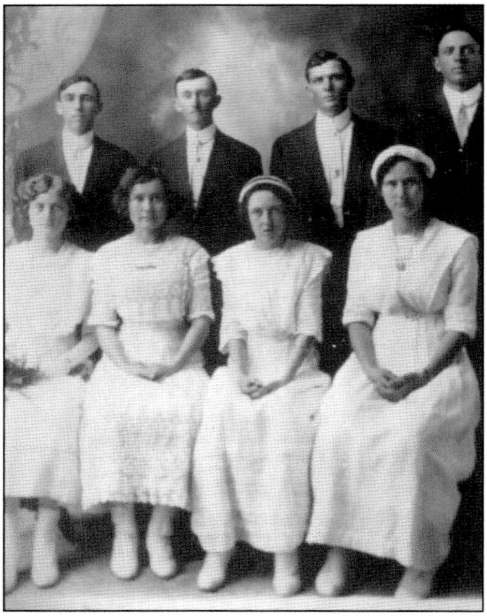

The class of 1912 missed some school due to a meningitis epidemic in which some Lancaster citizens died. The class of 1912 includes, from left to right, (seated) Virginia Graham, Freida Winniford, Ruby Parks, and Ethel England; (standing) Howard Ferguson, Earl Goforth, Holland Filgo, and Will Sears.

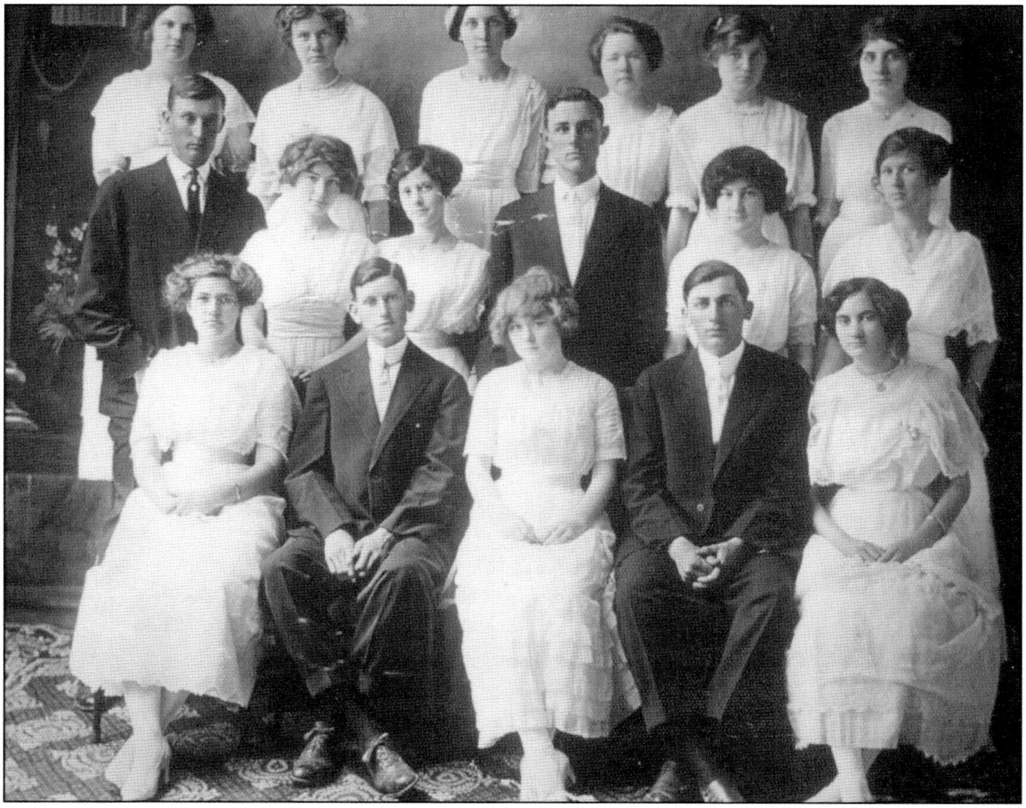

There were 439 students in the Lancaster schools in 1913. Pictured here is the graduating class from that year. From left to right are (first row)) Evelyn McCarty, Roy Waller, Geraldine Lavender, Lee Roy Filgo, and Fannie Graham; (second row) Burns Turk, Corinne Howell, Bess Moreland, Roy Bailey, Irene Scott, and Mary McCarty; (third row) Ruby Fonden, Nay Clark, Pansy Hood, Gladys Turney, Faye Graves, and Winnie Mitchell.

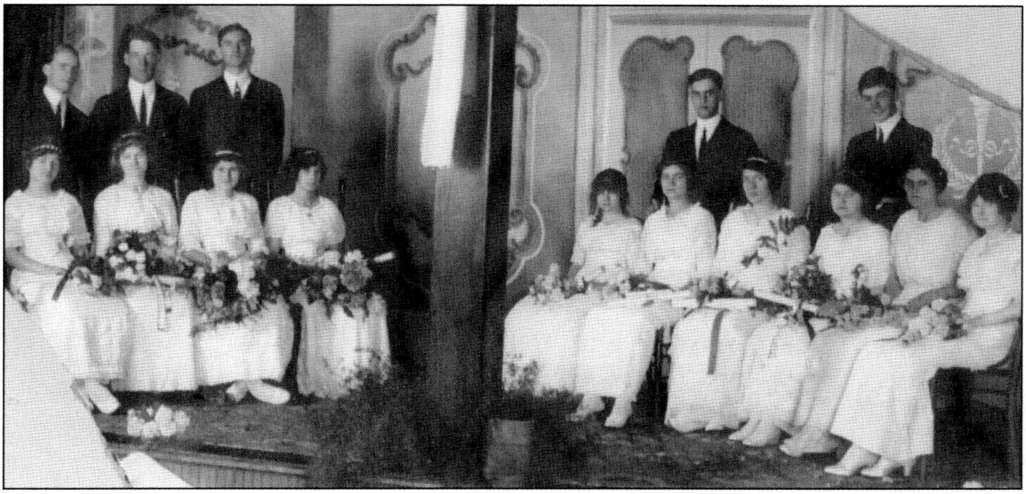

There were 430 students in the William L. White School, which made it very crowded. This 1913–1914 graduating class consisted of, from left to right, (seated) Ethel Barnes, Louise Lyon, Vic Solomon, Mattie Graham, Beth Guy, Nettie Fitzhugh, Mary Filgo, Nell Whaley, Lucille Summer, and Annie Morton; (standing) Will Randlett, Fred Gorham, Henry Brown, Lawrence Henry, and Taylor Dean.

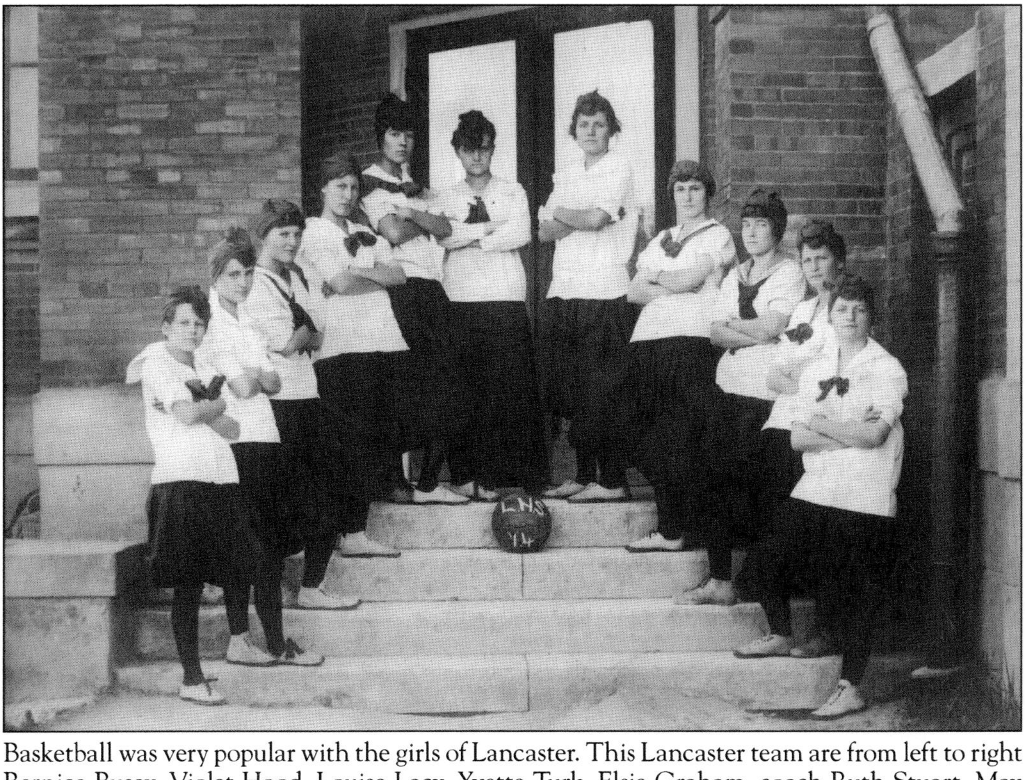

Basketball was very popular with the girls of Lancaster. This Lancaster team are from left to right Bernice Busey, Violet Hood, Louise Lacy, Yvette Turk, Elsie Graham, coach Ruth Stuart, May Hudson, Neva Dixon, Esther Hudson, Lillie Turk, and Lula May McIlheney.

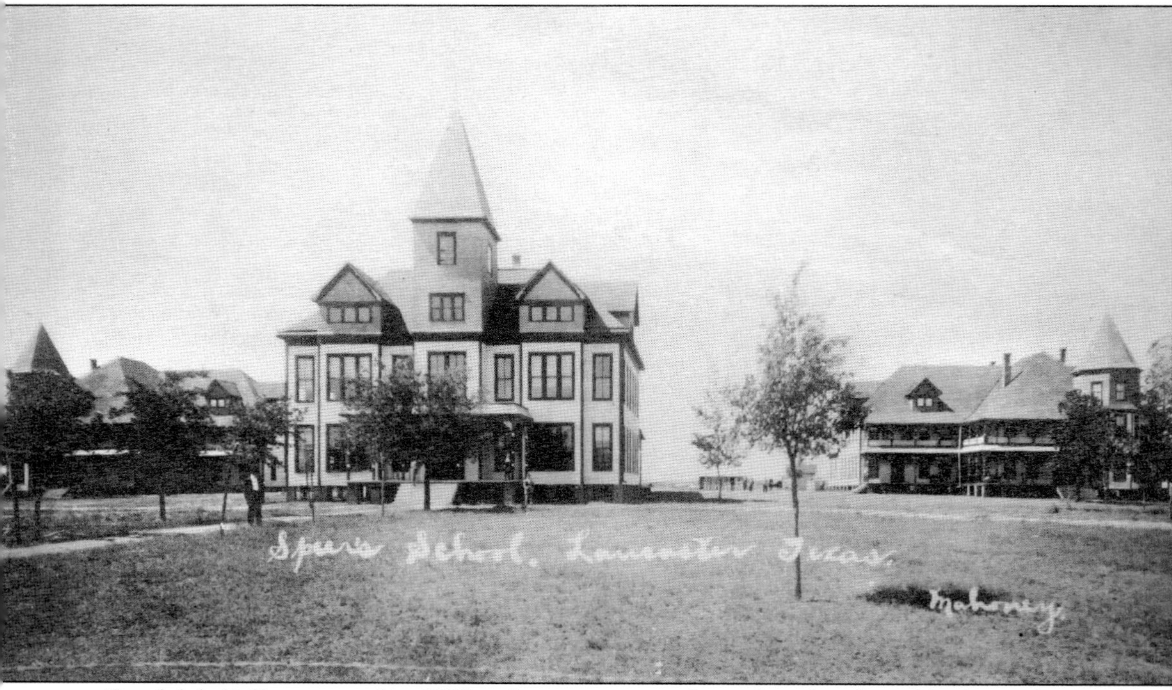

Randolph College opened in 1898 with nonsectarian classes but closed in 1901 due to financial difficulties. Randolph Clark, an ordained minister in the Christian Church, founded several other colleges connected with the Christian Church. This was probably the beginning of Texas Christian University. Henry College used the buildings in 1901 and 1902. Following that, the Lancaster Military Academy opened as a preparatory school, which was highly supported, although not financially, by the Baptist Church. Abandoned sometime after 1905, the buildings remained closed until 1911 when A. C. Speer opened Speer's College, which operated until the buildings burned in 1912. The education building was very up-to-date. The men's dormitory and the women's dormitory were located on either side. The Speer family lived in one of the dormitories when Speer's operated the school.

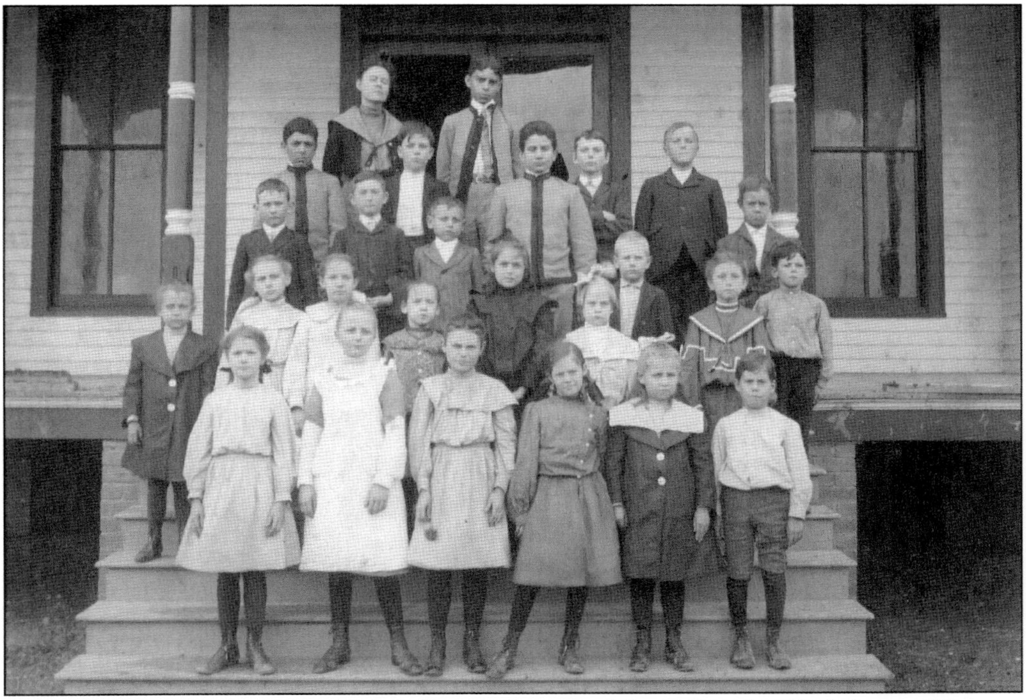

The abandoned campus of Randolph College took on new life in 1903 when Prof. George Wharton opened the Lancaster Academy, or Lancaster Military Academy. It was a first-class preparatory school. The Baptist churches highly recommended the school, and it is thought that Baptists used the school as their headquarters for meetings. The Lancaster Academy was a coeducational institution with military instruction for those who wanted it much like the ROTC. The preparatory school concept was very popular in the early 1900s.

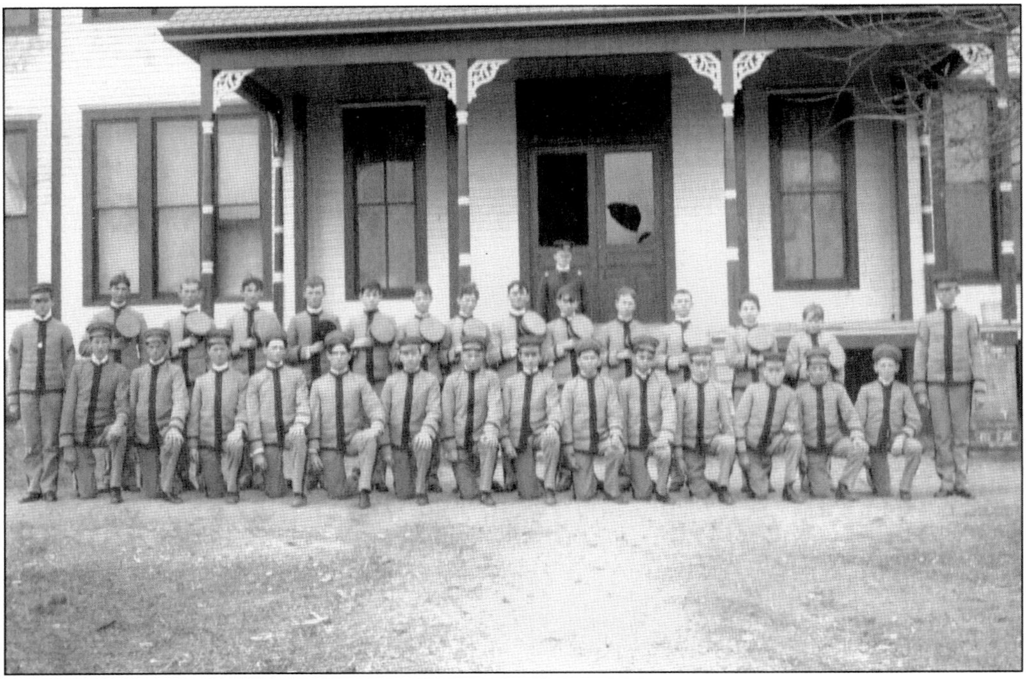

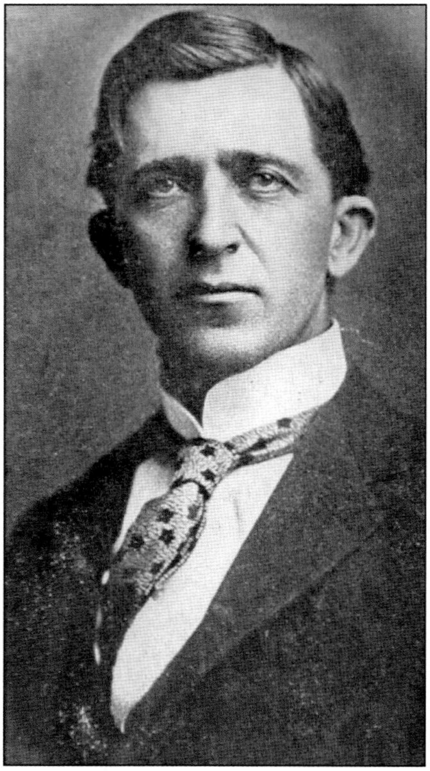

Prof. A. C. Speer lived in Ferris, Texas, but operated the Speer School in Lancaster from 1911 until the building burned in 1912. He then opened a school in Mount Pleasant, Texas, in an old hotel. The school advertised as a college preparatory school, but in truth, it was another high school, which closed its doors in 1914. Later Speer was associated with Southern Methodist University in Dallas.

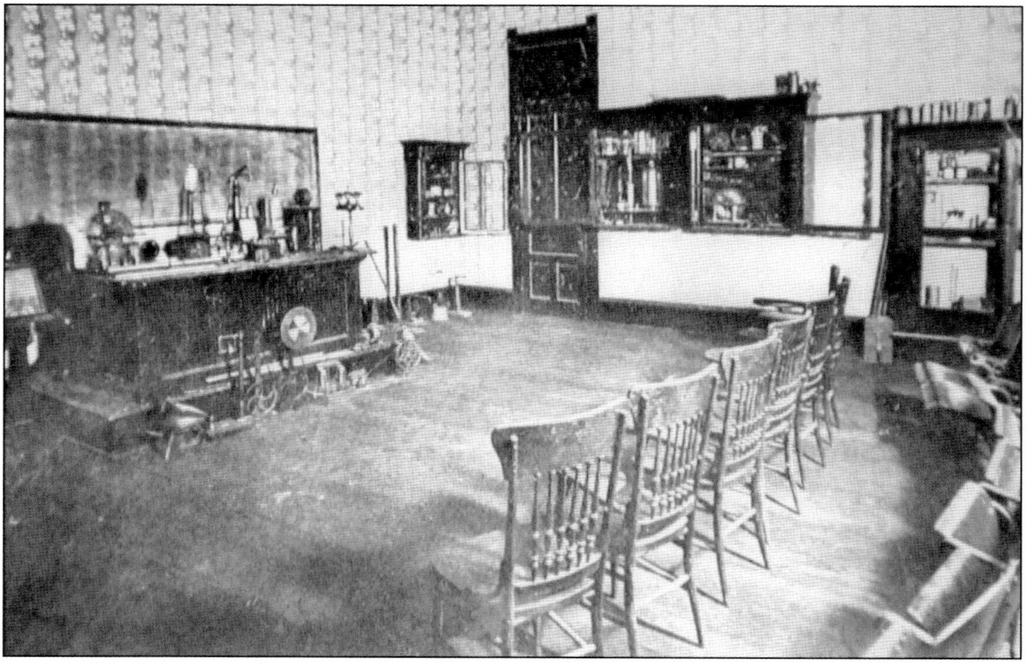

Speer offered many modern innovations such as this lecture room for science. One might notice the "soft seats" for the students. Remember too there was no air-conditioning and the students wore long-sleeved shirts and the females wore long skirts with lots of petticoats. It was in the early 1900s that females' education became more important.

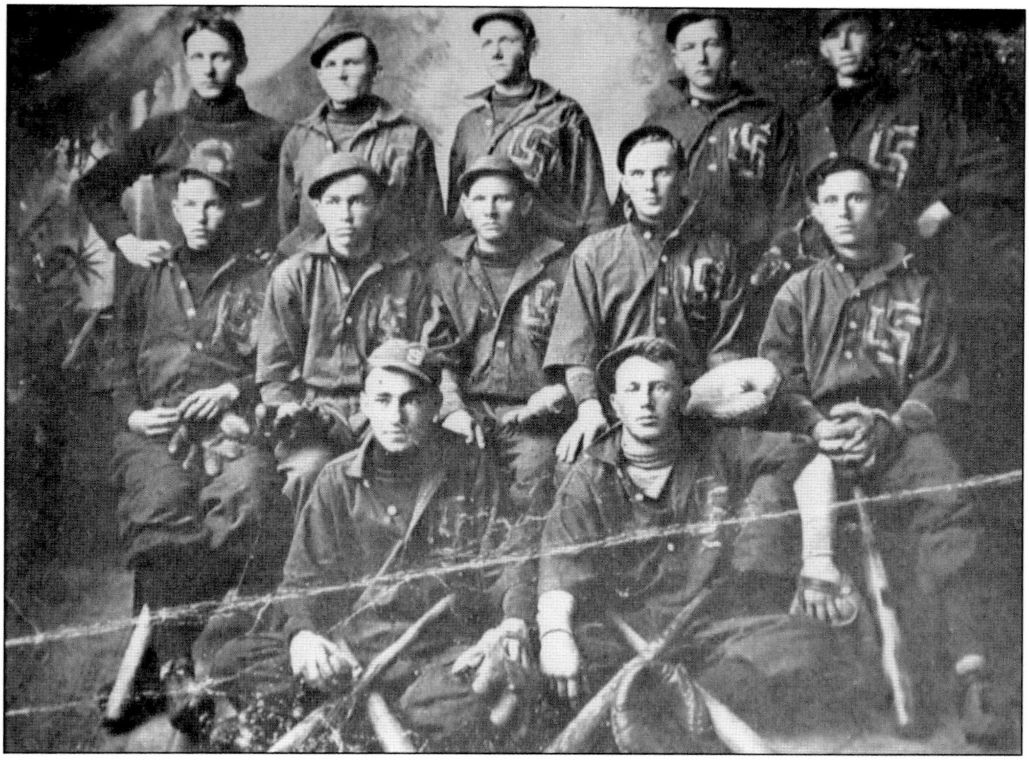

Speer School boasted of a full program, including sports and the arts. Baseball was a very popular sport in Lancaster before Speer School began. The team might have had several Lancaster players in the group. Football was not as popular as baseball in Lancaster but this team (below) appears ready to play.

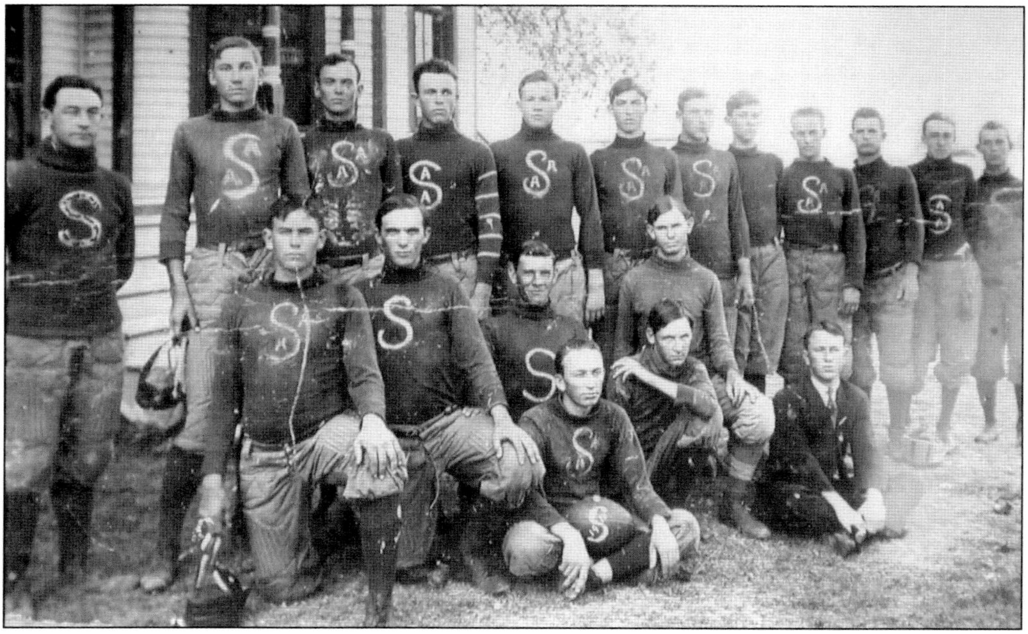

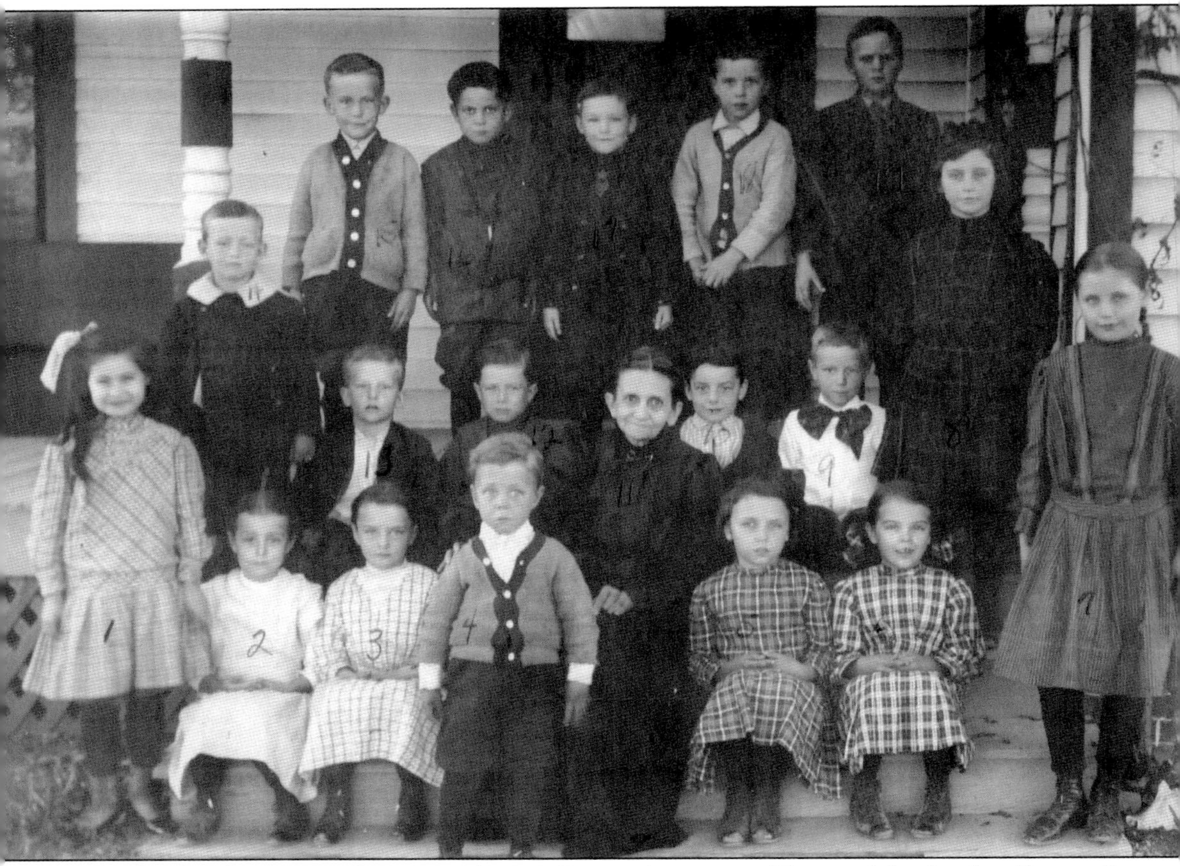

Schoolteacher Georgia Rogers was born in Georgia but came to Texas with her brother. Eventually she came to Lancaster and opened a school in the back of John Taylor's house and then taught in the public schools. She returned to Georgia for a short time but was brought back to Lancaster by one of her former students, Alex Rawlins, as his wife. Georgia Rawlins taught in the public school until 1896 when she opened a private school. Her school was located in the 300 block of South Dallas Avenue. In this picture, around 1908, Miss Georgia is sitting with her class in front of her school. From left to right are (first row) Ruth Orr, Irene Harris, Fay Ellis, Lester Hagan, Georgia Rawlins, ? Graham, Maxine Nowell, and Laura White; (second row) Hall Kirk, two unidentified, Jamie Randlett, Arthur Strain, and Evelyn Lavender; (third row) Arlen Winniford, Ray Winniford, and three unidentified.

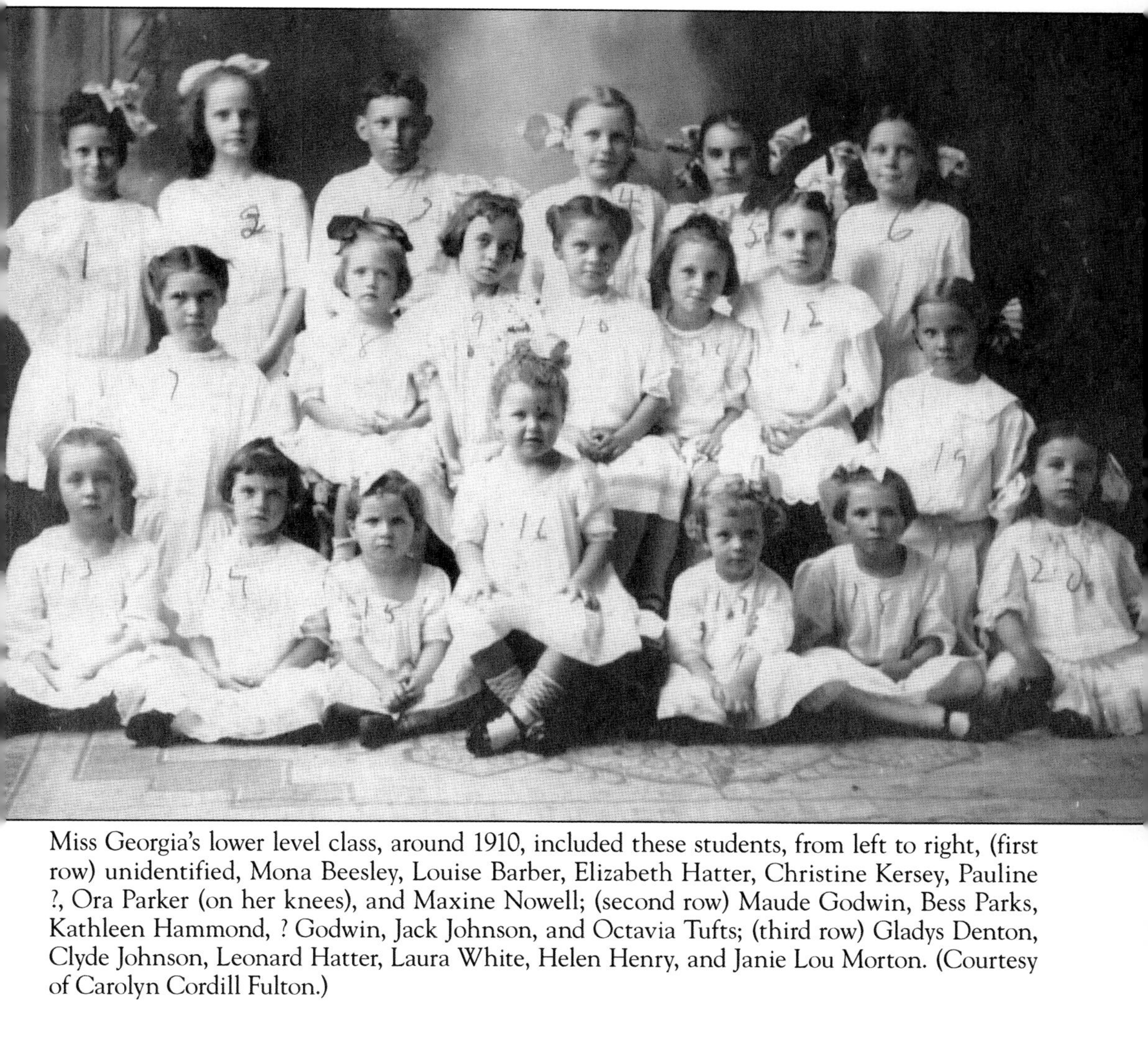

Miss Georgia's lower level class, around 1910, included these students, from left to right, (first row) unidentified, Mona Beesley, Louise Barber, Elizabeth Hatter, Christine Kersey, Pauline ?, Ora Parker (on her knees), and Maxine Nowell; (second row) Maude Godwin, Bess Parks, Kathleen Hammond, ? Godwin, Jack Johnson, and Octavia Tufts; (third row) Gladys Denton, Clyde Johnson, Leonard Hatter, Laura White, Helen Henry, and Janie Lou Morton. (Courtesy of Carolyn Cordill Fulton.)

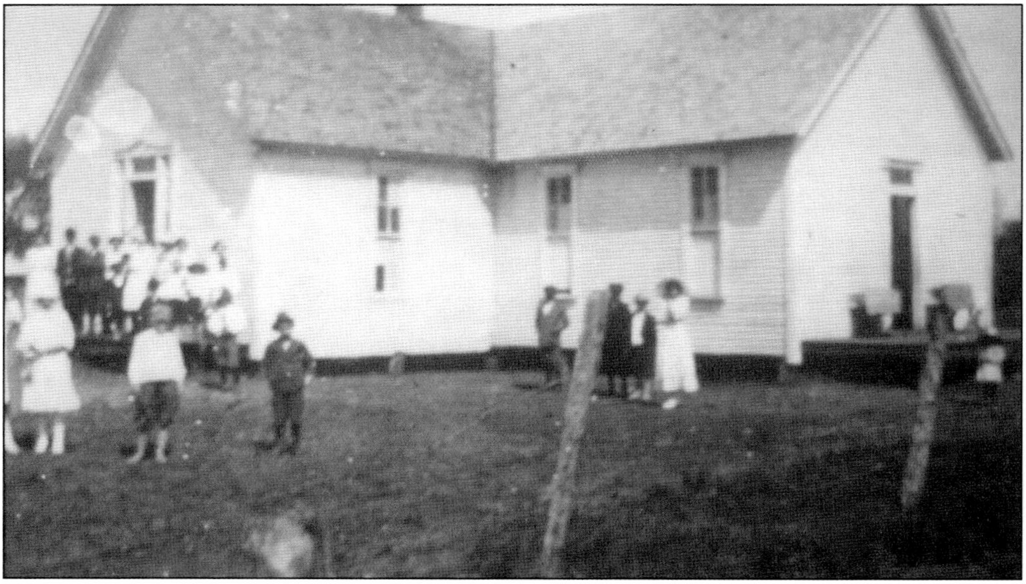

Lancaster boasted of a fine public school, colleges, a preparatory school, and Miss Georgia's private school but it also had more common school districts. Common schools were located in areas where students lived. The F. Rawlins School was first located close to where the Cold Spring Church of Christ is located on Main Street. This structure was a log house and had plank seats without backs. The school term lasted only two or three months. After this school burned, it was relocated to the northeast corner of Pleasant Run and Houston School Road. The new building was a wood-frame structure that also served as a church building.

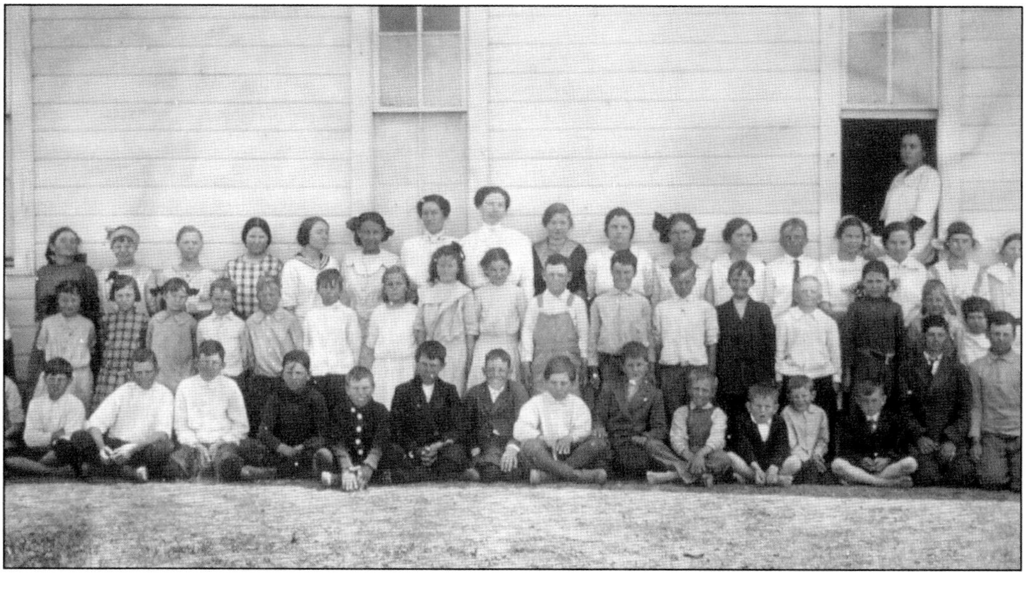

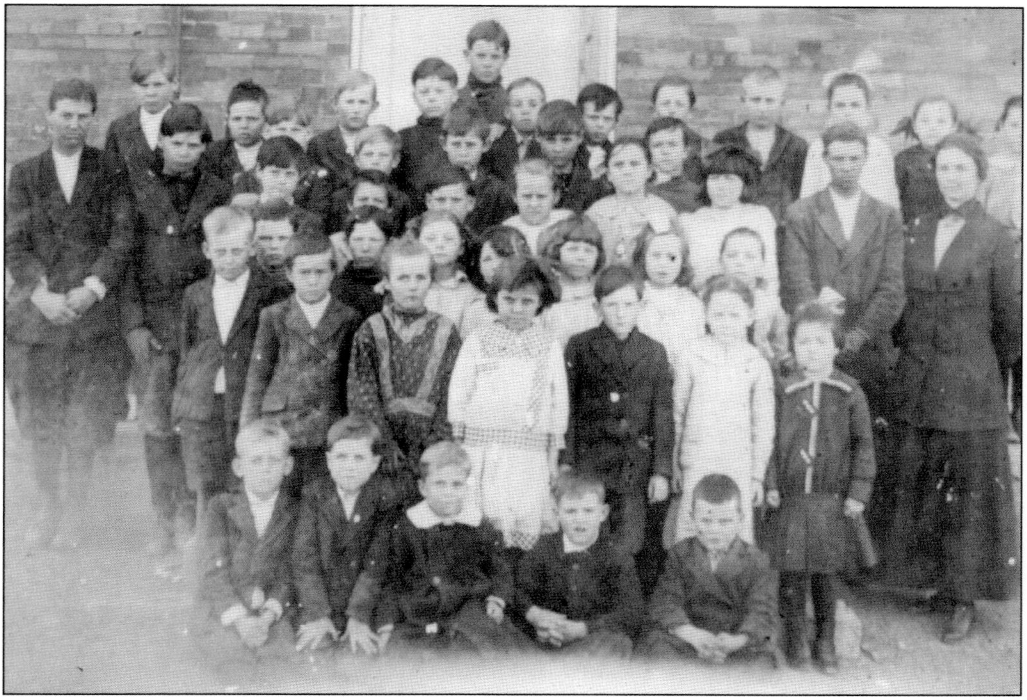

The George School was located on Nokomis Road, east and south of the Winniford home. There were many children that lived in this part of Dallas County and in the north section of Ellis County during this period and attended the George School (1899–1929). Later the George School and the Winniford School (Lower Bear Creek School) were consolidated into one.

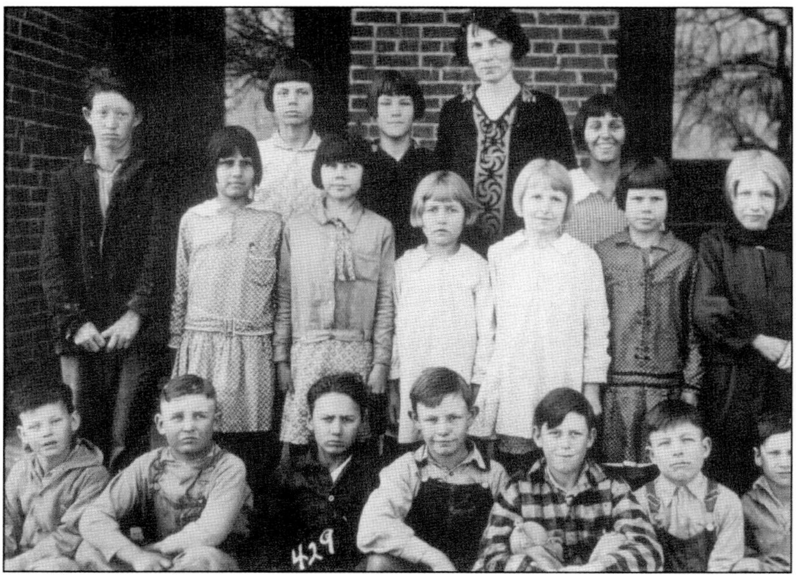

The Johnson Bank School (1885–1887) consolidated with the Bear Creek School (1885–1886), and the two schools were then referred to as Bear Creek School. It was situated on Houston School Road just south of Bear Creek Road but was actually in Ellis County. They had a wonderful brick school.

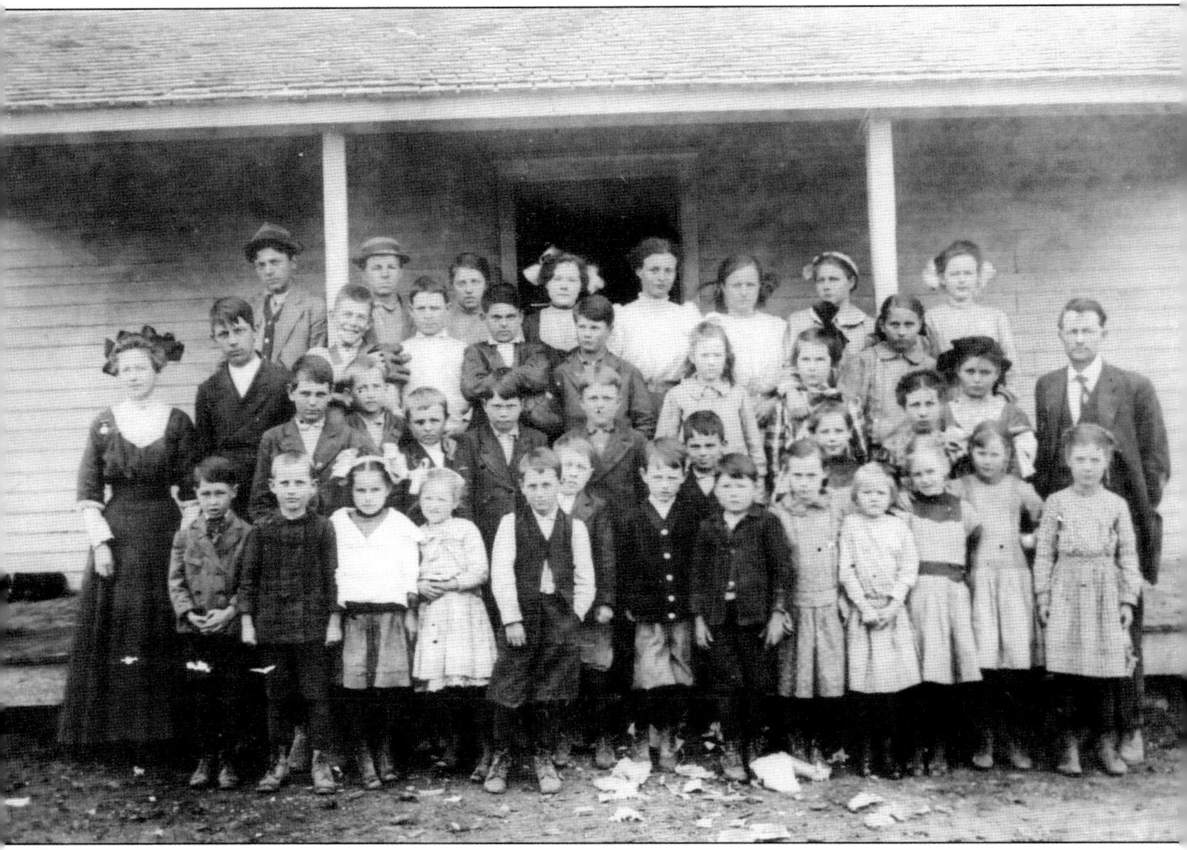

Independence School was located on Wintergreen Road near present day U.S. Interstate-45. The school was 2 miles from Hutchins and the smallest of the common schools. Dudley Chapman identified many of the students in the picture. From left to right are (first row) unidentified, Dudley Chapman, Roberta Mann (Mrs. Lenard Beard), Grace Turney, Jimmy Lacey, Turns Rawlins, Lawrence Green, two unidentified, Cleo Cook, and two unidentified; (second row) teacher Edna Turney, ? Lacey, unidentified, Buck Summer, Guy Green, unidentified, Fed Sears, Julia Cook (Mrs. Fred Wise), unidentified, Jimmie Lacey, Helen Smith, and teacher Ben Chapman; (third row) Renee Sears, Oscar Chapman, Bert Shisnand, Jim Sears, unidentified, Gladys Witt, and Adda Summer; (fourth row) Bill Sears, Elmo Smith, unidentified, Estelle Turney, unidentified Mosier, two unidentified, and Gladys Turney. The school closed in 1911, and the students went to Hutchins.

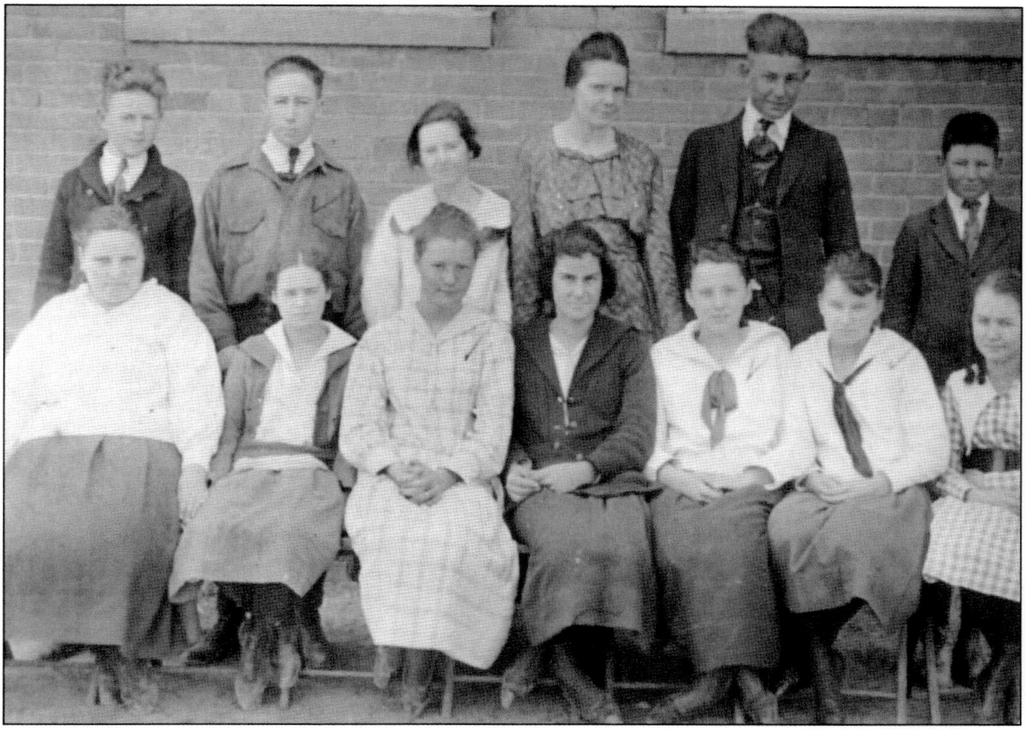

Houston School is located on Houston School Road at the intersection with Danieldale Road. A new brick building was constructed in 1915 and is currently used as a residence. Pictured are students in 1913 and their two teachers: (seated, from left to right) Ada Brownlee, Lucille Eastep, Estelle Greenwell, Bess Austin, Ruth Brown, Ruthe Weatherall, and Alience Langley; (standing, in no particular order) William Leaham, Imogene Estep, teachers Mary Murray and Hood Williams, William B. Austin, and Cal Case.

The Cross Roads School was at the corner of Sunrise and Beltline Roads near Wilmer, Texas. The land at that time belonged to Bill and Lucy Greene Curry. It is assumed the school began in the fall of 1882 and closed in 1900.

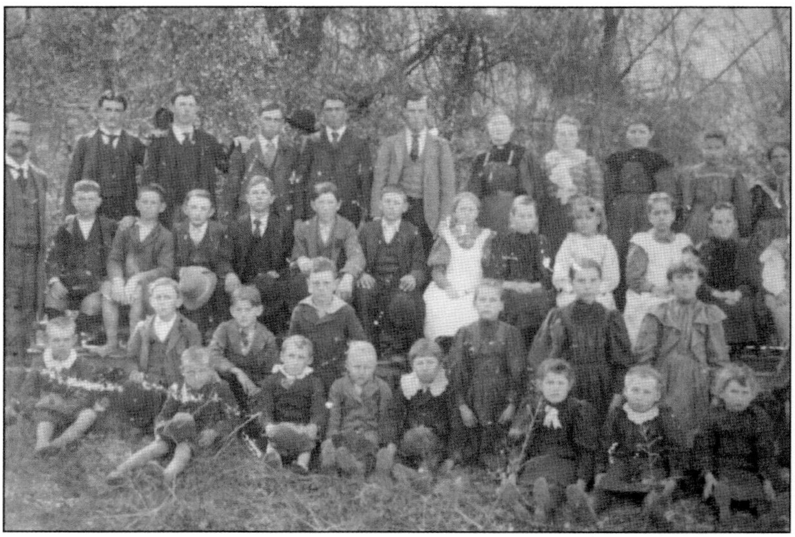

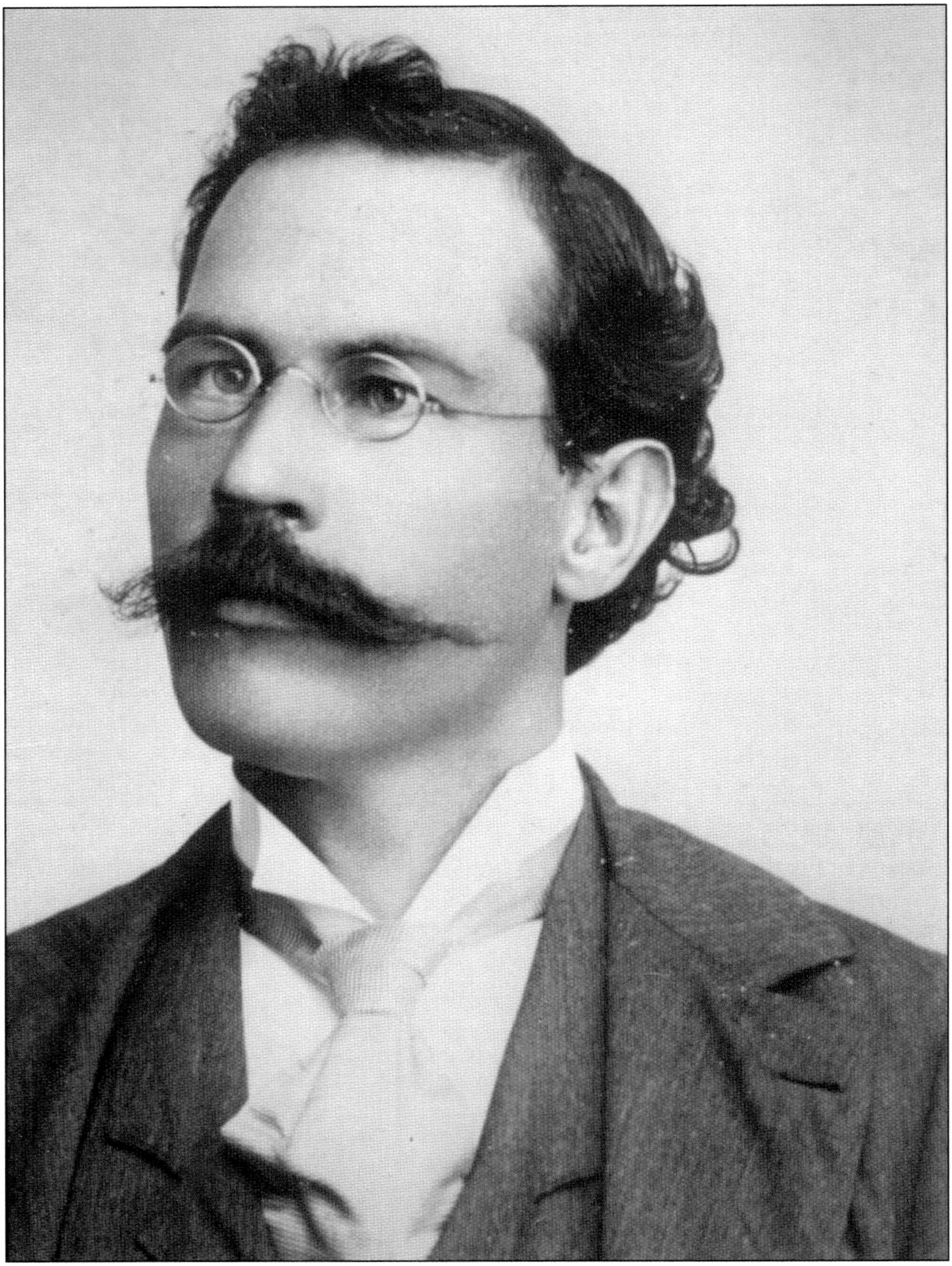

John Horton taught at the Cross Roads School around 1897. In the diary of Mary Margaret Greene, she mentioned several events that indicated the children often had fun. In one entry, Greene stated, "All of us went to Professor and told him that our parents did not care for us dancing and he let us dance." Many of the students had parents who opposed dancing and the children, therefore, told the professor a false statement.

Eight
Getting Around

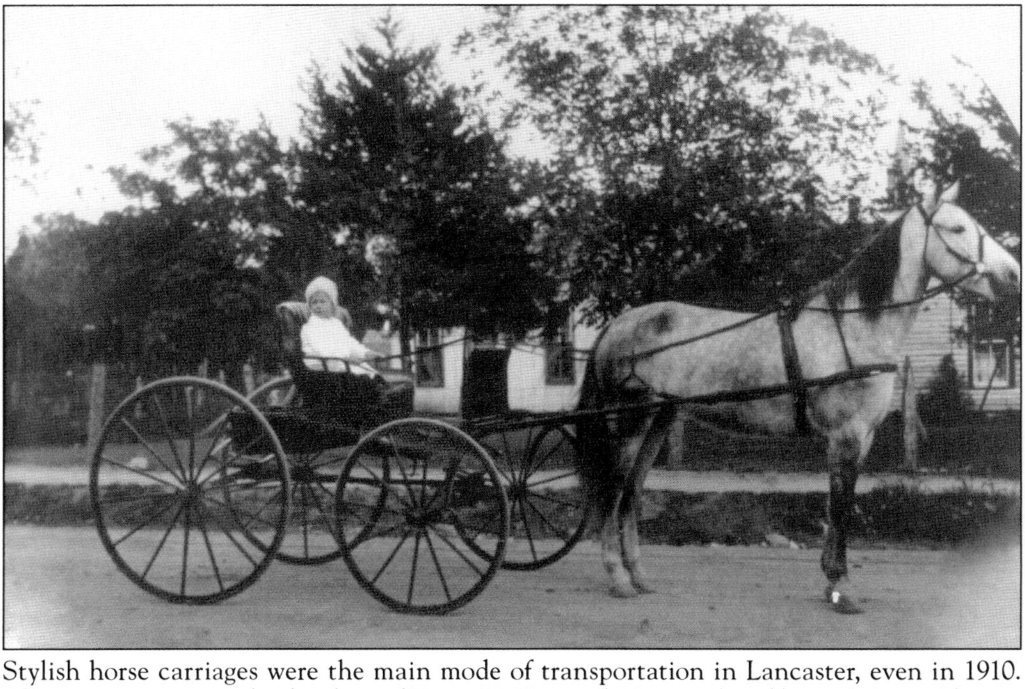

Stylish horse carriages were the main mode of transportation in Lancaster, even in 1910. Christine Keirsey was the daughter of Harry W. Keirsey (1879–1942) and his wife, Mary Eleanor Lowrey Keirsey (1882–1965), who was the daughter of early settlers, Seth Lowrey and Laura Moffett of Lancaster.

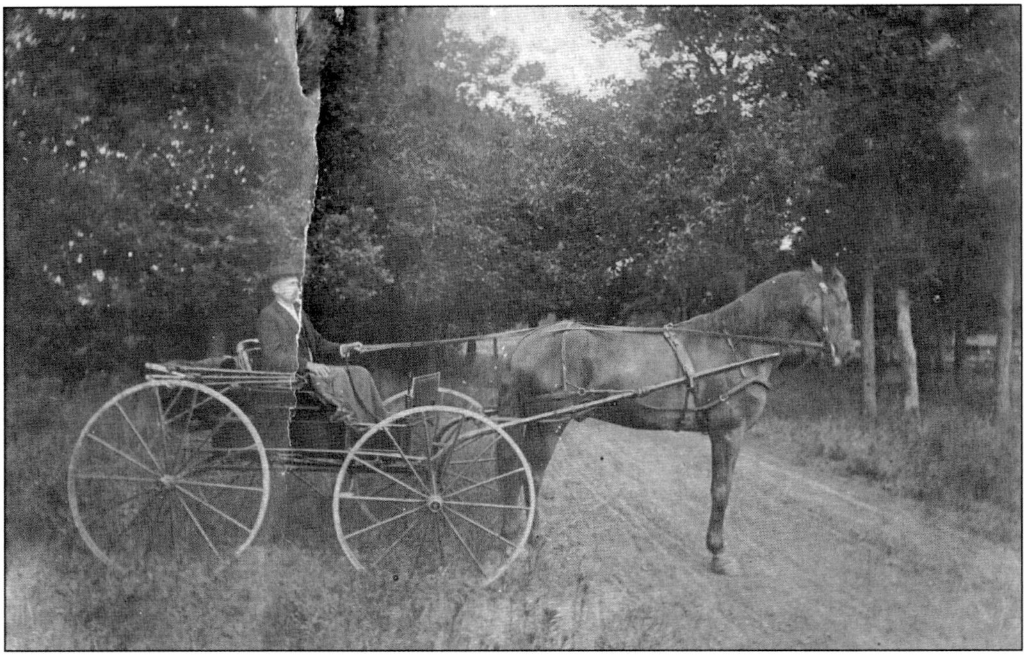

The citizens of Lancaster prided themselves on their fine horses. Ladies riding in carriages or surreys needed the right type of horse to carry them in style. Buggy accidents were not uncommon and were often fatal. The most frequent cause of the accidents was runaway horses, often resulting in overturned buggies. Here is an example of a fine horse, Rex, and his owner.

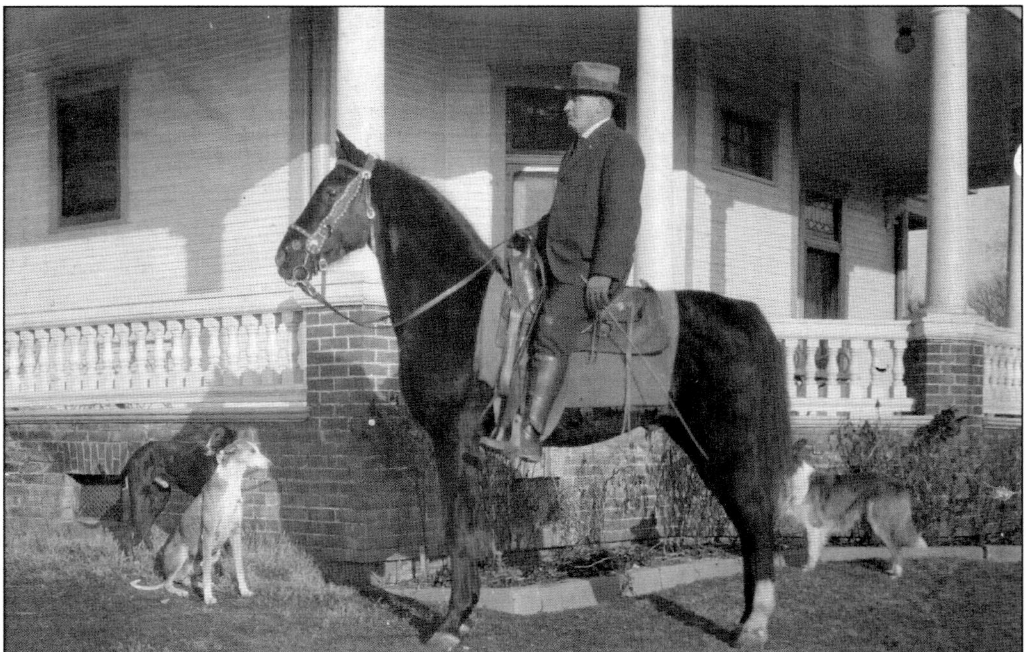

Hal White sits astride his fine riding horse on the east side of the White house at the end of Centre Street. White, an avid hunter, always had his dogs nearby. Hal White was involved in the operation of the White Bank and with the Baylor University's Board of Regents.

Will Smith was the son of Thomas T. Smith and Mary Francis Winniford. His grandparents raised him and his sister, Minnie, after his father and a cousin went hunting in East Texas and never returned. He is on his horse outside the home of his step-grandfather, Thomas S. Ramby.

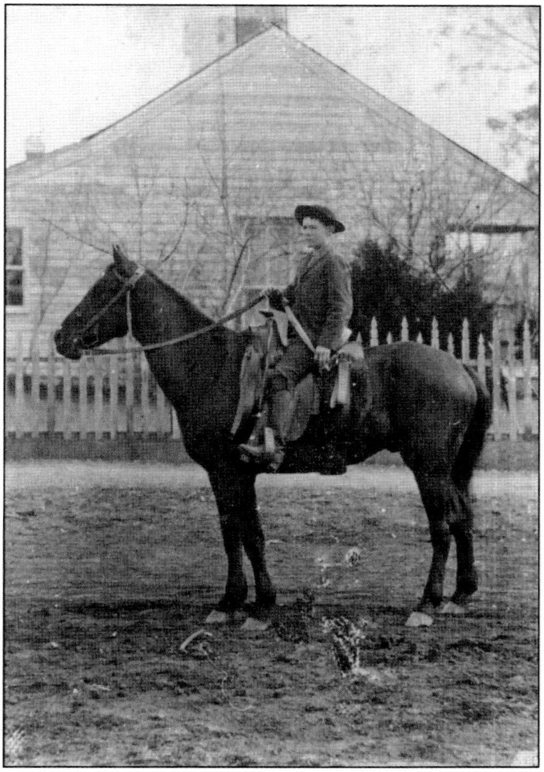

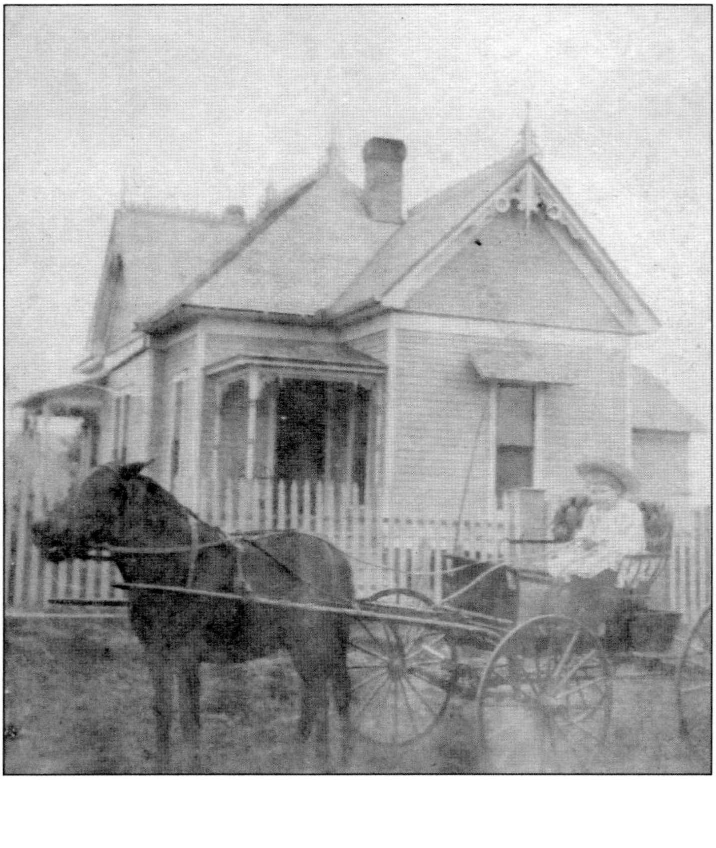

Laura White, daughter of Hal E. White, lived with her father and grandmother, Lou F. White. Her mother, Laura Gaston White, died when Laura was a baby. This was Lou White's home until 1907 when the large White home was built. This picture was taken when Laura was about four years old (1904). Later she married Leland Dupree, a Dallas banker.

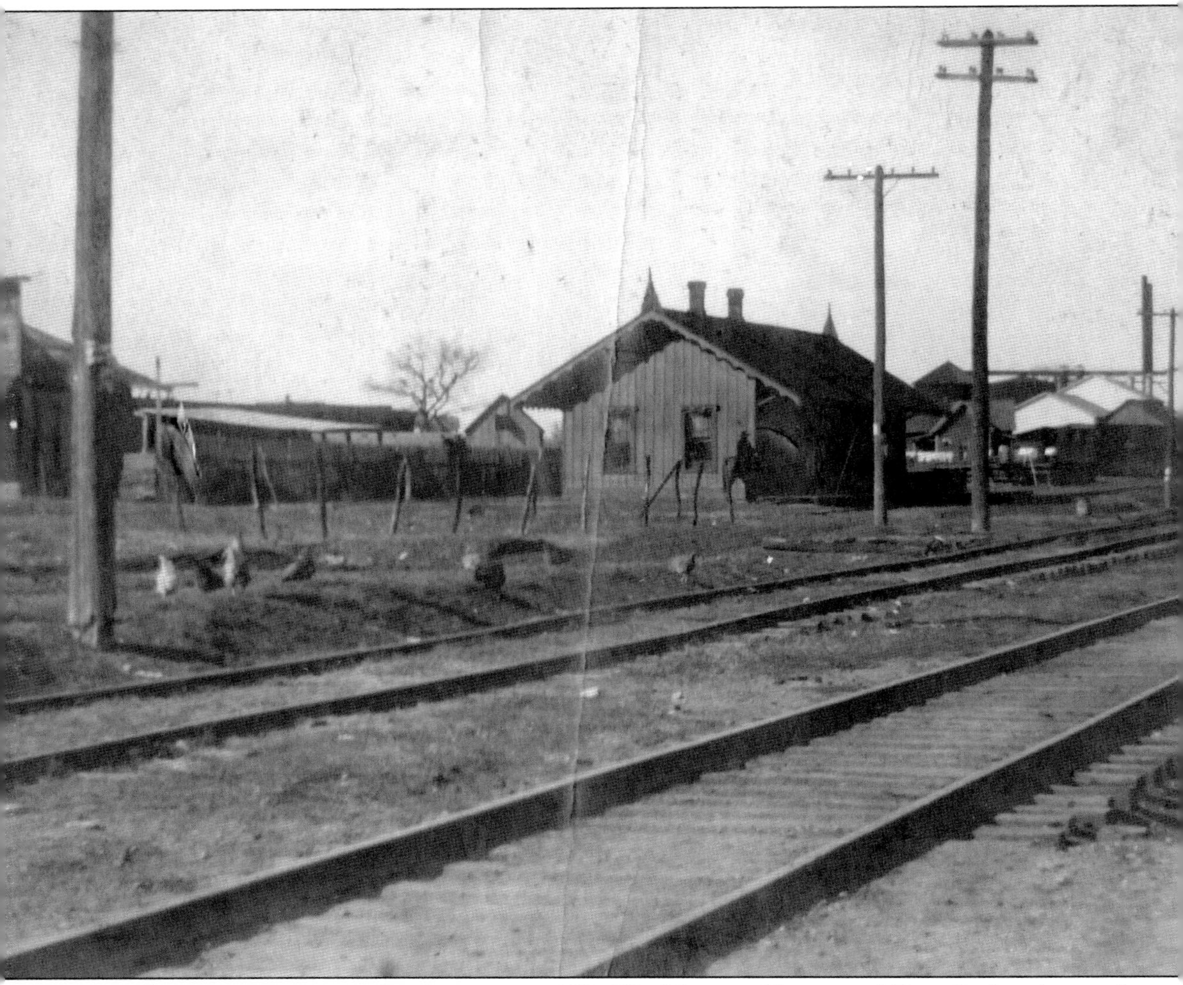

Rail transportation opened in Lancaster in 1889. The Missouri, Kansas, and Texas Railroad opened with a brass band and the firing of anvils. Note the telegraph poles. The railroads in the United States changed many lives. Products could be shipped across wide spans in very short time, and for Lancaster, the shipping of cotton, flour, and cattle helped the economy. Luckily standard time had been adopted in 1883 by the railroads. Before this, each city had its own time determined by the sun, which made railroad schedules next to impossible. Lancaster had been overlooked by the railways but had lines running as close as Hutchins. In 1885, a group of citizens banded together to bring a line to Lancaster with much of the right-of-way donated. Lou White did not want the line, but it had to cross her property. The tracks across this section were laid at night with several local men acting as watch outs.

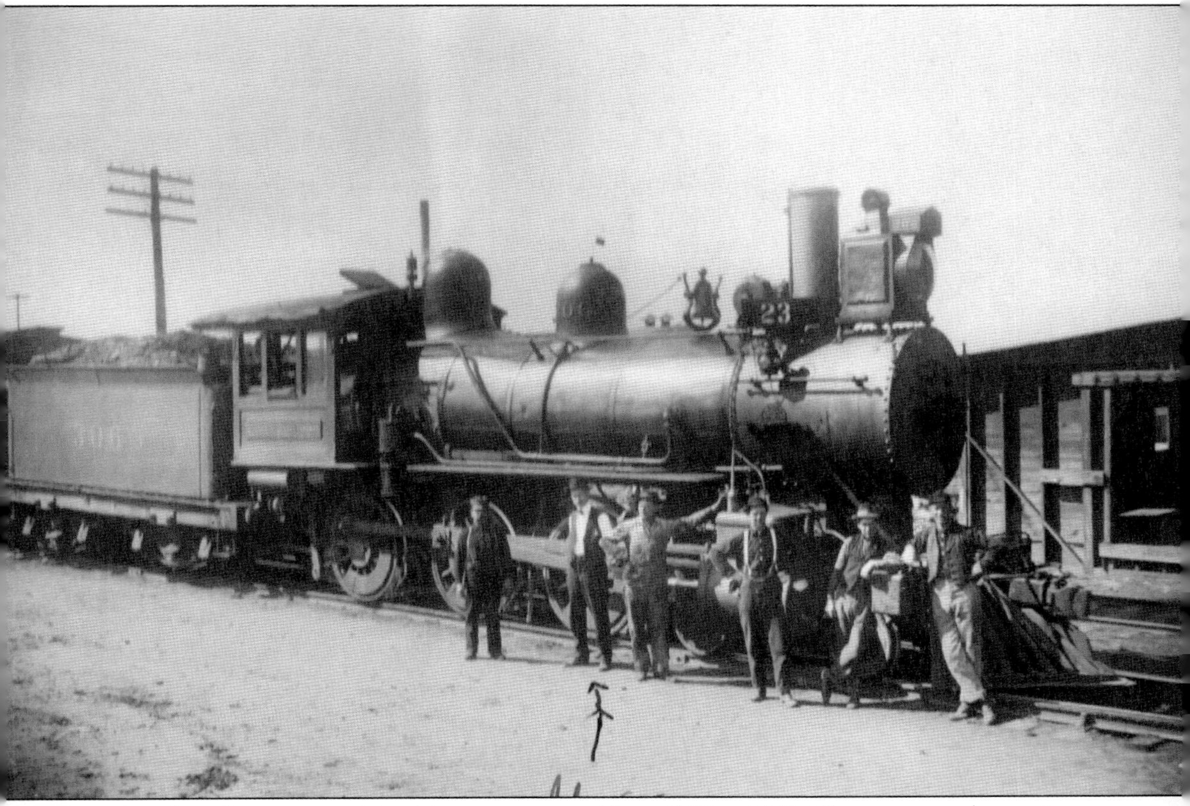

A tap line from Lancaster to Hutchins was operated from 1890 to 1905. The name on the engine read Houston and Texas Central. Mat Moreland was the engineer for this train. He was known for his ability to play a tune on the train whistle as it went down the tracks. Mat is leaning on the engine in the center. To his left is John Stuart. The Houston and Texas Central Railroad had the nickname "hell on Texas contractors" because contractors building the line had trouble collecting money for their work. The nickname "hen and ten chicks" came from the fact that in early days, one locomotive pulled 10 cars.

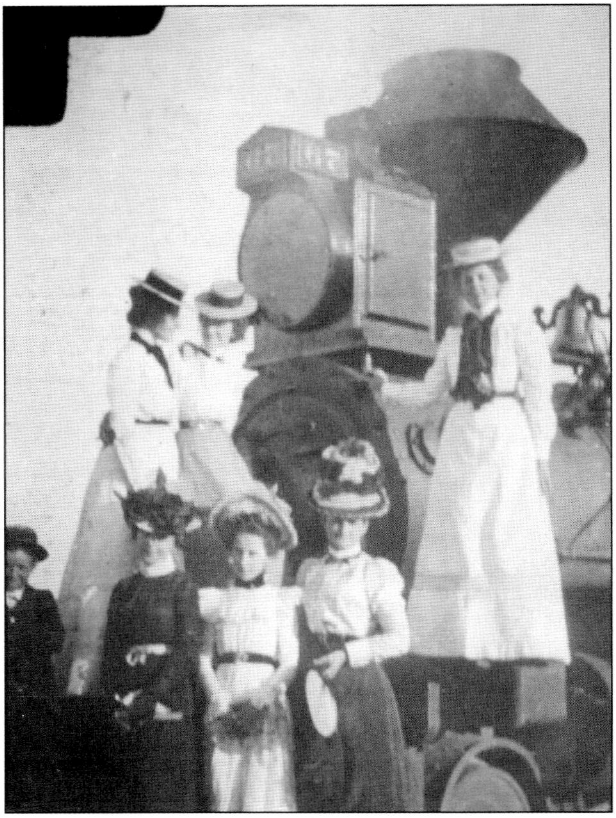

A dummy engine was much like today's bus line. The engine went to a specific spot, turned around, and returned. Mules pulled some early dummy engines but the one in Lancaster was a steam engine that burned coal. One of its connections allowed travel to the State Fair of Texas in the fall. The dummy traveled between Hutchins and Lancaster, carrying freight and passengers. At Hutchins, one could catch a train going many places. Lancaster Hutchins Road was eventually built on the right-of-way.

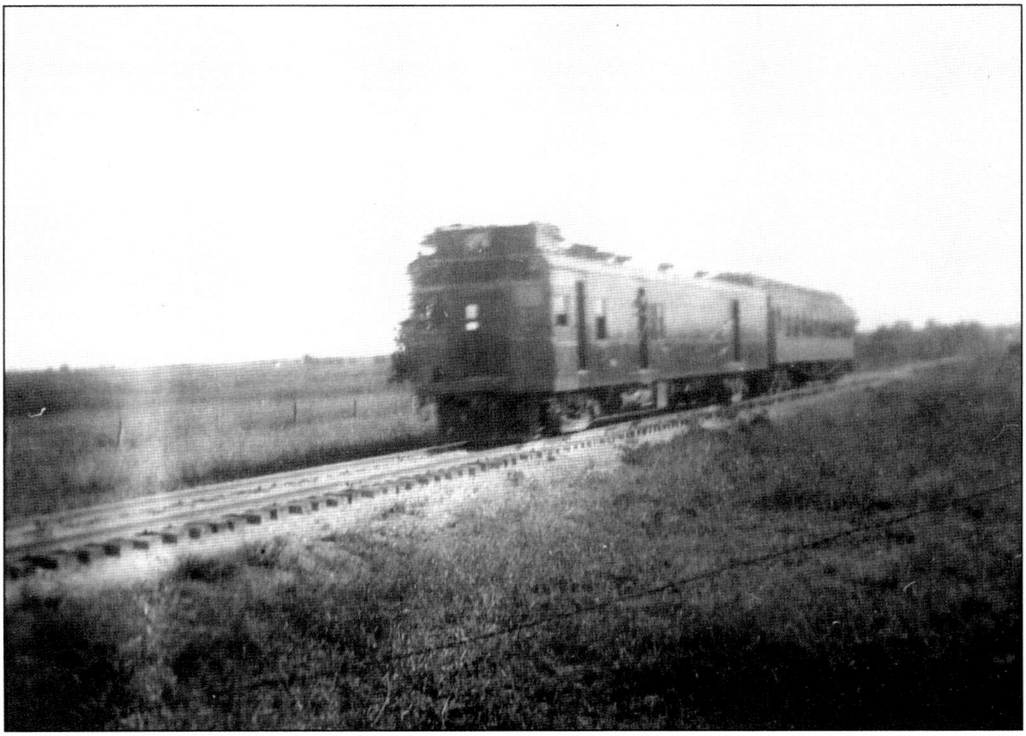

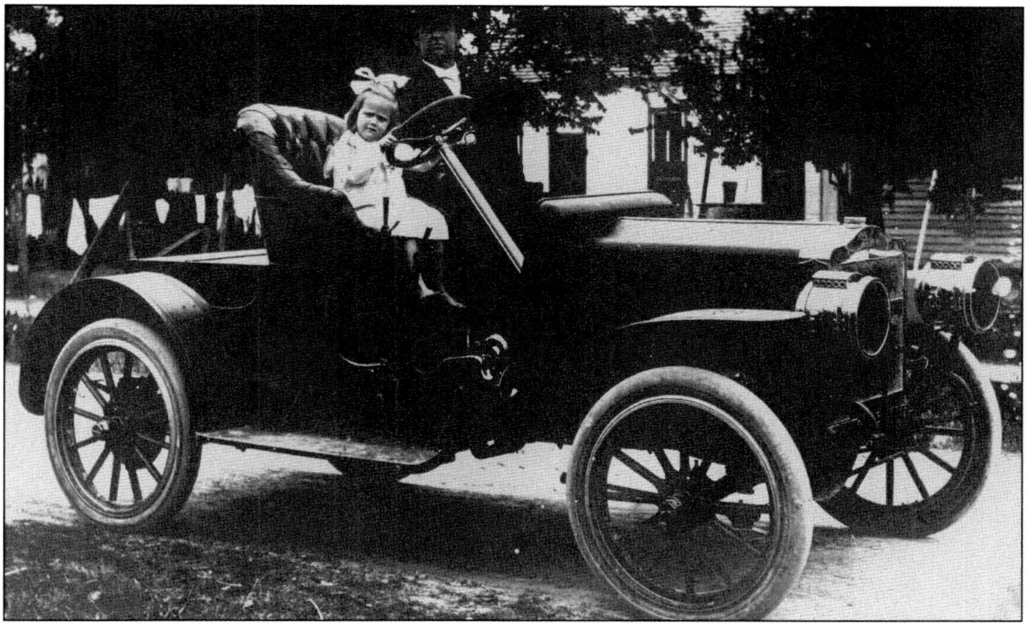

Mary Elizabeth "Bess" Parks (Mrs. Frank Cordill) and her father, Dr. George Parks, enjoy an outing in the family's new car, a 1909 Ford. Dr. Parks had the first car in Lancaster in 1902. His car was probably an Oldsmobile and a later model. Doctors were often the first in towns to purchase cars. Most babies were delivered at home. (Courtesy of Carolyn Cordill Fulton.)

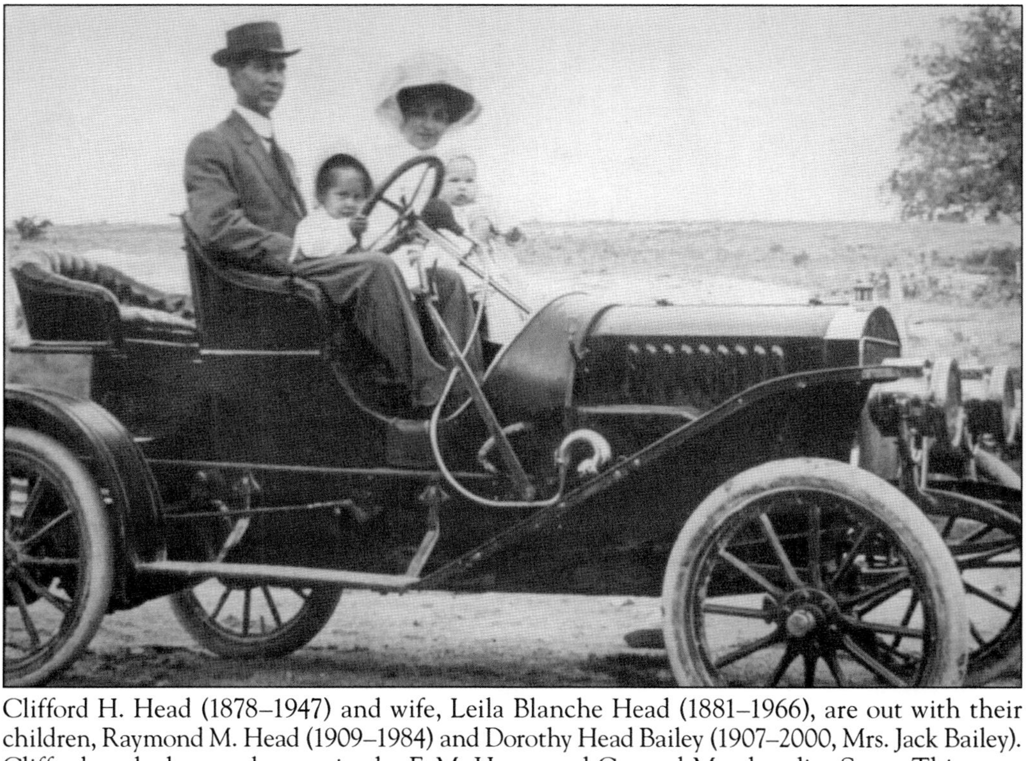

Clifford H. Head (1878–1947) and wife, Leila Blanche Head (1881–1966), are out with their children, Raymond M. Head (1909–1984) and Dorothy Head Bailey (1907–2000, Mrs. Jack Bailey). Clifford worked as a salesman in the F. M. Hammond General Merchandise Store. This store eventually became Heads and Son in 1945.

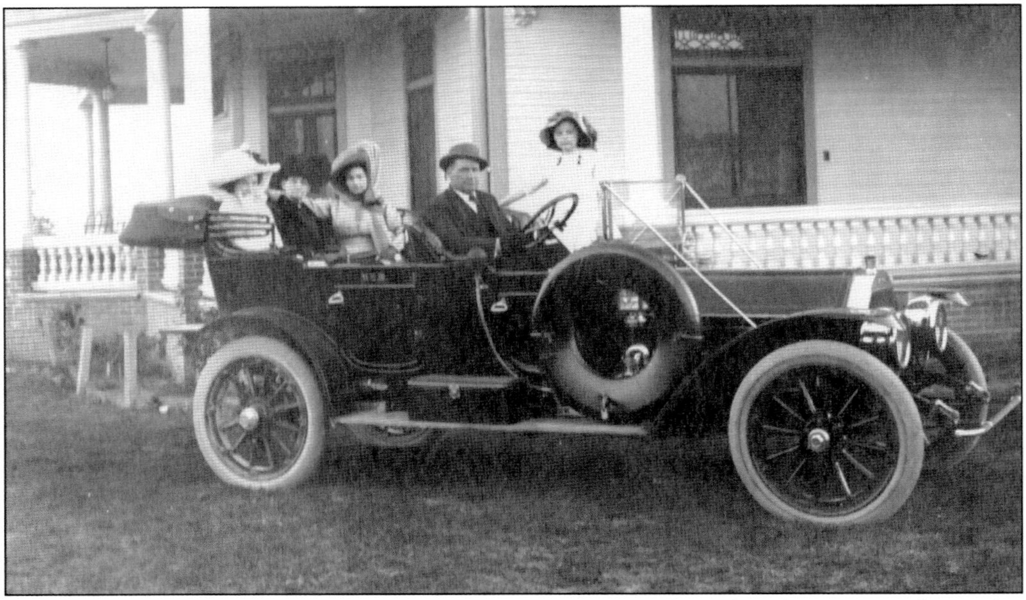

Hal White is in his 1914 Oldsmobile touring car in front of the White house. Standing is his daughter Laura White. Seated in the back are, from left to right, Lula Tubbs White (Mrs. Karl White), Lou White (Mrs. W. L. White), and Pearl White Harding (Mrs. R. D. Harding). Cars in this period were owned by the upper class.

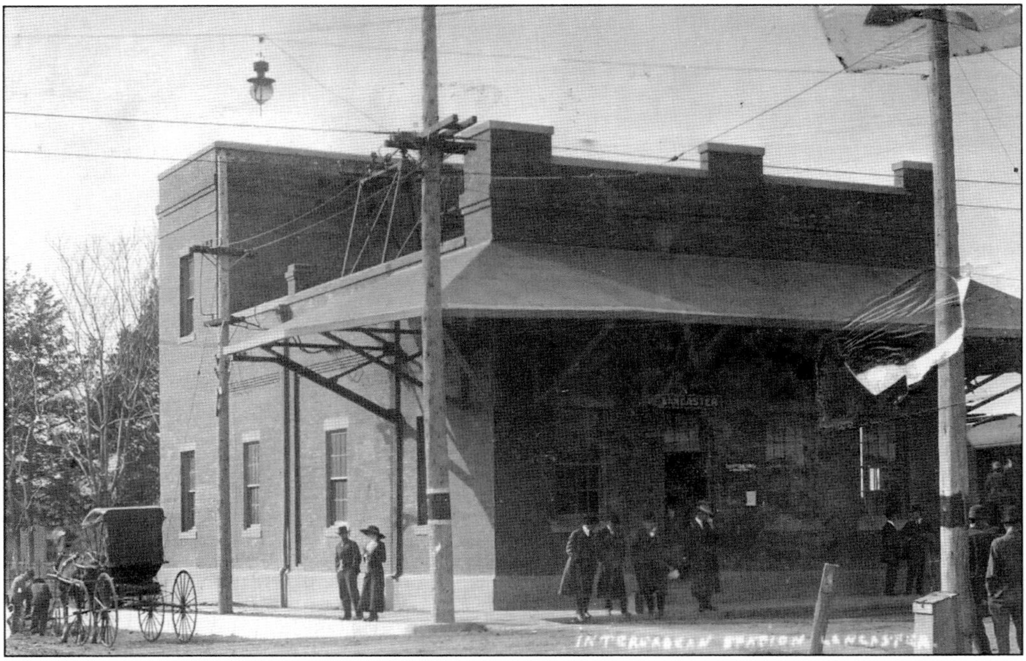

The first interurban in Texas was built in 1901 and others were gradually added. In 1911, J. F. Strickland had controlling interest in the Texas Traction Company. This company designated 28 miles of right away to build the Dallas Southern Traction company line from Dallas to Waxahachie. This is the station that served Lancaster on that line in fall 1911. It is currently being rehabbed into a Texas state museum of history and visitor's center for the city of Lancaster. (Courtesy of Winn Morton.)

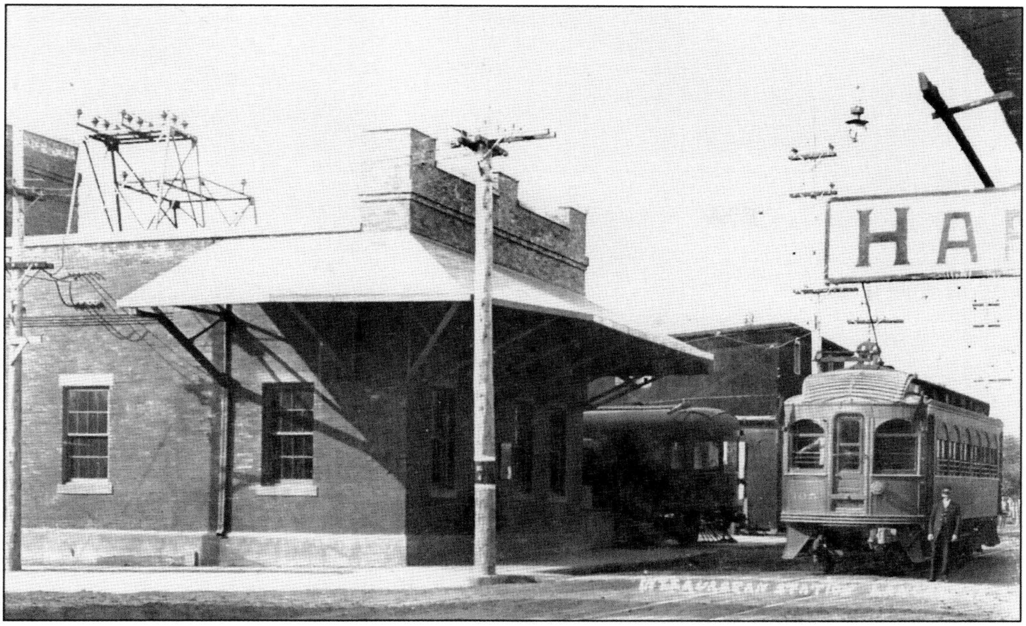

The opening of the Southern Traction Company in 1912 brought electricity to Lancaster and allowed easier travel to Dallas. In 1913, the line was extended to Waco, but Lancaster had to raise $12,000 to purchase the right-of-way needed. The interurban station was a busy place as businessmen and families traveled to Dallas or south to Waco to take care of business deals or visit relatives. Traveling by interurban was safer and quicker than going by carriage or car. (Courtesy of Winn Morton.)

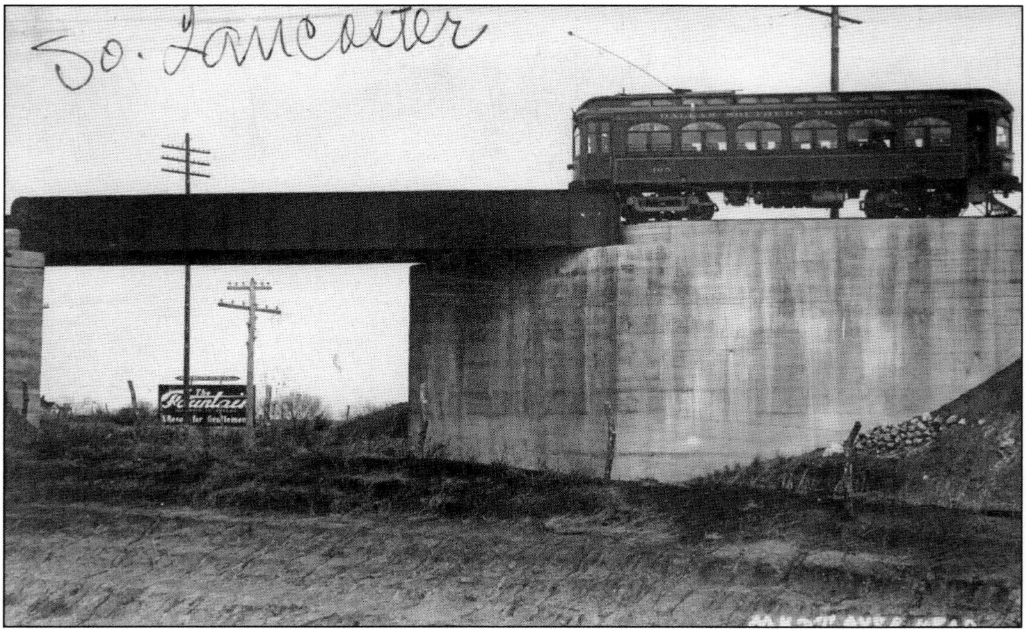

The Lancaster Pike that ran north and south through Lancaster had some changes due to the introduction of railways and interurbans. This is the overpass south of town that allowed the interurban to pass over the pike and keep cars and buggies from stopping for interurbans. This type of transportation often spooked horses near the tracks, making traveling more dangerous. (Courtesy of Winn Morton.)

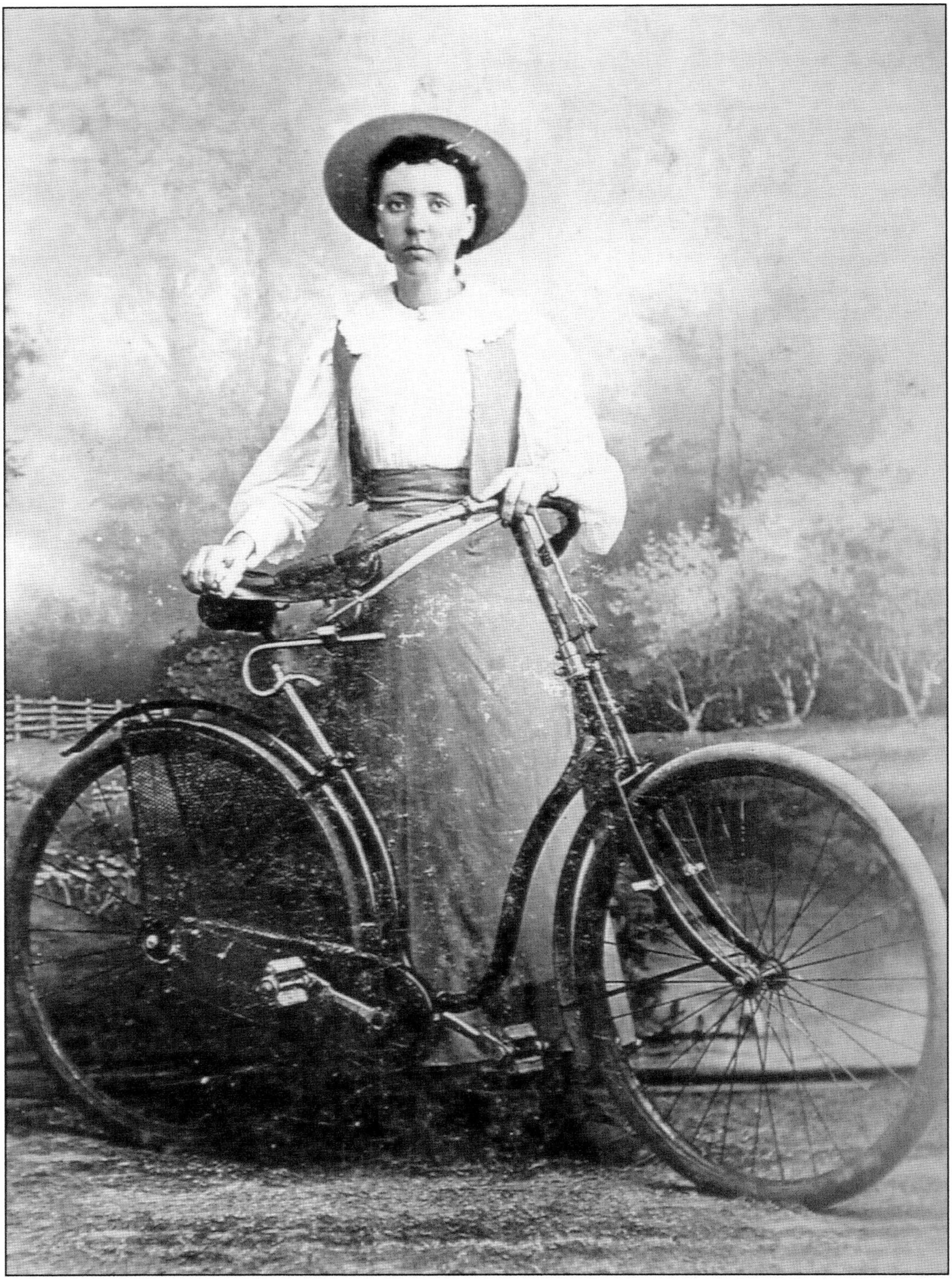

Bicycles were also an early form of transportation, especially for the young. Maude Hayden chose to have her picture made with her bike. Maude was trained as a musician during her youth. She participated in the music schools offered in Lancaster and learned piano and voice. She eventually studied violin with a teacher in Dallas. She trained some students in violin but taught piano for over 70 years. She retired at age 95 and died within six weeks of retirement.

Nine
Enjoying Life

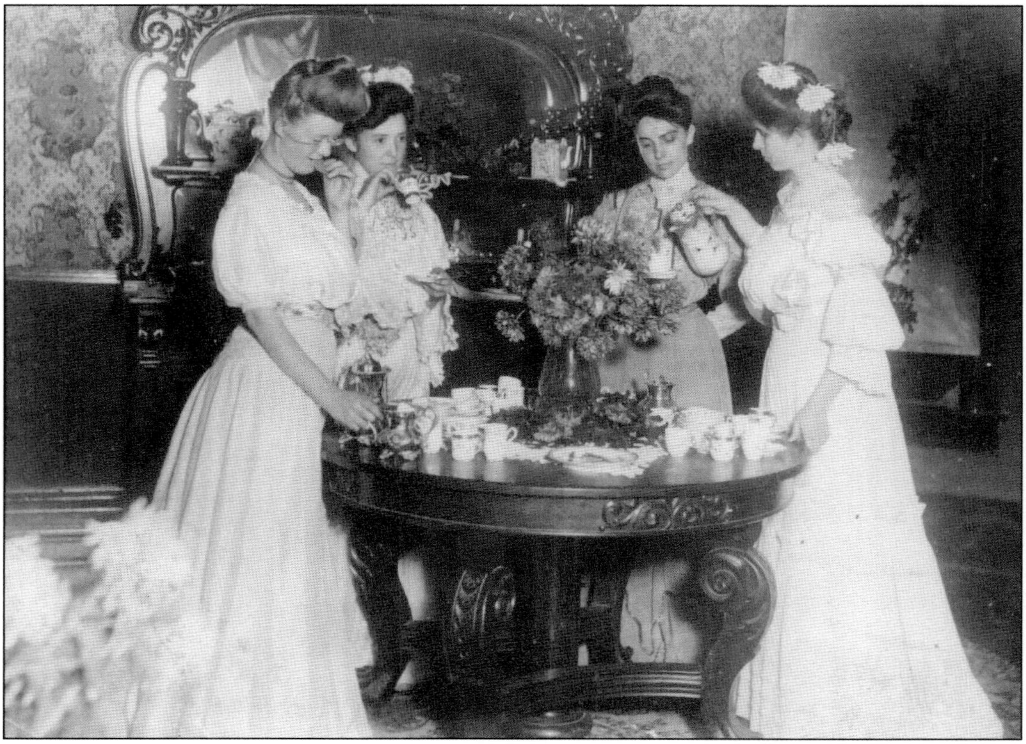

Teas were held for many occasions. One particular tea was held to announce the engagement of Myrtle Anderson to William Reynolds. The ladies are, from left to right, Berta Lee Rawlins (Mrs. James E. Thompson of Dallas), Hallie Magness (Mrs. Ross Ellis), Mamie Henry (Mrs. W. Turney White of Dallas), and the bride-to-be, Myrta Anderson.

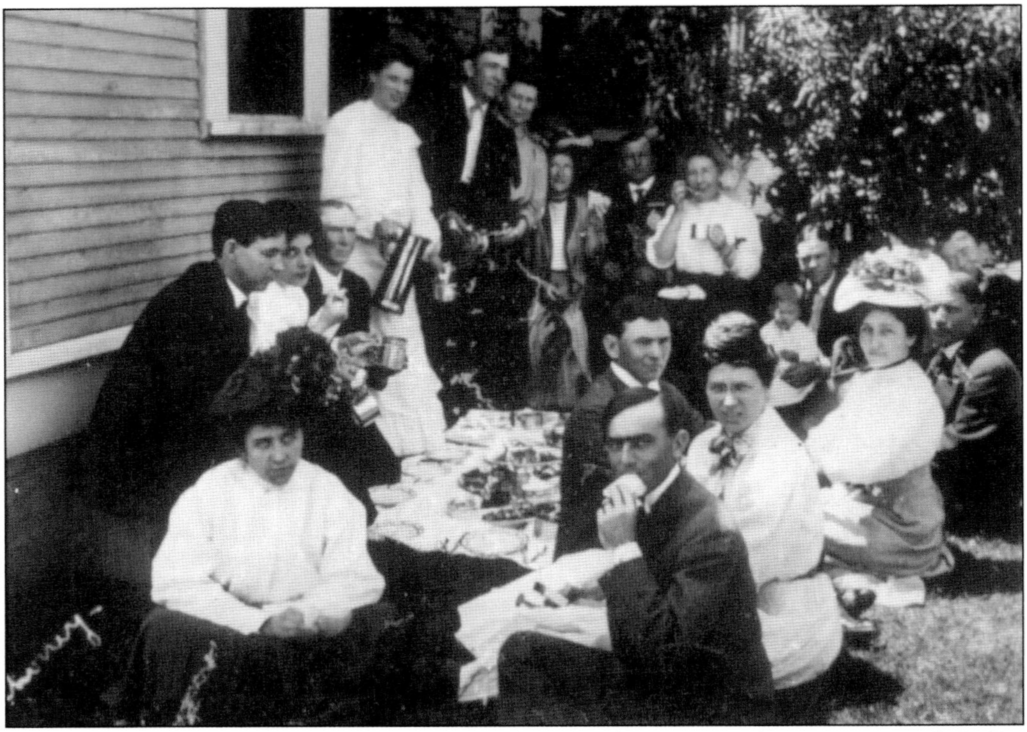

Great food and a great time with friends was often the theme at Head House on North Dallas Avenue. Those attending this picnic (starting at the lower left and moving clockwise) are Johnnie Barth, Cliff Head, Leila Head, Otis Durrett, Mary Kiersey, Will Moffett, Willie Moffett, Nannie Billingsley, Mr. Thompson, Bettie Taylor, Harry Kiersey with baby Christine Kiersey, Jack Billingsley, Will Hurst, Lena Guy, Will Batchler, Mary Johnson, and Paul Henry.

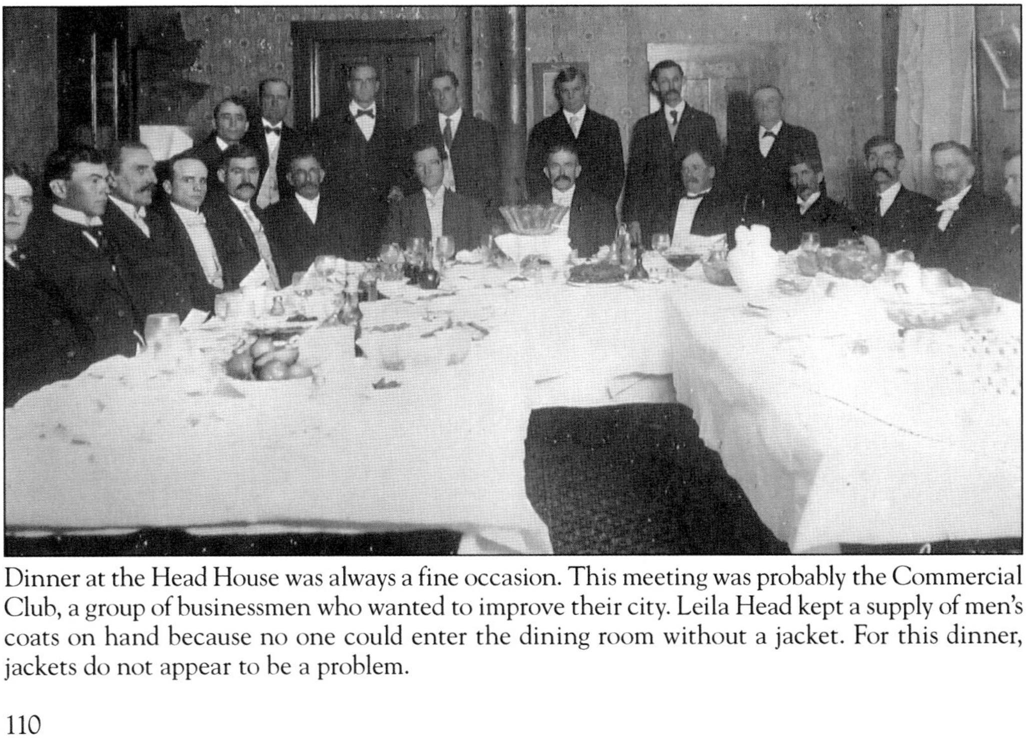

Dinner at the Head House was always a fine occasion. This meeting was probably the Commercial Club, a group of businessmen who wanted to improve their city. Leila Head kept a supply of men's coats on hand because no one could enter the dining room without a jacket. For this dinner, jackets do not appear to be a problem.

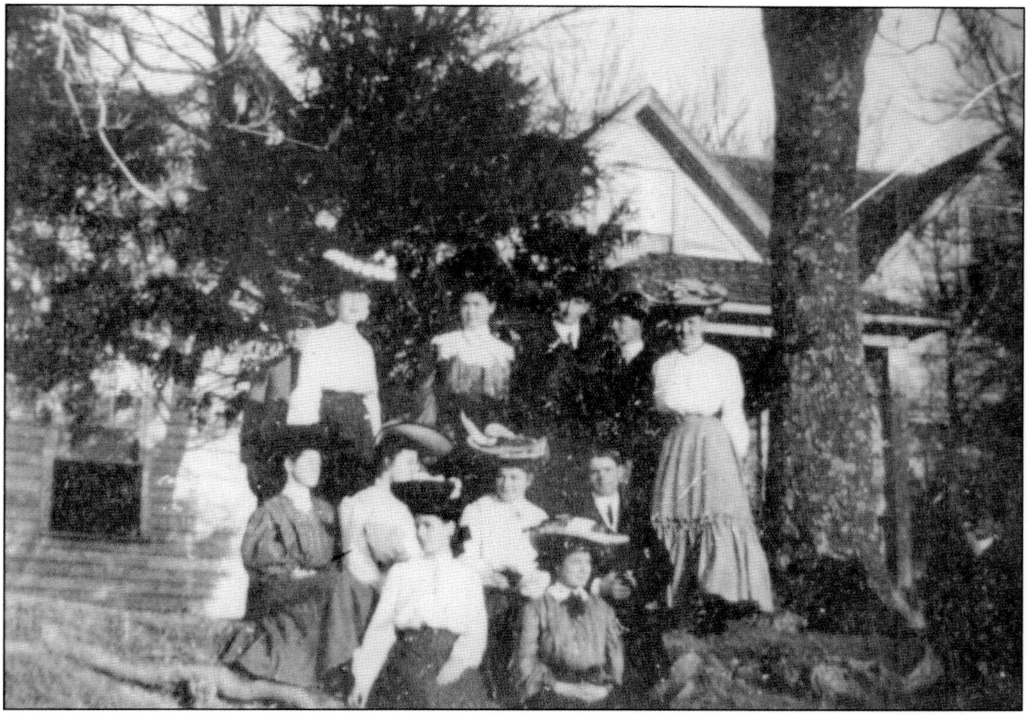

People of all ages called on friends and neighbors, primarily on Sunday afternoon. This group appears to be a social call for young people who came together for an afternoon of fun. Hats were part of the dress and they were often very elaborate.

On a hot Sunday afternoon in the 1900s, where would a person go to cool off? On the banks of Ten Mile Creek, where there were many trees and cool water in which one could relax and visit. Just imagine hot Texas days, wearing long dresses or pants most often made of wool, and trying to keep cool.

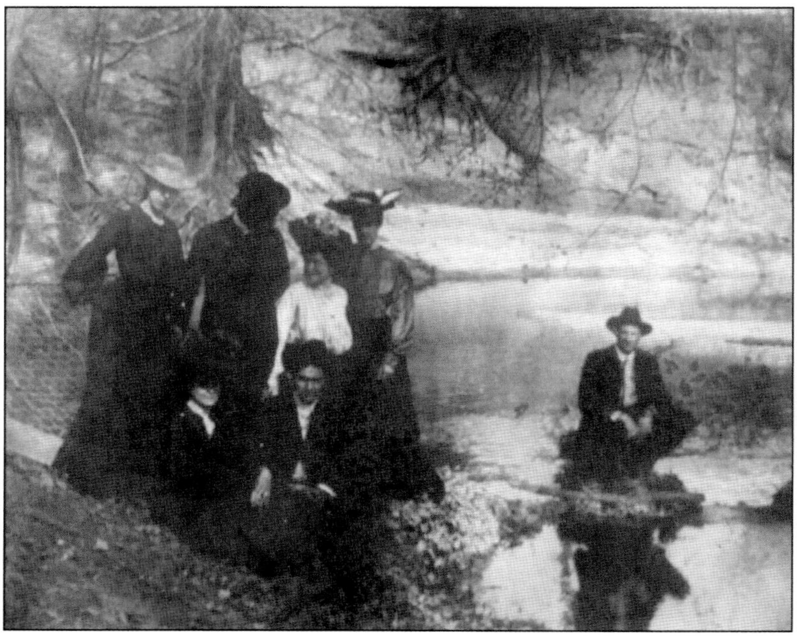

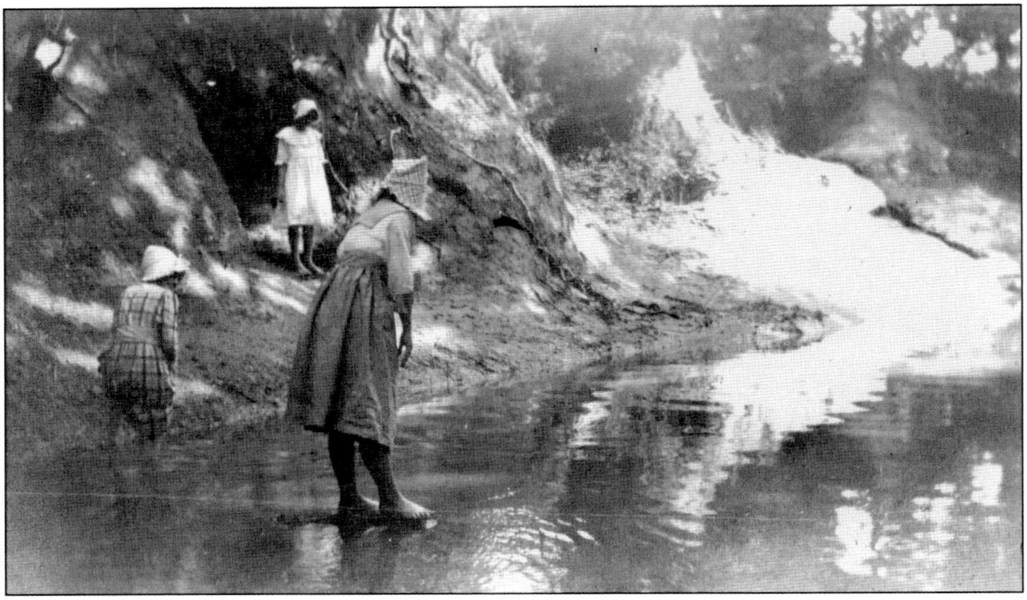

Wading in Ten Mile Creek was one way to cool down on a hot summer day in the early 1900s. Parents did not have as many dangers for their children as in today's society and kids were allowed to play unsupervised. Catching crayfish or crawdads by lowering a string with bacon on the end was great fun. Deeper sections of Ten Mile Creek were the place for baptisms. Some of the men went down to clear away debris and scare the snakes away before baptisms. (Courtesy of Carolyn Cordill Fulton.)

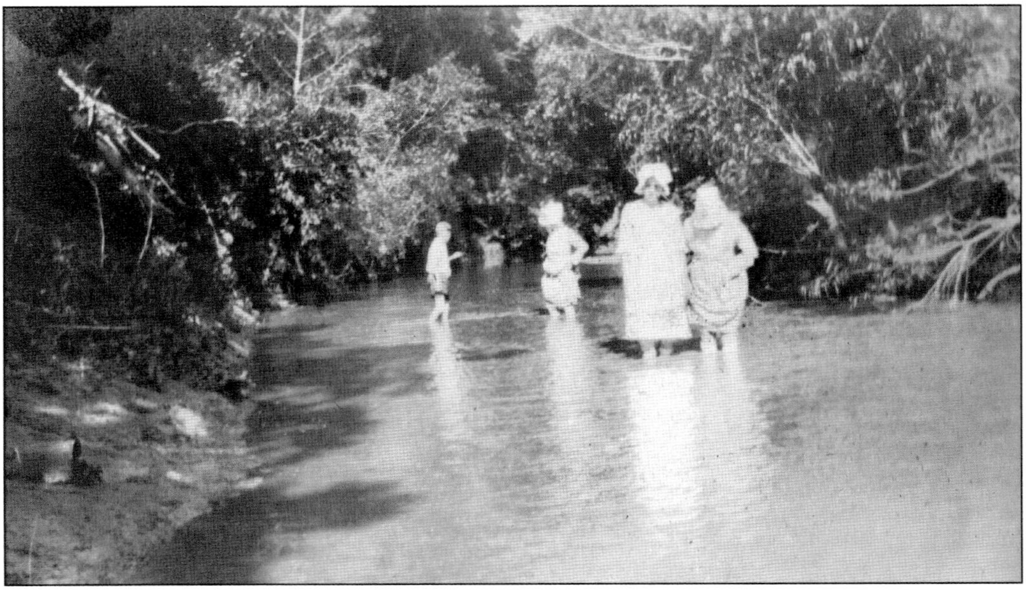

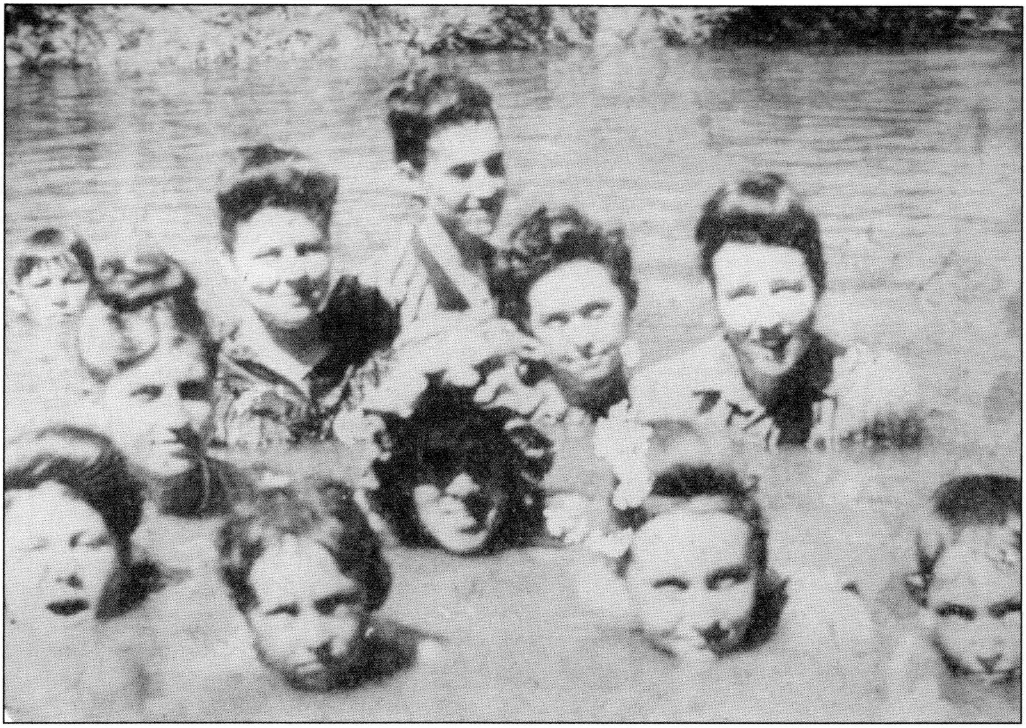

East of Nokomis Road in a bend in Ten Mile Creek is a large swimming area that had grapevine ropes on which one could swing and a stump to dive off of into the water. Many hours of fun took place at the swimming hole and probably some "skinny dipping" by the boys in the town. One day, a bull chased some unclothed youth from the swimming hole, according to old-timers.

Cooling off at Galveston, dressed in the latest swimming togs, are some Lancaster citizens around 1914. Pictured from left to right are (first row) Hal White; (second row) Laura White, Minnie White Strain, Arthur Strain, and Ellis Strain. Getting to Galveston in 1914 could be via car or train but not by buggy because of the lengthy ride. It would still take more than four hours to go to Galveston.

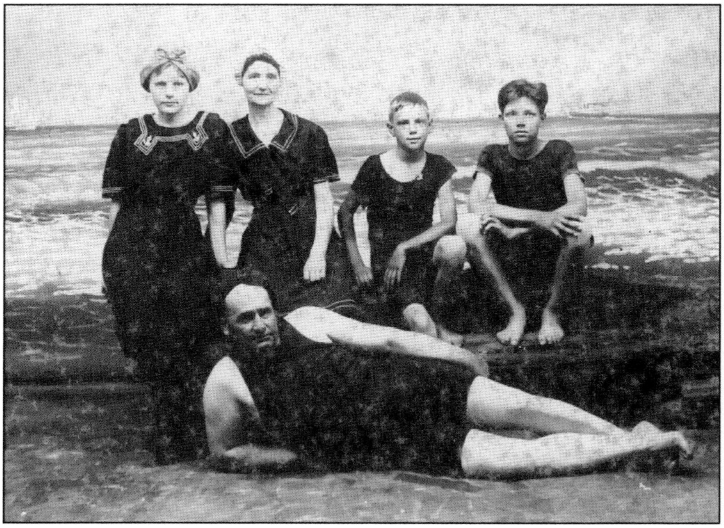

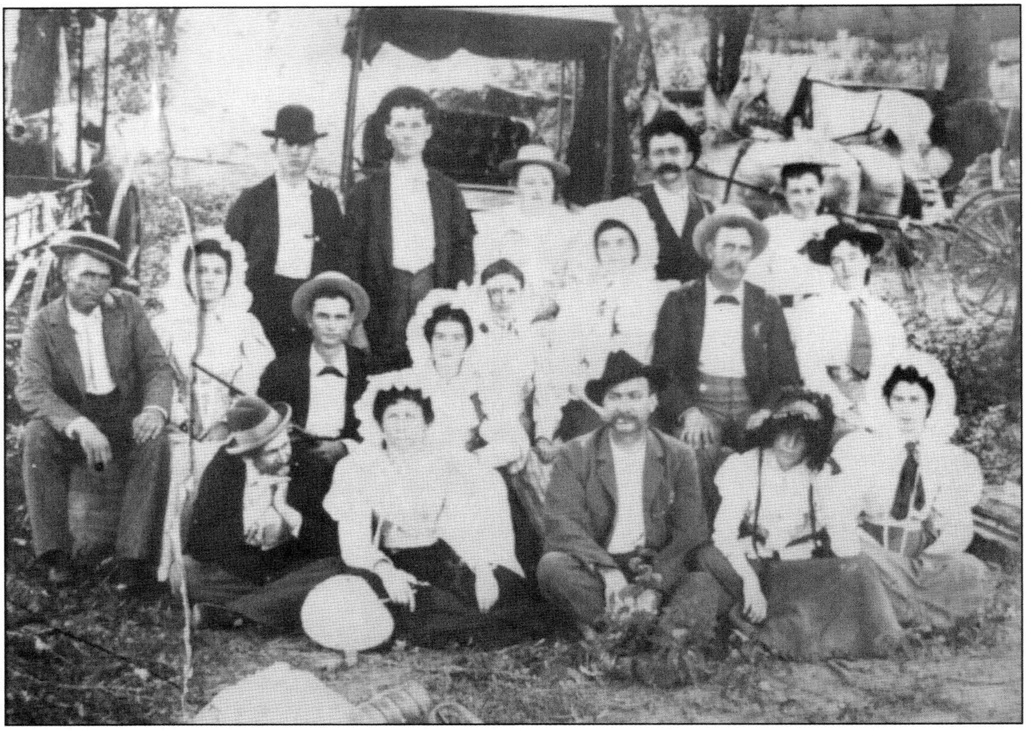

The huge oak trees in the grove just south of Beltline Road provided a perfect spot for community picnics and even Dallas County picnics for churches and political events. The oak trees still shade this often-used historic picnic area. Just west of this grove was Keller Branch, where one could cool off by wading.

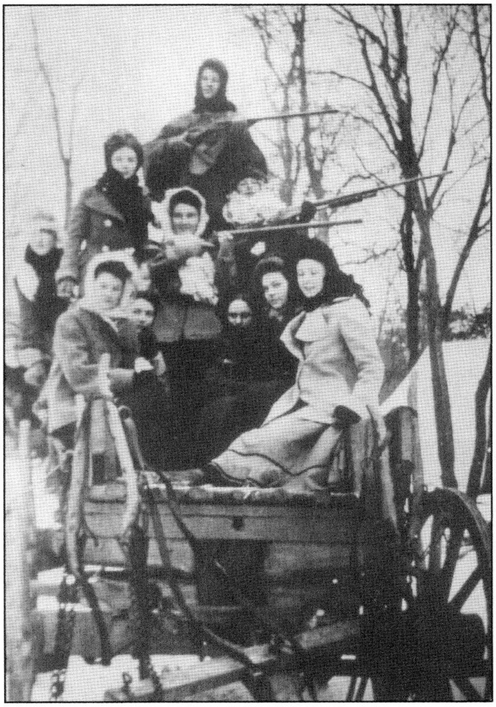

Girls hunting in the 1890s may have been looking for rabbits, turkey, or merely practicing their shot. The hitch is in front and there is no horse to pull the wagon, so they were posing for the photograph instead of planning to go somewhere.

Baseball was big in Lancaster around the beginning of the 1900s. Lancaster became divided into the north and south. Each side had its team and devised ways to guaranteed a win. The Cannibals team was from the south side. Not only did Lancaster teams play each other, but also other towns surrounding Lancaster played. Ferris, Hutchins, Wilmer, and Red Oak were only a few.

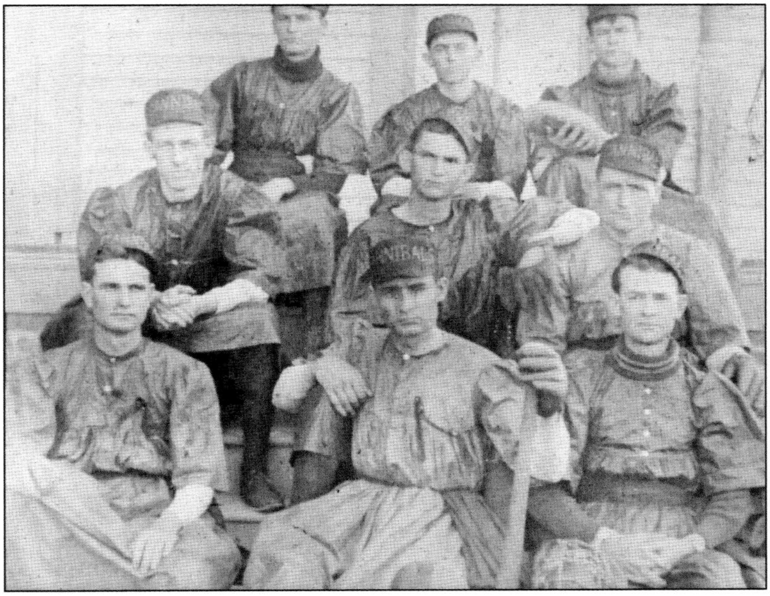

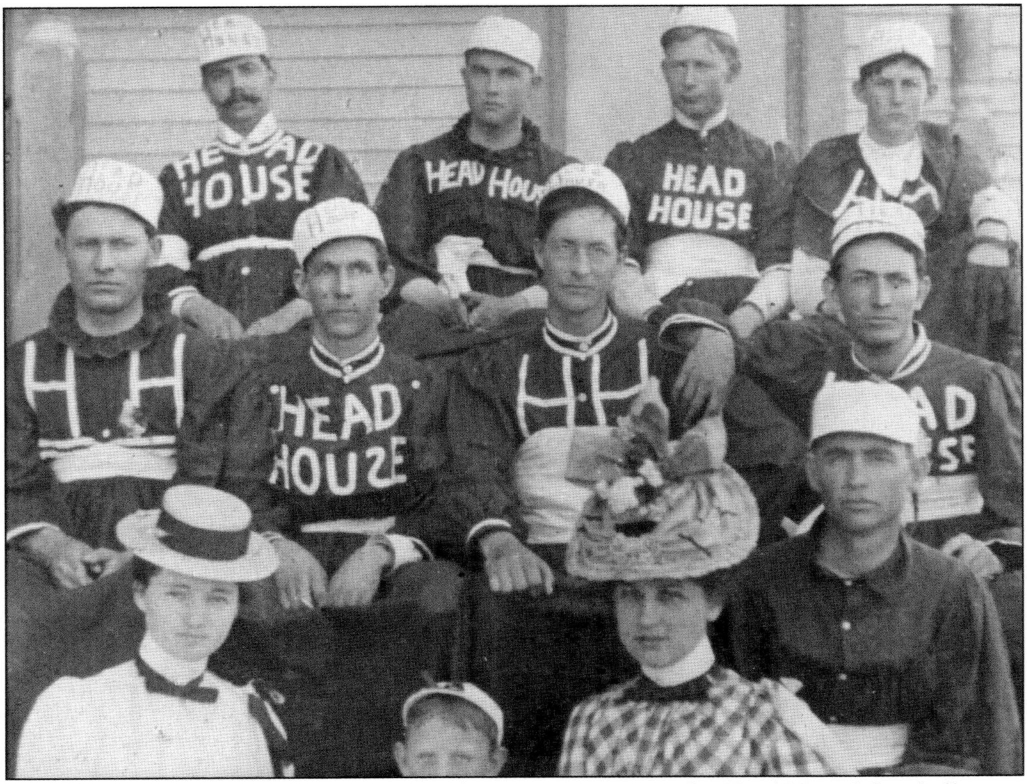

Businesses sponsoring teams is not a new phenomenon. Here is the Head House's baseball team. Other teams in Lancaster were called the Fats and Leans. To be on the Fats' team, one had to weigh 200 pounds or more. Ferris also had Fat and Lean teams, which played often.

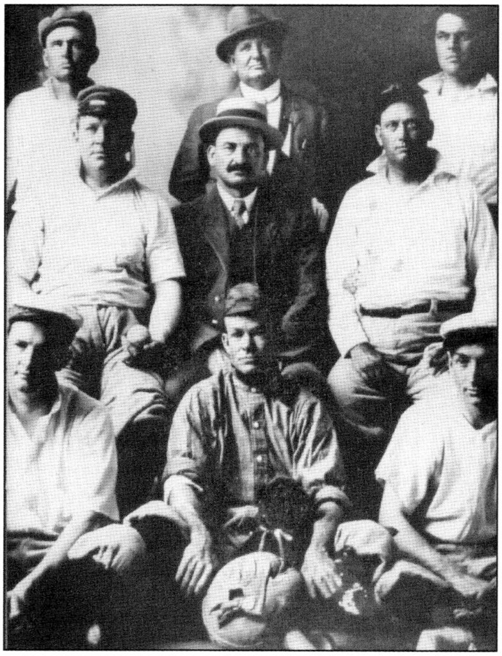

The Knights of Pythias was a service club established in many Texas towns in the early 1900s. This group represented Lancaster in matches with other Pythias teams in neighboring towns. Pictured are, from left to right, (first row) Lester White, Hutch McCurdy, and Will Moffett; (second row) unidentified, Will Perry, and Alex Mitchell; (third row) unidentified, Bud Wilson, and Earl Rawlins.

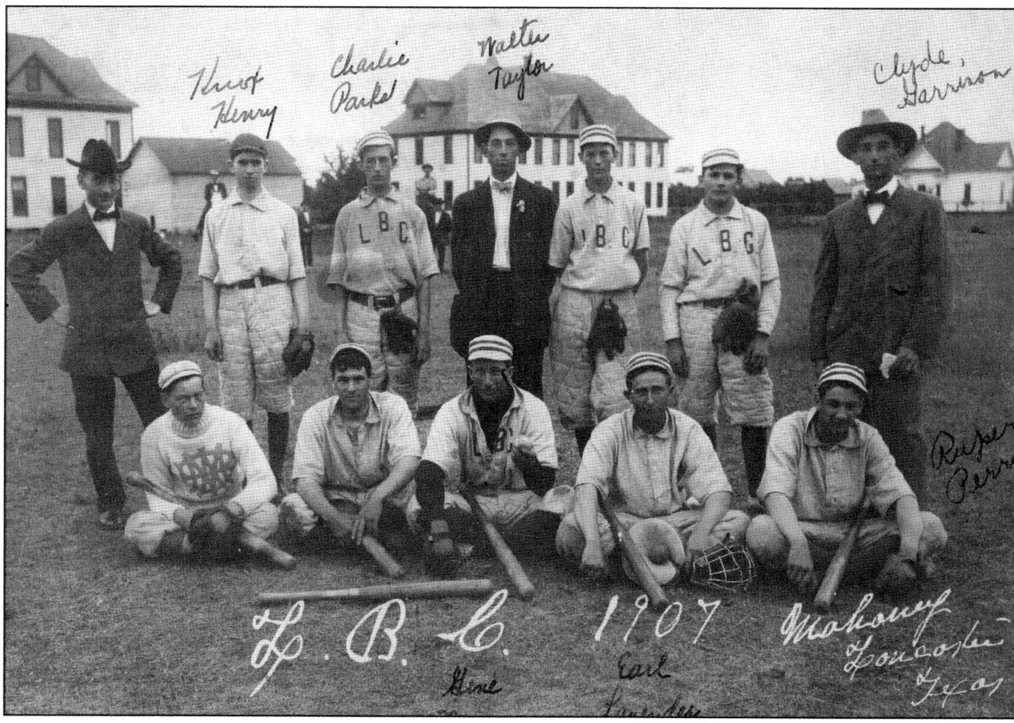

The Lancaster Baseball Club played on the fields of Speer's College. The dorms for the college can be seen in the background. On the right is the W. S. Strain house located on Wilson Street. Pictured here are, from left to right, (seated) two unidentified, Gene Moore, Earl Lavender, and Rupert Perry; (standing) Walter Hulbert, Knox Henry, Charlie Parks, Walter Taylor, two unidentified, and Clyde Garrison. Gene Moore later played professional baseball for the Pirates and the Reds from 1909 to 1912.

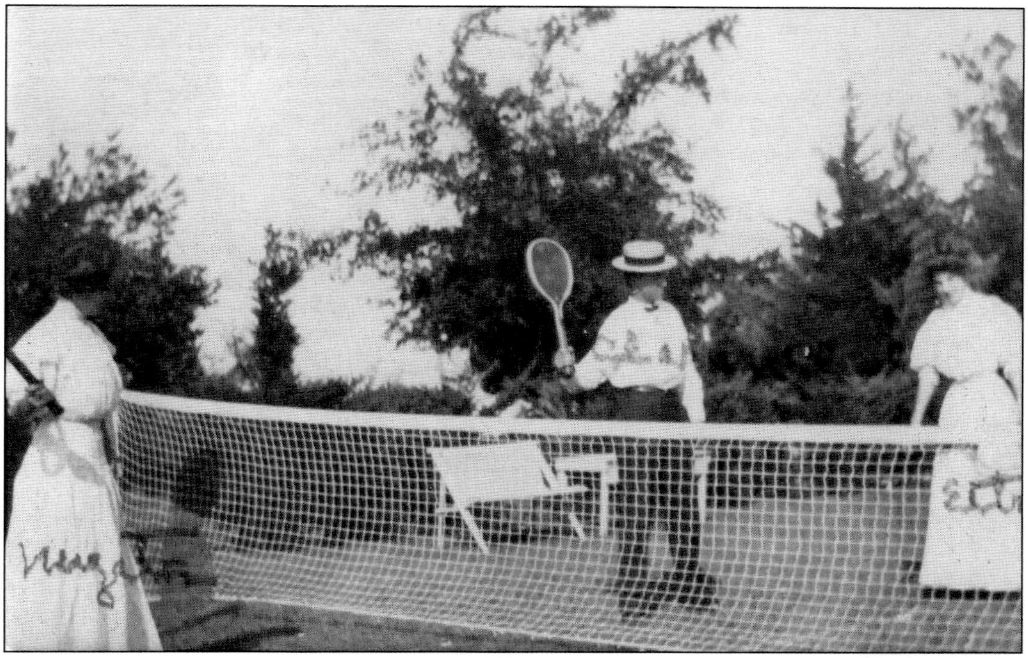

Tennis groups in Lancaster were small but very active. Courts were maintained by the members. In 1908, the club met at the Lancaster Drug Company. Sam Randlett was the president, Will Batchler served as vice president, while Paul Henry was elected secretary. Marvin Wills was captain of the grounds. There was also a tennis club for women that included Laura Groom White, Marian Randlett, and Addie Lavender.

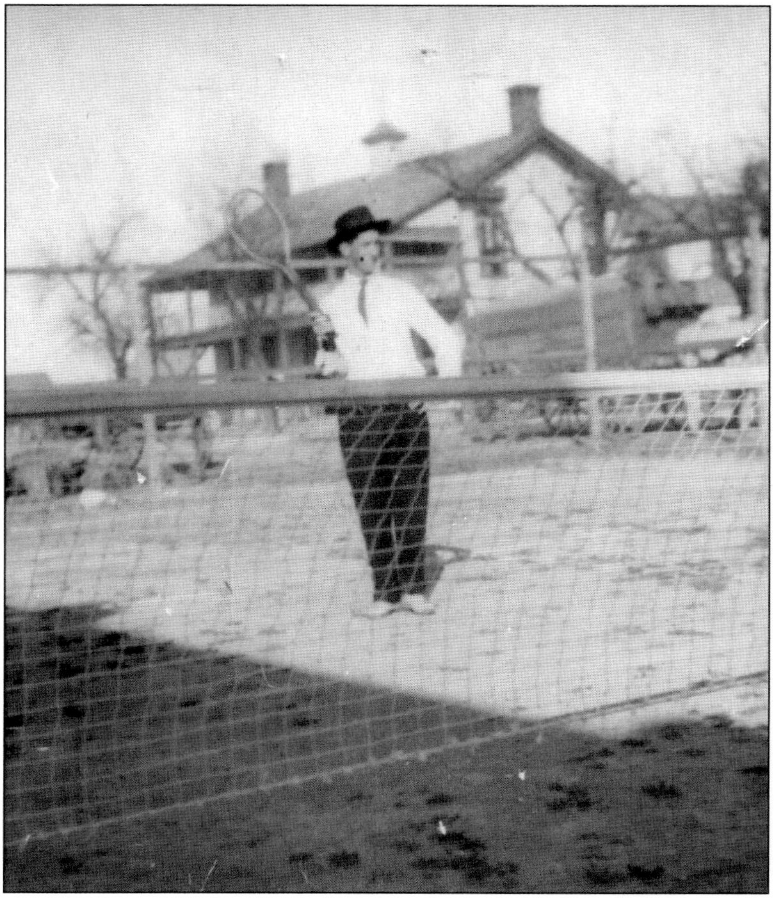

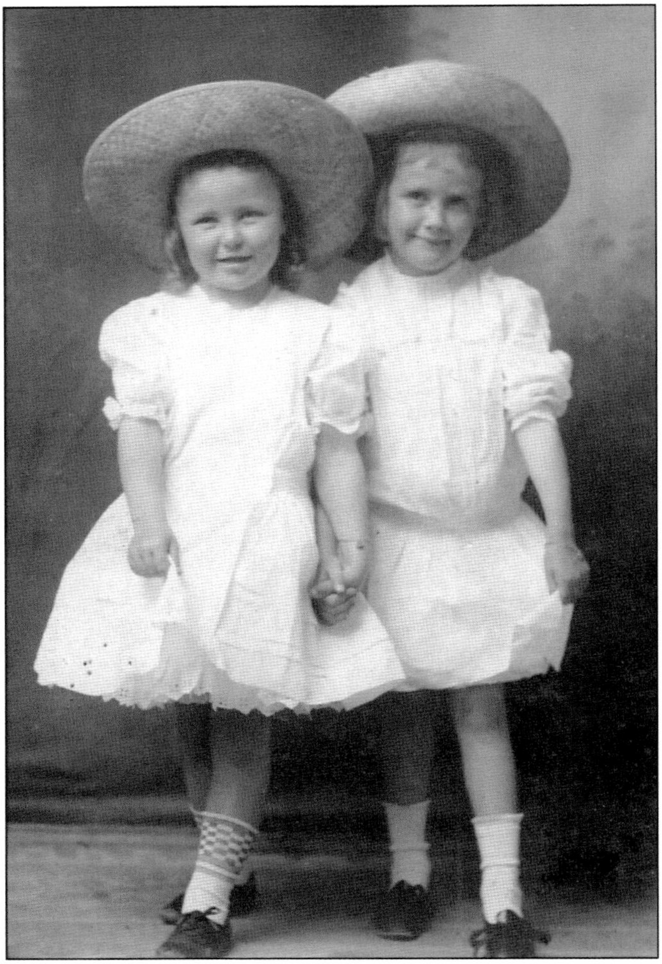

Two female friends show off their frocks. Bess Parks and Elizabeth Hatter stayed close friends the rest of their lives. Bess's father was Dr. George T. Parks, and the Hatters had a dry goods store. Below, Mary Elizabeth "Bess" Parks is in the tree overseeing the wash on the line. The laundress, Willie Norman, was washing clothes in the backyard of the Parks' house on Third Street. Wash day was an all-day job. (Courtesy of Carolyn Cordill Fulton.)

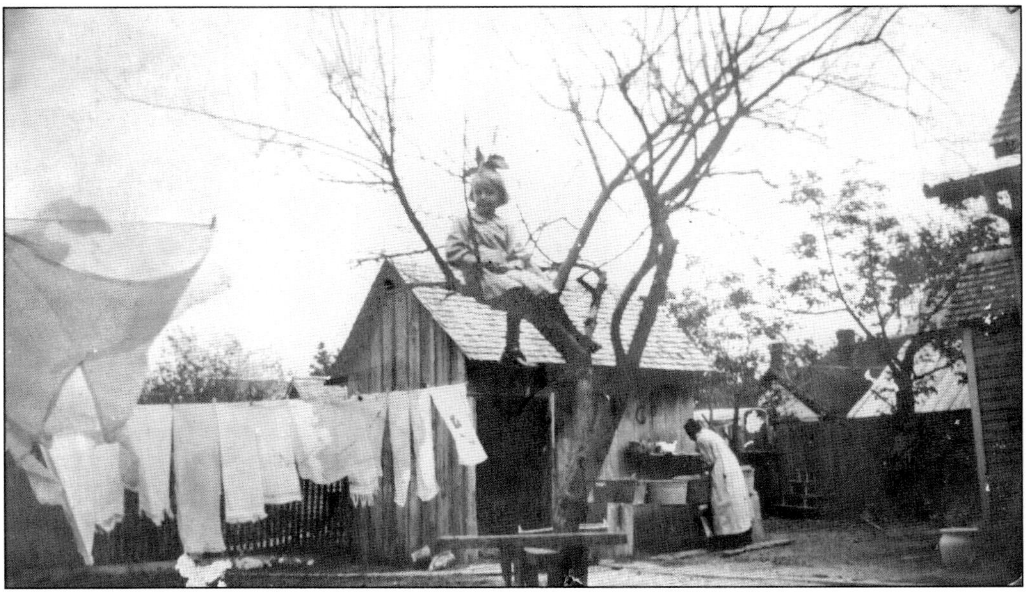

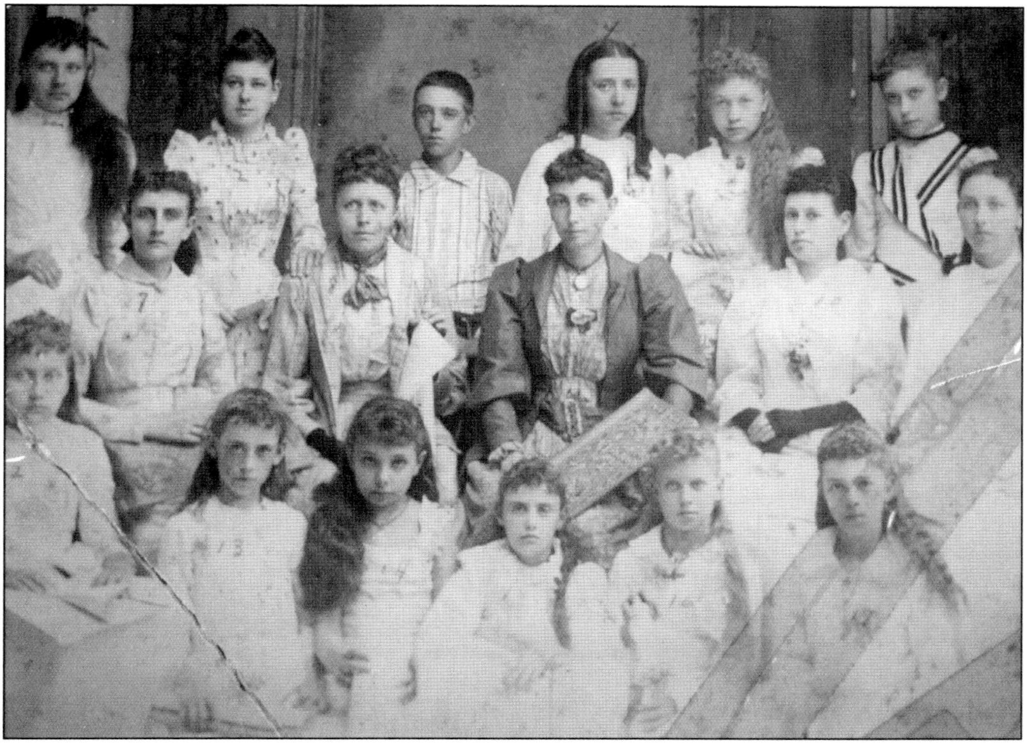

Music programs were often performed by the students of various teachers in Lancaster. Sometimes travel troupes passed through town but no matter what the program, Lancaster citizens supported the arts.

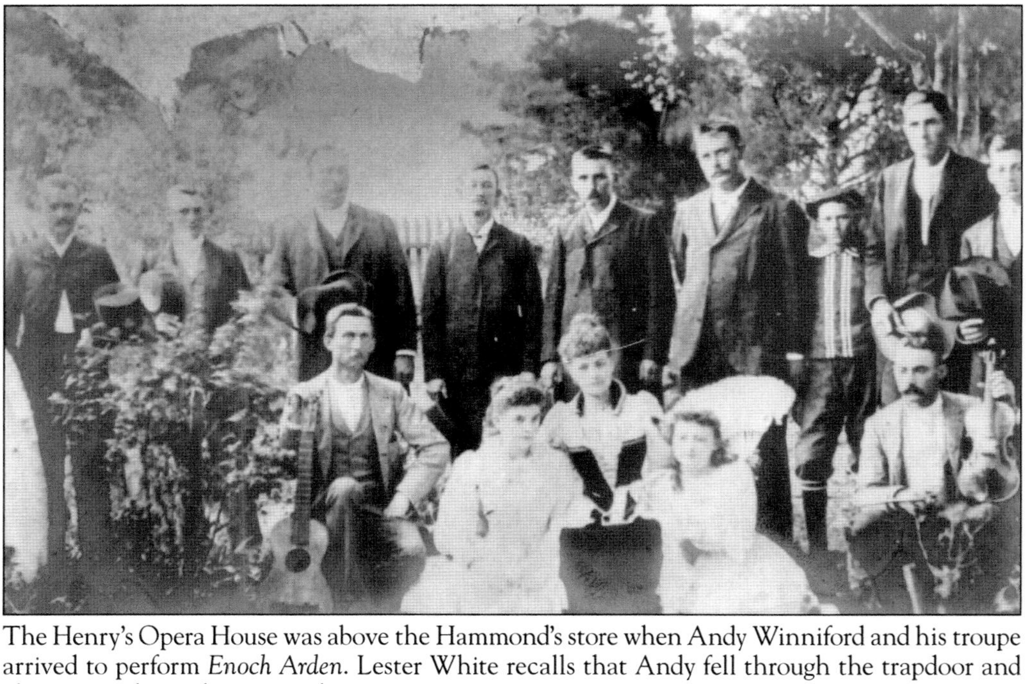

The Henry's Opera House was above the Hammond's store when Andy Winniford and his troupe arrived to perform *Enoch Arden*. Lester White recalls that Andy fell through the trapdoor and almost gave him a heart attack.

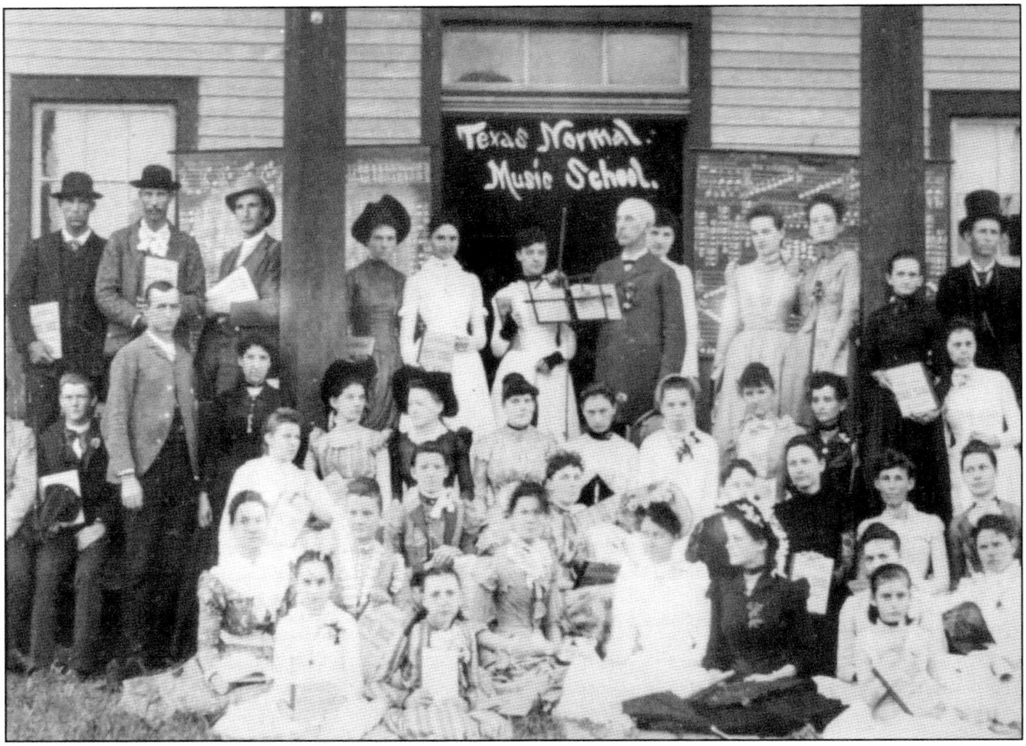

In the 1880s through the early 1900s, music schools were a part of children's education. These were located in towns or held by traveling music teachers in smaller communities. This was the era of barbershop quartets, and in most events, music was part of the program. This school was located at the Masonic hall and included students of all ages.

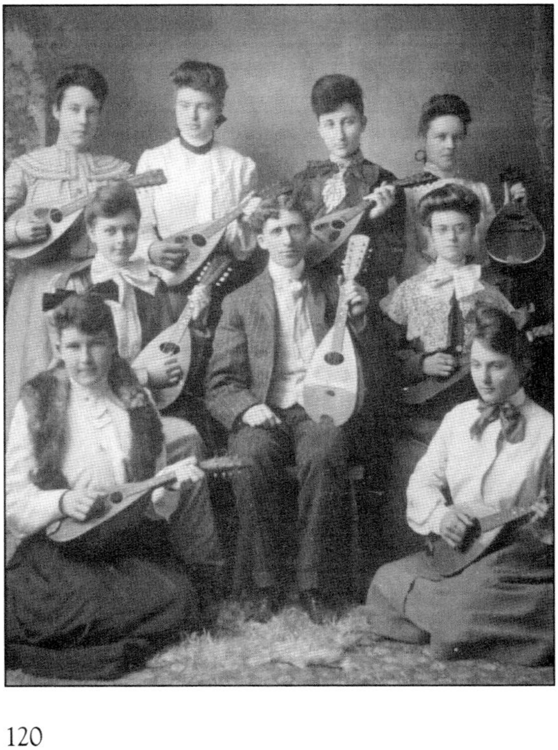

The members of this musical group are, from left to right, (first row) Addie Lavender and Myrta Anderson; (second row) Ressie Morton, teacher Oscar Quinn, and Daisy Rizer; (third row) Suzzie Parks, Lucille Curry, Mabel Batchler, and Lina Parks. The Mandolin Group would have performed at various community functions.

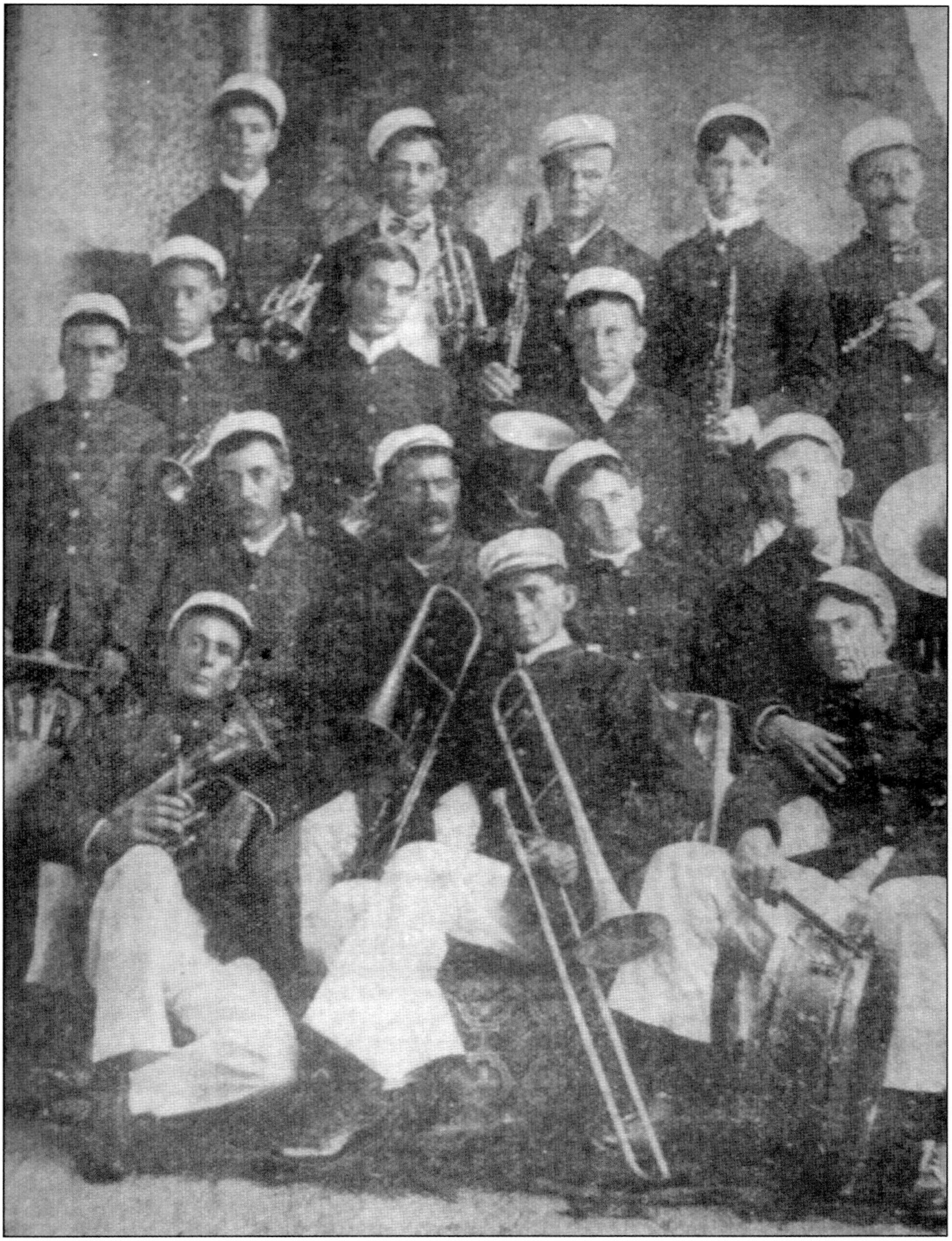

The Lancaster Brass Band probably performed at outdoor picnics and parades. From left to right are (first row) Al Hatter, Tuck Ellis, and Will Moffett; (second row) Johnnie Hatter, John Lott, Jim Hatter, Bert Lavender, and Cole Moffett; (third row) Charlie Strain, Horace Strain (leader), and Finis Holloway; (fourth row) Ollie Moore, Charlie Winniford, Will Brown, Clyde Lavender, and Henry Wetzel. Others who joined this elite group after the picture was taken were Hal White, Karl White, Byrd Earl White, Ross Ellis, Earl Ellis, John Winniford, Ben Miller, Will Rude, Eve Curry, Frank Hood, Carr Lowrey, Bob Moffett, H. E. Rawlins, and Lon Godwin. That must have been some band!

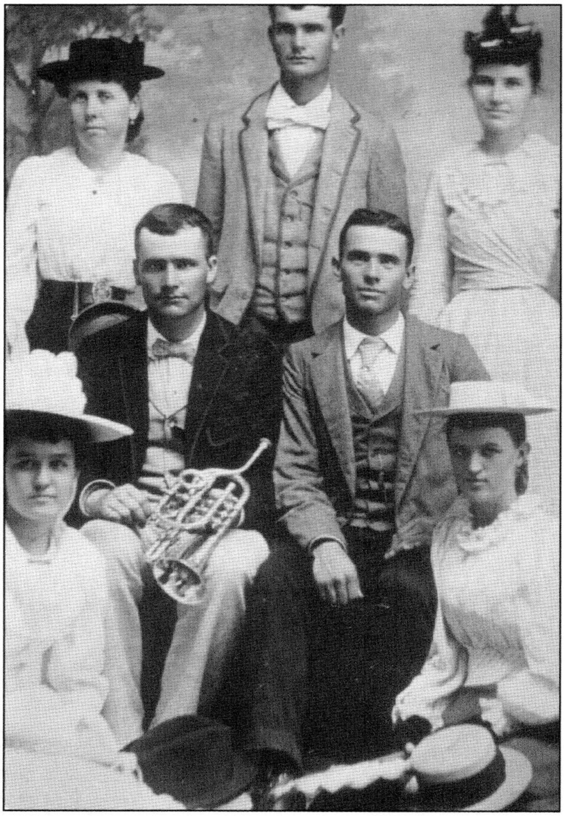

This group of young men and women of Lancaster must have included some type of musical entertainment. Pictured are, from left to right, (first row) unidentified and Lea Hunley; (second row) Hal White and Walter Beesley; (third row) Anne Graham, Karl White, and Lydia Lavender.

Forty-two was the game that was played at most social events whether it was a tea or an adult function. Ladies came in their finery and, of course, their hats. From left to right are (first row) Frances Guy, Janie Lacey Lavender, Lillian Little Lavender, Laura Croom White, Ella Howell, Mrs. Shaw, and unidentified; (second row) Maggie Lavender and three unidentified; (third row) two unidentified, Ada Rawlins, Mable Murphey, Lucille Curry, Stella White, and Julie Murphey.

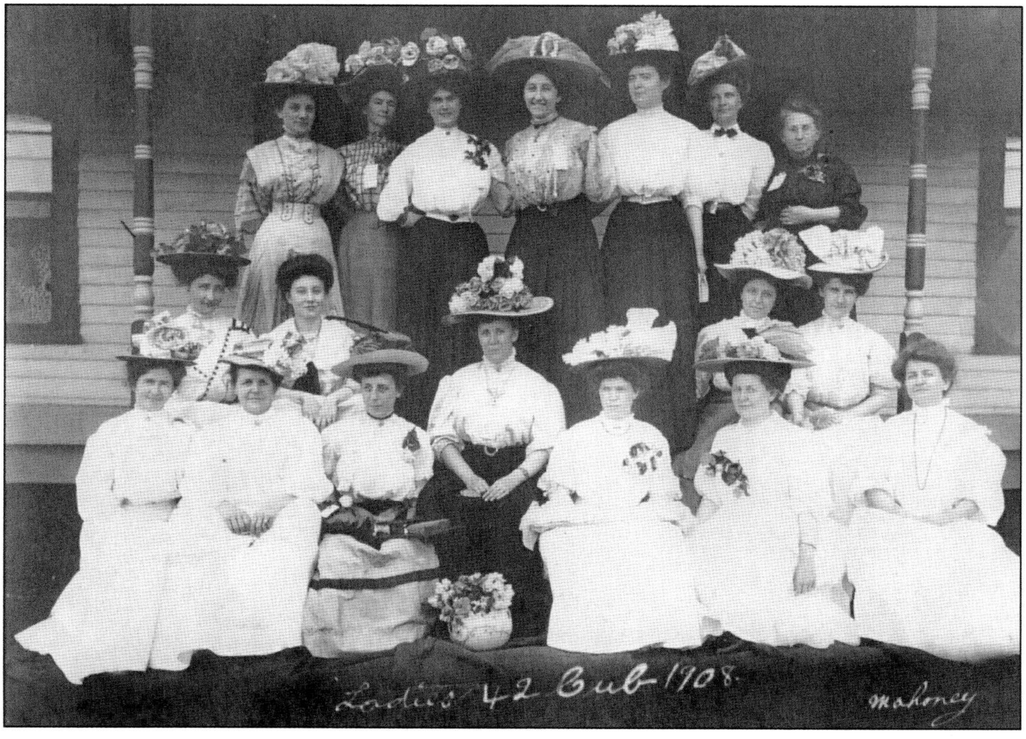

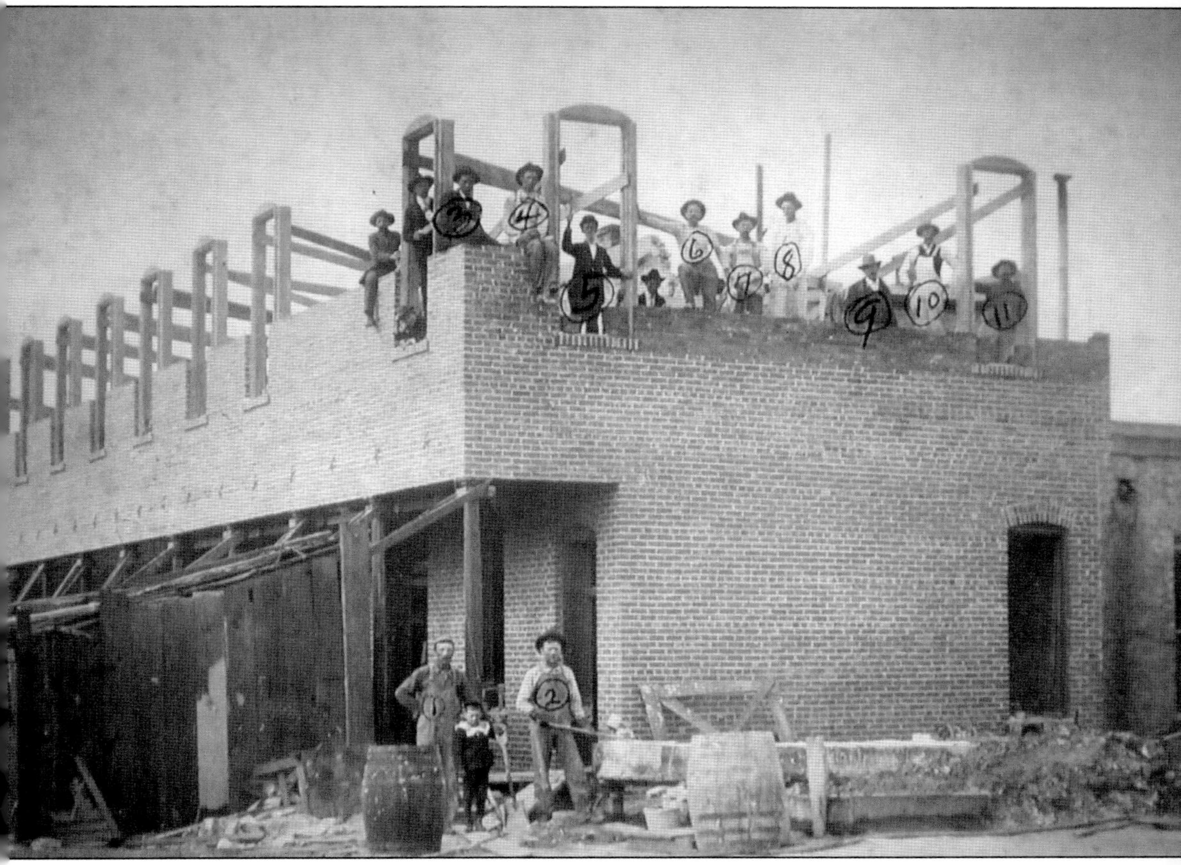

The Independent Order of Odd Fellows (IOOF) began in 1874 in Lancaster. A lot for the lodge was purchased for the building but nothing constructed until 1904 and then remodeled so the building fronted the square. The hall is still in use today. Pictured are, from left to right, (in front) Tom Barham, unidentified boy, and John Flemming; (on top of front wall) two unidentified, John Lott, Charlie Moore, George White, two unidentified, Allen Bandy, John Long, J. E. Hamilton, Lon Goodwin, Bill Moore, and Bernard Howell.

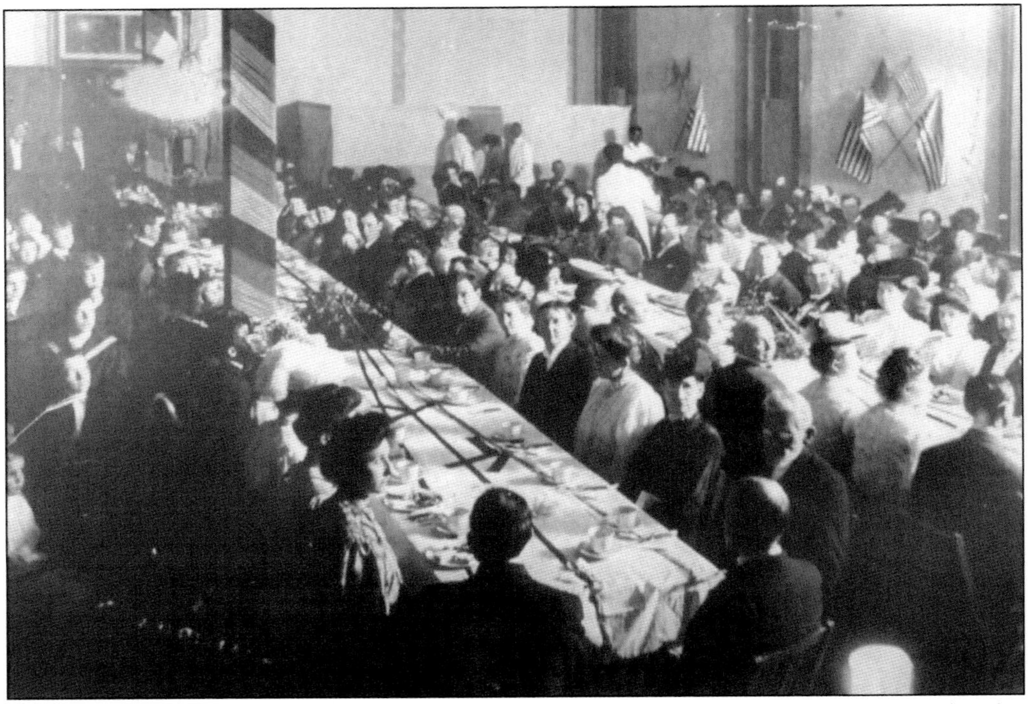

The Lancaster Masons Lodge No. 160 hosted a mid-summer meeting for the Texas Grand Lodge of Texas (all lodges under one organization) August 8–19, 1905. George White, Past Master of the Lancaster Lodge, is seated at the first table, first person on the right. Masons from all parts of Texas came by train and other vehicles. Fred J. Wilson was the current Grand Master of the Lancaster lodge. The lodge was granted a dispensation to form on October 4, 1854, and is still active in the community.

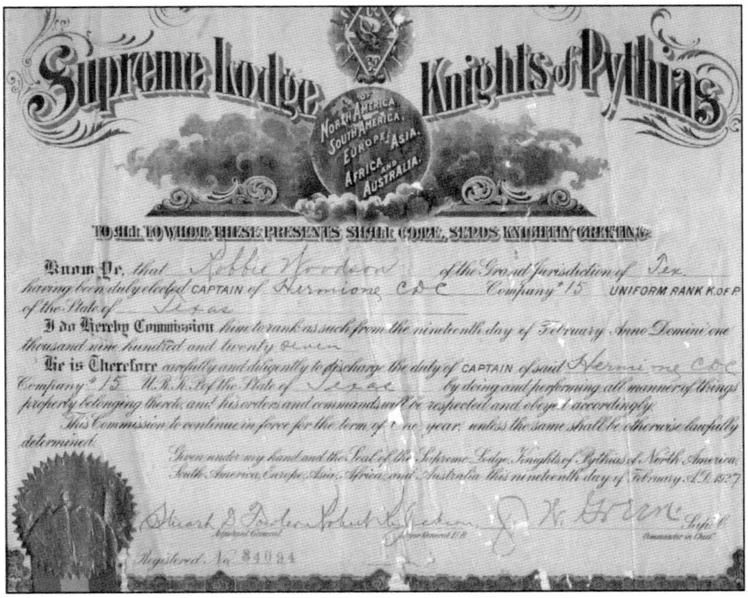

Supreme Lodge Knights of Pythias

of North America, South America, Europe, Asia, Africa and Australia.

TO ALL TO WHOM THESE PRESENTS SHALL COME, SENDS KNIGHTLY GREETING:

Know Ye, that Robbie Woodson of the Grand Jurisdiction of Tex. having been duly elected CAPTAIN of Hermione CDC Company #15 UNIFORM RANK K. OF P. of the State of Texas

I do Hereby Commission him to rank as such from the nineteenth day of February Anno Domini one thousand nine hundred and twenty seven

He is Therefore carefully and diligently to discharge the duty of CAPTAIN of said Hermione CDC Company #15 U. R. K. P. of the State of Texas by doing and performing all manner of things properly belonging thereto, and his orders and commands will be respected and obeyed accordingly.

This Commission to continue in force for the term of one year, unless the same shall be otherwise lawfully determined.

Given under my hand and the Seal of the Supreme Lodge Knights of Pythias of North America, South America, Europe, Asia, Africa and Australia this nineteenth day of February A.D. 1927

Adjutant General

Commander in Chief

Registered No. 34094

The Knights of Pythias was organized all over North America, South American, Asia, Europe, Africa, and Australia as a fraternal lodge. Robbie Woodson gained the rank of captain of Hermione CDC. Robbie Woodson was in an African American Knight of Pythias lodge. The registration number for her appointment was 34094. (Courtesy of the Ralph Wright family.)

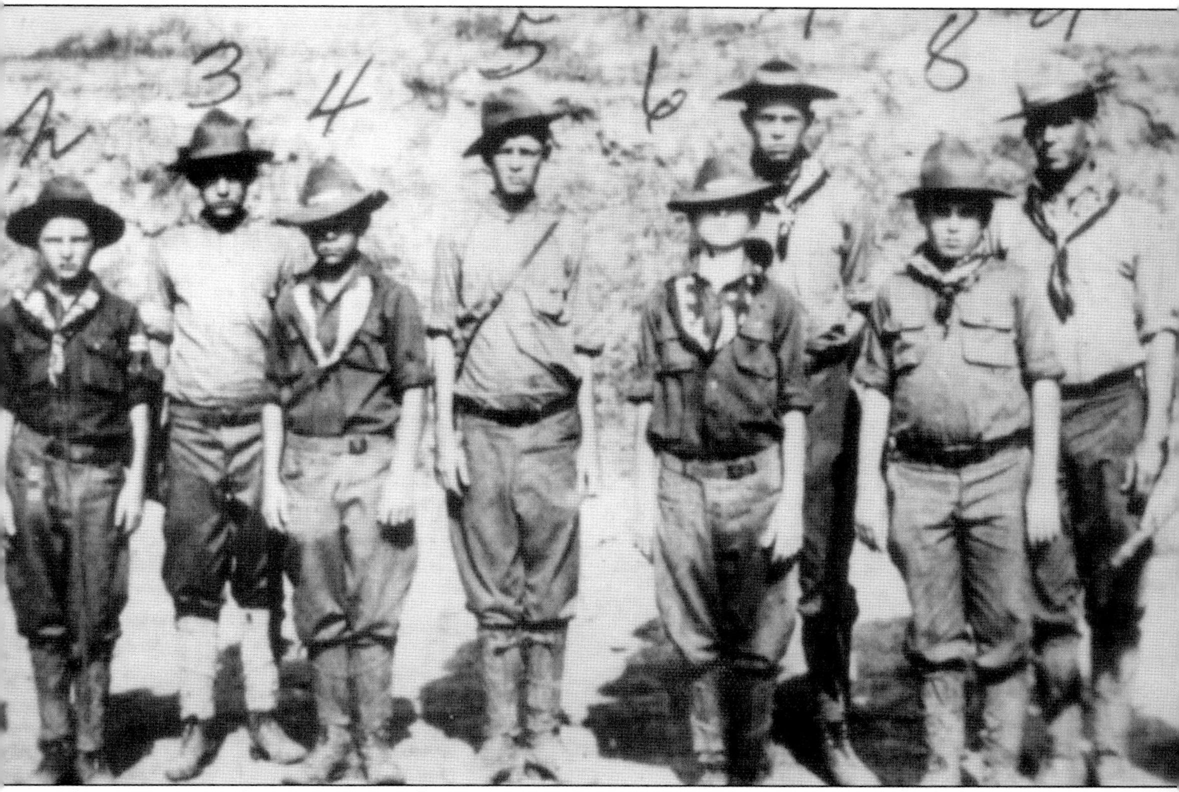

The Boy Scouts of America Troop from Lancaster went to the Brazos River in 1914. The Reverend Spencer Mitchell was one of the leaders of the group. Shown in the picture are John Foster, F. M Hammond, Raymond Curry, Sam Curry, Conner Hammond, ? Mitchell, Henry Ellis, and Marion Randlett.

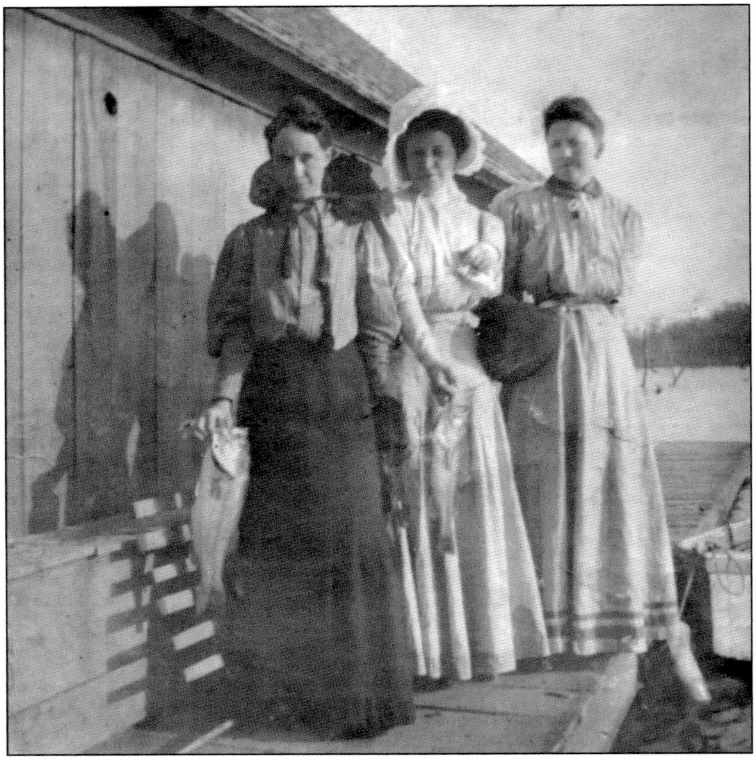

Ellen Julia Campbell Parks (1867–1951), Katie Lee Brailey Lavender (Mrs. James Lavender), and Janie L. Lacey Lavender (Mrs. Eber Lavender) enjoyed going to the Rod and Gun Club to fish with their families. This was not only fun but fresh fish were not often available in the stores. (Courtesy of Carolyn Cordill Fulton.)

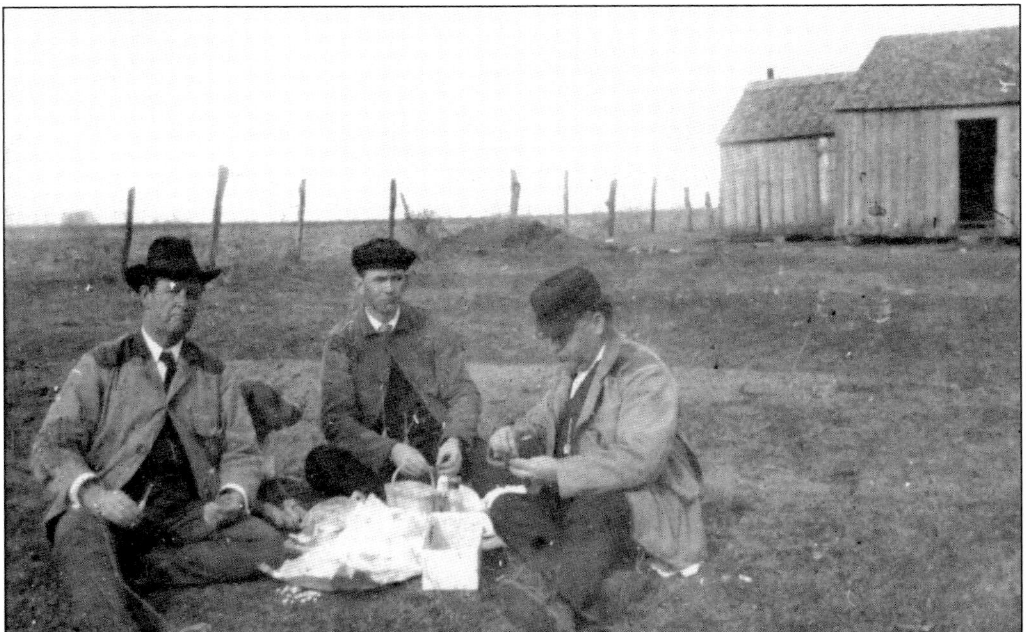

Dr. Nate Parks, James Lavender, and Eber Lavender enjoy a picnic at an outing where everyone fished and had good fellowship. There were several lakes around Lancaster where citizens could fish and hunt or relish in a day away. Many were to the east of Lancaster toward the Trinity River. (Courtesy of Carolyn Cordill Fulton.)

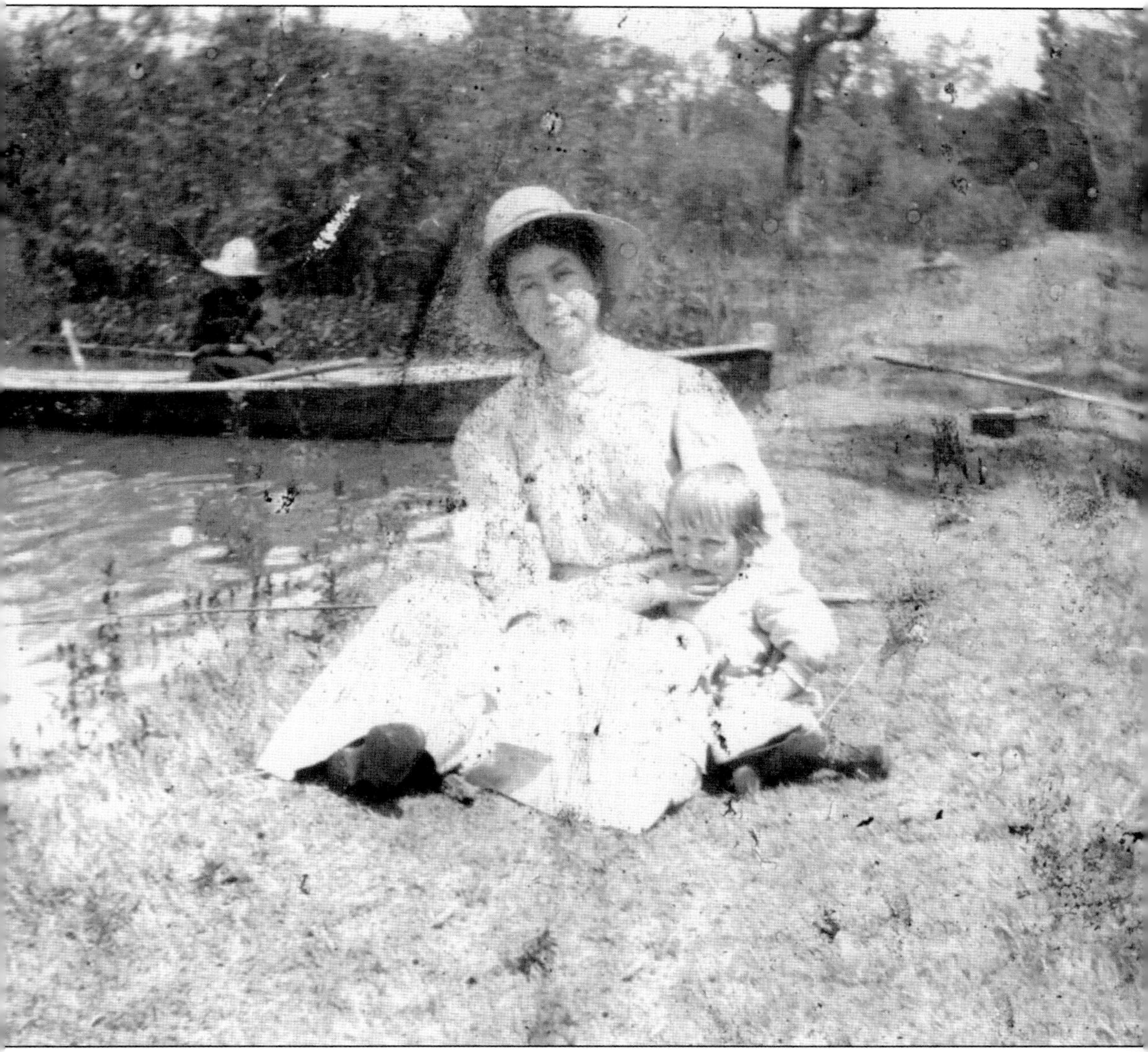

A day at the Rod and Gun Club was not only relaxing but the fish that were caught made a wonderful meal. In these early years of Lancaster, life was taken at a slower pace. Church and community were important to its citizens. Neighbors helped neighbors and families spent time together. Maybe this was the good life! (Courtesy of Carolyn Cordill Fulton.)